Urban Informality and the Built Environment

FRINGE

Series Editors

Alena Ledeneva and Peter Zusi, School of Slavonic and

East European Studies, UCL

The FRINGE series explores the roles that complexity, ambivalence and immeasurability play in social and cultural phenomena. A cross-disciplinary initiative bringing together researchers from the humanities, social sciences and area studies, the series examines how seemingly opposed notions such as centrality and marginality, clarity and ambiguity, can shift and converge when embedded in everyday practices.

Alena Ledeneva is Professor of Politics and Society at the School of Slavonic and East European Studies of UCL.

Peter Zusi is Associate Professor of Czech and Comparative Literature at the School of Slavonic and East European Studies of UCL.

Urban Informality and the Built Environment
Infrastructure, exchange and image

Edited by Nerea Amorós Elorduy, Nikhilesh Sinha and Colin Marx

First published in 2024 by
UCL Press
University College London
Gower Street
London WC1E 6BT

Available to download free: www.uclpress.co.uk

Collection © Editors, 2024
Text © Contributors, 2024
Images © Contributors, 2024

The authors have asserted their rights under the Copyright, Designs and Patents Act 1988 to be identified as the authors of this work.

A CIP catalogue record for this book is available from The British Library.

Any third-party material in this book is not covered by the book's Creative Commons licence. Details of the copyright ownership and permitted use of third-party material is given in the image (or extract) credit lines. If you would like to reuse any third-party material not covered by the book's Creative Commons licence, you will need to obtain permission directly from the copyright owner.

This book is published under a Creative Commons Attribution-Non-Commercial 4.0 International licence (CC BY-NC 4.0), https://creativecommons.org/licenses/by-nc/4.0/. This licence allows you to share and adapt the work for non-commercial use providing attribution is made to the author and publisher (but not in any way that suggests that they endorse you or your use of the work) and any changes are indicated. Attribution should include the following information:

Elorduy, N.A., Sinha, N. and Marx, C. (eds) 2024. *Urban Informality and the Built Environment: Infrastructure, exchange and image*. London: UCL Press. https://doi.org/10.14324/111.9781800086265

Further details about Creative Commons licences are available at https://creativecommons.org/licenses/

ISBN: 978-1-80008-628-9 (Hbk)
ISBN: 978-1-80008-627-2 (Pbk)
ISBN: 978-1-80008-626-5 (PDF)
ISBN: 978-1-80008-629-6 (epub)
DOI: https://doi.org/10.14324/111.9781800086265

Contents

List of figures and tables   vii
List of contributors   xi
Series editors' preface   xv
Acknowledgements   xvii

1   Introduction: foregrounding the built environment   1
Nerea Amorós Elorduy, Nikhilesh Sinha and Colin Marx

2   Informality and infrastructure   19
Swati Chattopadhyay

3   Informalities of exchange   33
Fran Tonkiss

4   The image of informal settlements   41
Kim Dovey

5   The role of change maker painters: graffiti and street art in Accra, Ghana   49
Claire Tunnacliffe

6   Informal everyday water infrastructures in the in-between territories of Galicia   73
Lucia Cerrada Morato

7   A morphogenetic approach to informality: the case of post-socialist Tirana   89
Blerta Dino

8   Informal structures of welfare: emerging spaces of social reproduction in Athens   107
Isabel Gutiérrez Sánchez

9   Rhythmanalysis as exploration of urban informality in
    Havana, Cuba   125
    Susan Fitzgerald

10 The death and life of Jian-Cheng Circle: a negative lesson for the
    built informality of urban places   141
    Chin-Wei Chang

11 Informality as pedagogy: collective design in the Mariamma
    Nagar settlement   155
    Nicola Antaki

12 Informality as an urban trend in mainstream architectural
    publications   173
    Fani Kostourou and Paul Goodship

13 Conclusion: foregrounding positionality   189
    Nerea Amorós Elorduy, Nikhilesh Sinha and Colin Marx

Index   199

List of figures and tables

Figures

5.1	Photograph of wall art 'Politics, patriotism and post no bills'.	49
5.2	Photograph of wall art 'Don't urinate here'.	51
5.3	Photograph of wall art 'The story of Ghana'.	55
5.4	Photograph of work bench.	57
5.5	Photograph of wall art 'African unity'.	61
5.6	Photograph of wall art 'Peaceful elections'.	65
5.7	Photograph of wall art 'After the floods'.	66
6.1	Photograph of a household water deposit connected to the *traída* in Pedrouzos, Galicia, Spain.	75
6.2	Photograph of one of the *traída* collective water deposits in Pedrouzos, Galicia, Spain.	76
6.3	Map of the Atlantic axis of Galicia-north Portugal.	77
6.4	Photograph of an upgraded catchment point at the *traída* A Malata, Abegondo, Galicia, Spain.	80
6.5	Photograph of the new technologies to monitor water quality in a catchment point, Galicia, Spain.	83
7.1	Photograph of former public space converted informally into parking space. Tirana, Albania, 2016.	93
7.2	Photograph of an extension to an early 1990s apartment block showing an appropriation of public space by cafés.	94
7.3	Diagrams showing the change from 1989 (left) to 2016 (right) in pedestrian and vehicle circulation as well as access points to buildings in the Kombinati case study, Tirana, Albania.	97
7.4	Diagrams showing land use distribution (left) and morphological evolution (right) up to 2016 in the Kombinati case study, Tirana, Albania.	97
7.5	Diagrams showing the change from 1989 (left) to 2016 (right) in pedestrian and vehicle circulation as well as access points to buildings in the Shallvaret case study, Tirana, Albania.	98

7.6	Diagrams showing land use distribution (left) and morphological evolution (right) up to 2016 in the Shallvaret case study, Tirana, Albania.	99
7.7	Map of overlaid urban growth in 1989 and 2016, Tirana, Albania.	101
7.8	Photograph of an extension to an early 1990s apartment block showing conversions to non-domestic land use on the ground floor in Tirana, Albania.	102
7.9	Photograph highlighting high demand for commercial units in Tirana, Albania.	102
7.10	Photograph of Tirana, Albania.	103
8.1	Diagrammatic depiction of *O Allos Anthropos Social Kitchen*, Athens, Greece.	113
8.2	Diagrammatic depiction of *Athens Community Polyclinic and Pharmacy*, Athens, Greece.	113
8.3	Diagrammatic depiction of *City Plaza Refugee Accommodation Centre*, Athens, Greece.	115
9.1	Photograph of street view outside Julio's garden in La Habana Vieja, Cuba.	129
9.2	Photograph of harvested plants in Julio's garden in La Habana Vieja, Cuba.	130
9.3	Photograph of customers on the street outside Julio's garden waiting to buy plants in La Habana Vieja, Cuba.	131
9.4	Photograph showing views from above of Julio's garden in La Habana Vieja, Cuba.	132
9.5.	Graphic representation of rhythms, networks and activities from 12 to 2pm any given day in a specific section of La Habana Vieja, Cuba.	136
9.6.	Graphic representation of rhythms, networks, and activities from 4 to 6pm any given day in a specific section of La Habana Vieja, Cuba.	137
11.1	Photograph showing the contextual plurality of the surroundings of Mariamma Nagar, Mumbai, India.	159
11.2	Photograph showing children setting off on their neighbourhood walkabout.	162
11.3	Two photographs showing the classroom where the class create their map of the settlement using printed photographs they had taken, drawings and annotations.	163
11.4	Photograph of children's map of learning in Mariamma Nagar, made in cloth, ink and paper, 3x3m.	164

11.5 Four photographs depicting the process of making the
      children's map of learning in Mariamma Nagar, cloth, ink
      and paper, 3x3m.   166
11.6 The finished tapestry.   168
12.1 Graph showing the evolution of the total number of
      keyword searches for all magazines selected between
      1960 and 2015 (in absolute numbers). Superimposed is
      the average frequency trend line showing percentage of
      keywords present among total number of results.   178
12.2 (Left) Graph showing the evolution of the total number of
      keyword searches for all magazines selected between 1960
      and 2015 broken down to each of the seven mainstream
      magazines. (Right) Graph showing the average evolution of
      the concurrence of keywords (percentage) in six mainstream
      magazines between 1960 and 2015 (excluding *Ekistics*).   178
12.3 Area graphs for 31 keywords referenced between 1960 and
      2015 (absolute numbers).   179
12.4 (Left) Graph showing the concurrence of the *favela* keyword
      in seven mainstream magazines between 1960 and 2015.
      (Right) Graph showing bibliography on the *favelas* of Rio
      de Janeiro together with number of publications per year
      between 1900 and 2002. Sources: Valladares, 2008 and
      URBANDATA, Brasil, 2004.   180
12.5 Standardised line graphs of the evolution of informality as
      an urban trend in the mainstream press (average without
      taking into consideration *Ekistics*).   182

Tables

12.1 Table showing list of the selected seven magazines with
      their estimated total number of issues for the period
      1960–2015. The table includes the year each magazine was
      founded and its country of origin.   176

List of contributors

Nerea Amorós Elorduy is guest professor on Settlements and Shelter at the UIC-Barcelona and managing director of think-and-do-tank Creative Assemblages. She is an architect and urbanist, with a PhD (UCL) on the built environment of long-term refugee camps published as her latest book, *Architecture as a Way of Seeing and Learning* (2021).

Nikhilesh Sinha is professor of economics and finance and chair of research ethics at the Hult International Business School in London. He holds undergraduate and postgraduate degrees in economics, a Master of Laws and a PhD (UCL) in Development Planning. Nikhilesh's research spans the fields of urban studies, institutional economics, law and development studies.

Colin Marx is professor of urban development planning at the Bartlett Development Planning Unit, UCL. He has a master's in town and regional planning and PhD in geography. Colin has studied urban injustice and inequality since 1991 and is currently researching concepts of informality and urban land dynamics to understand Sub-Saharan African cities outside of Eurocentric theories. He co-edited *The City in Urban Poverty* (2015).

Nicola Antaki is a senior architect at Turner Works and a postdoctoral researcher at the University of Sheffield working on developing a civic pedagogy toolkit based on her doctoral research. Her research is situated in Mumbai, looking at the links between architecture and learning.

Lucia Cerrada Morato is an architect and urban designer. After 10 years in private practice, she joined the public sector in 2017. Lucia combines her practice with an academic career. She holds a PhD from the Bartlett School of Planning where she taught for eight years. Lucia was awarded an ESRC Fellowship, and she will be joining King's College London as a postdoctoral researcher.

Chin-Wei Chang has a PhD in architectural and urban history and theory from the Bartlett School of Architecture, UCL. Chin-Wei's research addresses the social production of spatial forms within non-architect consequences, everyday landscapes and their conflicts with modernity in the contemporary built environment.

Swati Chattopadhyay is professor of history of art and architecture at UC, Santa Barbara and visiting professor of architectural history at Manchester School of Architecture. Swati is an architect and architectural historian specialising in modern architecture, urbanism and the cultural landscape of the British Empire. Her latest publications include the *Routledge Companion to Critical Approaches to Contemporary Architecture* (2019).

Blerta Dino works as an urban design consultant and researcher. She completed her doctorate in 2019 in the Space Syntax Laboratory at the Bartlett, UCL, where she worked as a researcher before joining AECOM (London). She is based in Tirana where she continues to work and write on urban issues.

Kim Dovey is professor of architecture and urban design and director of the Informal Urbanism Research hub at the University of Melbourne. He is an architect with a PhD from Berkeley. His research focuses on theories of place, power and urban informality. His latest titles include *Urban Choreography* (2018) and *Mapping Urbanities* (2018).

Susan Fitzgerald is design director of FBM and an associate professor at Dalhousie University in Halifax, Nova Scotia, Canada. Her design work has received many accolades including the Canada Council for the Arts's Professional Prix de Rome and the Governor General's Medal in Architecture.

Paul Goodship is research and impact data analyst at the Bartlett, UCL, measuring the impact of research with data. Previously he worked as a data scientist at Atkins, analysing built environment data for development opportunities. Paul holds a PhD in urban morphology and sociospatial analysis from the Bartlett School of Architecture, UCL.

Isabel Gutiérrez Sánchez is a researcher and educator with a background in architecture and anthropology. Her work situates across the fields of urban anthropology, critical geography and feminist political theory. She is a postdoctoral fellow at the Spanish National Research Council. She did her PhD at the Bartlett School of Architecture, UCL, and taught there.

Fani Kostourou is associate lecturer at UAL and urban computation specialist at Grimshaw Architects. She was previously associate director at Theatrum Mundi and has taught in the United Kingdom and Europe. She holds a PhD from UCL, and her research interests include spatial data and theories, housing, informality and urban cultures.

Fran Tonkiss is professor of sociology and head of the sociology department at the LSE. Her focus is the fields of urban and economic sociology, studying urban inequalities, urban development and design, social and spatial divisions and the socio-economic organisation of urban space. She is currently managing editor of *Economy and Society*.

Claire Tunnacliffe (Sé Mali) is a writer and researcher completing a PhD on queer practices of placemaking at the Bartlett School of Architecture, UCL. Their creative writing explores queer embodiment and the urban and natural environment.

Series editors' preface

The UCL Press FRINGE series presents work related to the themes of the UCL FRINGE Centre for the Study of Social and Cultural Complexity.

The FRINGE series is a platform for cross-disciplinary analysis and the development of 'area studies without borders'. 'FRINGE' is an acronym standing for Fluidity, Resistance, Invisibility, Neutrality, Grey zones, and Elusiveness – categories fundamental to the themes that the Centres support. The oxymoron in the notion of a 'FRINGE *Centre*' expresses our interest in (1) the tensions between 'area studies' and more traditional academic disciplines; and (2) social, political, and cultural trajectories from 'centres to fringes' and inversely from 'fringes to centres'.

Focusing on informality, global informal housing and urban development, *Urban Informality and the Built Environment* follows on from the contributions of earlier volumes in the series such as *Invisible Reconstruction, Comparative Approaches to Informal Housing, Re-Centring the City* and *The Global Encyclopaedia of Informality*.

The book resonates with the core objectives of the FRINGE series both theoretically and empirically. It studies phenomena that are fluid and resistant to articulation. It focuses on the built environment as a visual manifestation of processes that are illegible or invisible to outsiders. Its case studies promote a cross-fertilisation between disciplines, lenses, geographies and methodologies. An international team of economists, anthropologists, urban planners, architects, sociologists and political scientists brings together research from Accra, Havana, London, San Francisco, Tirana and others.

The main argument of the proposed volume is the need to re-centre the study of informality away from state-centric approaches that define the informal vis-à-vis the state. With a focus on the built environment, this volume puts forward considerations of materiality, form, function and meaning, shifting attention to the relational in informal spaces and embracing the varying components of the urban infrastructure.

Alena Ledeneva and Peter Zusi
School of Slavonic and East European Studies, UCL

Acknowledgements

A book like this would have been impossible without the support and generosity of a great many people. We'd firstly like to thank our contributing authors for putting their faith in us, and their patience through this long process. Swati Chattopadhyay, Kim Dovey and Fran Tonkiss in particular gave generously of their time at a formative stage of the project. A huge debt of gratitude is due to Alena Ledeneva, Peter Zusi and all of the members of the Fringe series editorial board. We'd also like to thank all the members of the Bartlett Doctoral Informality Initiatives, which provided a forum where we were able to discuss our ideas, and where the idea of this book first took shape.

The project was only possible due to the financial support of the Bartlett Doctoral Initiatives Fund and the inspired leadership of Stephen Marshall. We'd like to thank the Fund for agreeing to support the Doctoral Informality Network, and the conference that allowed us to bring all the contributors together.

1
Introduction: foregrounding the built environment
Nerea Amorós Elorduy, Nikhilesh Sinha and Colin Marx

To examine urban informality is to be concerned with socio-spatial marginalisation, uncertainty, the control and use of physical space, the categorisation and distribution of resources, the forms of regulation and much more in human settlements. Urban informality has come to be associated with the means to analyse and counter the injustices and inequalities so deeply entrenched in many urban environments. In this way, urban informality has emerged as a potent touchstone in the scholarship and activism of struggles over the future forms of equitable and sustainable cities. However, in this process, one key element has become relegated to a side issue: the built environment.

It appears that contemporary studies and policies related to urban informality focus on the built environment somewhat incidentally. They frame the built environment as either a result of informal processes or a starting point of studies that rapidly shift focus to political, economic or governance aspects. Such approaches might consider an informal settlement the outcome of the lack of formal planning. Or, an informal market, as an entry point into socio-economic dynamics inevitably loaded against a specific social group. In examples like these, the built environment is present seemingly only as background to the 'real' consequential processes that have either happened or are about to.

The most likely reason for this state of affairs is that influential strands of scholarship and activism of urban informality – mostly in the 1990s – foregrounded how urban informality was bound up with the political economies of cities. This scholarship took place at a time when architects and urban planners around the world were being enticed by, and were drawing inspiration from, the morphologies of the 'self-built'; a time when international developmental agencies were focusing on transforming the morphologies of the 'informal' cities to change their socio-political conditions. In that landscape, the scholarship that foregrounded the political economies of cities explicitly rejected attempts to treat the built environments labelled 'informal' as objects to be transformed. Powerfully articulated by Ananya Roy and Nezar AlSayyad (2004, 296–304) this critique exposed how a narrow focus on the morphology and image of the built environment could lead to epistemic injustice, the aestheticisation of poverty and colonial interpretations of 'rationality'. In other words, how such a narrow focus stripped informal urban phenomena of the political economies it constituted and mediated.

However, pushed too far, such approaches miss out on the ways that the built environment is itself political, social and economic – giving rise to and shaping politics, societies and economies. Hence, building upon those critiques articulated by Ananya Roy (2005), Oren Yiftachel (2009) and others, this book argues that it is worth revisiting the relationship between urban informality and the built environment for engaging with contemporary urban injustices. More specifically, we propose to foreground the built environment as a socio-political relational power in our analysis of urban informality.

In doing this, we can draw on examples like Ghertner's (2015) work that takes the aesthetic qualities of the built environment to study urban governance and Caldeira's (2016) examination of how autoconstruction can characterise distinctive modes of urban production. Both authors identify reciprocal relations with notions of urban informality informing understandings of the built environment and *vice versa*. Both examples conceive of the built environment as saturated in, and expressive of, politics, culture and history. In its materiality and physicality, the built environment cannot be separated from the unequal social and economic relations that it gives rise to and that it conditions.

This book is an attempt to revive the discussion about urban informality to keep it relevant for urban phenomena now and in the near future. Hence, we seek to contribute to and enable the further decolonisation of the urban studies field with our approach. In our contribution to decolonising the field, this volume brings a variety of disciplines and situated knowledges to the making and studying of the built environment, including various contexts and a range of voices. That is why the purpose of this book is to offer a framework to study urban informality: to add nuance and richness to methods of understanding phenomena that have been categorised as informal, rather than offer a new, all-encompassing definition of urban informality. This book aims to provide understandings of urban informality useful to various authors and settings without automatically universalising knowledge.

We now look at how the built environment allows different urban processes to interact and how it groups elements together. We propose to explore urban informality by analysing the infrastructures that compose it, the exchanges it enables and the diverse images it makes and unmakes. In line with the Fringe series, and in its willingness to inspire new research, readers can approach this book by using the bookmarks on the three themes of image, infrastructure and exchange. These can act as parts that stand by themselves, and as an interwoven and intricate testament to the continuing relevance of the informal in understanding the urban. Finally, key to our argument, we propose the need to decentre the State in the analysis.

Moving past state-centrism

This book is born in the acknowledgement that informality, as a category, has come to signify such a large set of phenomena that some scholars dismiss it as unhelpful (Sindzingre 2004). In this context, there have been several examples of different ways in which 'urban informality' can still be helpful (Boudreau and Davis 2017; Marx and Kelling 2019; Banks, Lombard and Mitlin 2020). Despite differences across these examples, we identify two consistent themes. First is recognising the value of understanding urban informality relationally. In other words, as always constituted by multiple, overlapping relations with other social phenomena that go on to shape what can be said and done in performative feedback loops. Second, the State has remained a fundamental point of reference for any phenomena considered informal. In our view, to make space to analyse the relations of the built environment and urban informality, we need to build on, but move past, state-centrism.

What we term state-centrism emerges from the ways in which urban informality has been fundamentally tied to definitions of the formal. The formal has widely been understood to signify activities, relations and systems regulated by state authorities. According to this understanding, the specifics of the rule systems applied, forms of regulation, the nature of the State and the legitimacy of its power have not influenced this categorisation. While state actors can engage in informal activities, the State remains an embodiment of the formal. Roy's (2009) insights have been influential in demonstrating how states routinely employ informality strategically, and that informality can be a tool of the State. Consequently, the view has endured that formality is a foundational feature of the State, and by extension any activity, relation or mechanism can only be deemed to be formal by the State.

The implication is that if, as we build on an understanding of urban informality as 'an organising logic [and] a process of structuration that constitutes the rules of the game' (Roy and AlSayyad 2004) and as 'grey spaces of permanent temporariness' (Yiftachel 2009), we need to hold open the possibilities for other factors to be influential. While recognising the State, we do not need to automatically reach for understandings of urban informality as exceptions, different, exotic, or rebellious vis-à-vis the State. State-centrism has enabled deep and fascinating insights into informality. Yet, in our view, it carries two constraining consequences.

One of the consequences of foregrounding the State, explicitly or implicitly, is that it is difficult to then disentangle power hierarchies from a single vertical structure, making all other power relations at best subsidiary and at worst invisible. The entire gamut of informal phenomena tends to be clubbed together. The extent of informality becomes a measure of the strength or weakness of the State to provide and control, or of the other actors to be co-opted, be oppressed or rebellious. The primary relationship is with the State. Therefore, all analysis tends to focus on this dynamic of informality produced by the State and/or responses to, and by, the State. This assumption hinders considerations of urban life beyond the parameters of state governance systems and structures. For example, much urban informality scholarship operates with the governance terminology and modes of thought that characterise the State. That is that nations consist of individuals who live in (discrete) households, in neighbourhoods, municipalities and regions that make up the nation. Under the state-centrism framework, it is difficult to think of life as circuits and flows (Simone 2003) or different hierarchies or clusters with minimal reference to these state structures of governance.

Another consequence is that state-centric approaches imply an acceptance of an underlying convention of what the State is. European and Anglo-American academics and organisations have been the primary creators of this convention. Thus, a continuous duality exists in this body of literature between urban areas in former colonies and those in colonising states. De-centring the State allows us to move away from both limiting epistemological filters.

Recent work has challenged the heavy leaning towards a state-centric lens. Seth Schindler notes that 'a focus on the state can hinder our understanding of informality' (2017, 249). Schindler demonstrates the vital role of a myriad of other actors in creating urban informality. Specifically, he explains the purpose of middle-class associations in regulating informal street trade and waste collection in Delhi. Another example is Antonia Settle (2018) as she examines Pakistan's land market, where informal transactions are not a reflection of a lack of faith in state institutions or an attempt to evade regulatory authorities but a response to the uncertainties of global financial flows. Settle highlights that the motivating factor is a desire for liquidity, which parallels the imperative behind liquid financial trading in the west. These two instances use an economic entry point to highlight the value of considering a non-state-centric approach. This collection does so by focusing on the built environment and analysing infrastructures, exchanges and images.

Urban informality, the built environment and relationality

This volume seeks to explore urban informality's relational nature in an attempt to move away from dichotomies that tend to be understood more statically. We explore dichotomies such as powerful/vulnerable, regulated/unregulated, legal/illegal to pay attention to the multiple sets of actors involved in their creation and break up linear approaches to power and agency such as top-down and bottom-up. In focusing on the built environment, we aim to give clarity, contextualisation and richness to the concept of urban informality. We question some of the adjectives accumulated through the state lens, which constrain the study of the urban informality phenomena making them less legible such as opaque, convoluted, confusing and complex.

We understand the built environment as all the physical elements constructed by humans to interact with each other and their surroundings, and that it often exceeds the intentions of its constructors. Elaborating on that, we conceive built environments as sets of overlapping relations: the social links that physical space affords; the economic ties that produce built forms; the physical connections between components and materials that ensure stable structures. These relationships affect many aspects of social life, not least how people make sense of what can be done by who, when, where and why. While relations are not the only way to understand different aspects of the built environment, they are a dominant and useful one for understanding urban informality. Hence, our volume asserts that urban informality is a relational concept; processual, reflective of inequalities, impossible to isolate from other urban dynamics and intrinsically related to the physical manifestations it takes.

The different relationships work through institutions, infrastructures, people, materials, forms and developments. These links shape and define phenomena in urban settings understood as formal or informal, with different consequences for their inhabitants. In this volume, we try to dissect and understand what the useful, relevant relations of situated urban informality are.

We focus on relationality. An ever-present feature of urban informality scholarship is that it cannot be understood outside of its binary relation to other social phenomena: economic transactions, social interactions, work, health and well-being, access to services and housing. This relational quality of urban informality has been central to understanding its diverse causes, effects and manifestations. Two recent academic contributions have explicitly recognised this relational quality: Boudreau and Davis (2017) and Marx and Kelling (2019). Both works focus on a relationship with two co-constitutive forms. One is an identifiable relation – either tangible or intangible. The other is how the link establishes and distributes meaning and value across the related entities. An example of a tangible association would be a road connecting point A (a house) to B (a place of work). An example of an intangible relation would be the stigma associated with that house, work and road set in an 'informal neighbourhood'.

Given the relational nature of urban informality, it is unsurprising its dominant analyses draw on aspects suited to understanding linkages. In this volume, the three that we focus on are exchange, infrastructure and image. Infrastructure, in relating two or more points, might be tangible (pipes, roads, cables) or intangible (ideas, power, culture). Exchange requires two entities between which to pass material, energies, goods, money, ideas and beings. And the image has symbolic, ideological, cultural and relational aspects. It also entails an exchange – between its producers and its consumers.

Focusing on these three relational features – which offer a particular way of grasping urban informality relations – is just an entry point. We do not pretend to offer an all-encompassing perspective but rather draw inspiration from Healey's (2012) conceptualisation of the contingent universal. We want to demonstrate the utility of including a variety of contexts and perspectives that are attentive to the local and query the universal. We incorporate discourses of diverse urban actors and the voices of those who participate in creating these urban spaces. The point is to steer clear of conventions and all-encompassing assumptions.

Infrastructure, exchange and image: the structure of the book

At the start of this piece, we highlighted how previous scholarship identified the pitfalls of a narrow approach to studying the built environment – in particular, the potential for epistemic injustice, the aestheticisation of poverty, and colonial interpretations of 'rationality'. Acknowledging that the physicality of the built environment cannot be separated from unequal social and economic relations that it creates and influences, the focus shifts to what enables urban processes to interact, and what binds phenomena together. Here three cross-cutting themes have been employed to triangulate the social relations that constitute and are given rise to by the built environment: infrastructure, exchange and image. The themes emerged during a workshop involving the contributors at UCL in 2016. They serve both as organising categories and threads that bind the pieces together.

The 13 chapters of this volume interrogate the relational aspects of infrastructure, exchange and image to seek new understandings of urban relationships and urban informality. We believe that the relational aspects of infrastructure, exchange and image can provide a lens to isolate and analyse these relationships and contribute to understanding urban informality in a plural and intersectional way.

Firstly, the physical manifestations of infrastructure embody specific social ties and often reflect the global aspirations of the urban middle classes (Chattopadhyay). The appropriation of these physical infrastructures for unintended purposes creates new landscapes and disrupts encroached social relations – privileging previously invisible actors and infrastructures composed of feelings, social relationships, culture and exchanges (Simone 2008; Chattopadhyay 2012). Secondly, informal exchanges are conceived as paramount in urban space production and provisioning the basis for urban life. Physical spaces become durable settings and platforms for informal exchange in more or less obvious ways. In addition to the process of coming into being through negotiation, invention, creation and exchange, it is mainly the aesthetic, the morphology and the materiality of these spaces that makes them conventionally understood as formal or informal, which brings us to the third theme, image. Finally, the visual appearance of certain kinds of urban informality, such as informal settlements or street vending, violate common visions of the modern city (see Chattopadhyay, p. 19 and Dovey, p. 41 in this volume). With the nation as an imagined community often coalescing around urban imagery, aesthetic judgements operate within a field of power composed around 'symbolic capital'. Studying the morphogenesis and the material and visual characteristics of urban informality presents a rich and relatively unexplored line of inquiry.

The three initial chapters of this book by Swati Chattopadhyay, Fran Tonkiss and Kim Dovey shed light on multiple readings of infrastructure, exchange and image. The following eight chapters speak to these three themes in diverse and intertwined ways, contextualising the book's ideas and operationalising them at different scales and with different perspectives. The final chapter provides some thoughts on the new perspectives engendered by this approach and the way forward. The 13 chapters in unison serve as a testament to how using the built environment as an entry point and exchanges, infrastructure and image as lenses, one can create new situated understandings of urban informality rooted in the stories of varied human and non-human actors. They include the views and voices of young children, software, neoliberal business models, refugees, citizens, literature or inhabitants of the sprawl. They are located in diverse geographies, Albania, Cuba, Greece, Ghana, Taiwan, India, and many others.

Infrastructure

The cross-cutting theme of infrastructure straddles two distinct notions. One relates to the physical infrastructures, those that human and non-human actors use, appropriate, encroach and transform through informal processes. The other recognises social and optical infrastructures as the enablers of informal exchanges, growth, negotiation, encounters and dialogues. Swati Chattopadhyay reframes informality as an infrastructural condition, one that is caught between the dual problem of invisibility and hypervisibility, both representing a failure to read. She sets out how a relational focus addresses this failure to read by rethinking the commonly held notions of infrastructure, whose dominant form is synonymous with institutionalised infrastructure put in place by the State or corporations. Conventionally, infrastructure is understood as the physical infrastructure: roads, railways, telecommunication towers, airports and the like. These represent the dominant institutionalised form put in place by government authorities and large corporations. In her chapter, Chattopadhyay calls attention to the duality of these physical infrastructures. They serve as channels for economic exchange and represent 'sinews of power, lines of control' (Chattopadhyay, p. 20).

This duality is tested in Cerrada Morato's chapter about water supply infrastructure in the low-density areas in Galicia, Spain. In the Galician case, authorities favour one overarching system over the pre-existing, traditional and rooted-in-the-context infrastructures, to simplify the whole and gain remote control. Her work challenges both the assumed dichotomies urban–rural as well as the formal–informal. Through her entry point on water infrastructure, Cerrada Morato aims at countering the conventional notion of urban sprawl as fragmented, scattered and unsustainable. These adjectives are implicit in a state view that assumes a lack of density wastes resources; one that assumes that as resources are centralised, it is challenging to reach low-density areas. She dialogues with Chattopadhyay's contribution emphasising that infrastructure is not just a relationship of various technical devices, but a set of human and non-human actors, relations, beliefs and assumptions. Cerrada Morato explains how the urban-centric modernistic approaches to planning in Spain have classified the traditional regional water systems as informal, complicated, uncontrollable and unsafe. The regional government tries to exclude the local actors and systems over a simplified, centralised approach, with implications for sustainability, self-management and accessibility. However, Cerrada Morato argues that the traditional infrastructures seem to better serve the physical qualities of the low-density built environments of semi-rural territories.

Chattopadhyay's 'lines of control' contribute to a particular socio-spatial logic. They serve as a means for exchange, provision of services and expropriation. Inhabitants, private developers and other actors may repurpose and appropriate these lines and grids, giving rise to unplanned new landscapes. Isabel Gutiérrez's study in Athens is an example of how the broken state-led welfare system is appropriated into a citizen-led welfare system that uses and transforms the built environment of central Athens to provide for refugees, migrants and the urban poor. Gutiérrez speculates that these forms of practical informality might pave the way towards a potential new political and urban horizon, in which social reproduction could be placed at the centre of the social and urban life, substituting formerly institutionalised welfare infrastructures such as the government or the family unit.

Blerta Dino's chapter, which focuses on the urban development of Tirana since the end of the communist bloc, illustrates the rapid morphological, material and functional transformation that individuals and groups of private developers are bringing to the urban infrastructure. Through a spatial analysis, she illustrates how these actors transmuted the rigid architectures that embodied and reflected authoritarian power structures. The contemporary citizens are 'undoing' the former fixed infrastructure and intuitively adopting a mixed-use oriented development through built environment interventions.

Chattopadhyay (2012) suggests that wall writing, and urban festivals, are a form of optical infrastructure for subaltern populations, especially in postcolonial cities. Re-engineering the current conceptions of infrastructure, Chattopadhyay makes optical infrastructures visible in the context of informal spaces. She allows tracing connections between popular culture, subalternity and international, national and local authorities. Claire Tunnacliffe incorporates these notions of optical and social infrastructures in her chapter about the street art scene in the neighbourhood of Nima in the north of Accra. It is a study of the multifunctional use of the wall as a communication tool and site of exchange; an investigation into the use of surfaces to create space for potential new social and political forms. Drawing on Chattopadhyay and Simone's notions of optical infrastructures, Tunnacliffe finds that – viewing urban informality through the lens of the built environment – graffiti and street art reposition the power of those living within informal settlements. It mediates their image by subverting infrastructure and hence negotiates the image of themselves to the rest of the city. Informal urban activity involves the utilisation, appropriation and alternative use of urban spaces and surfaces, bypassing regulations.

For Nicola Antaki, the process of mapping Mariamma Nagar, an informal settlement in the heart of Mumbai by school children who live in the settlement represents a cataloguing of socio-spatial pedagogical characteristics, rooted in time, locality and people. A psycho-geographical reading of the landscape and built environment transforms both aspect and experience of the settlement. The physical and social infrastructure of the settlement form an integral part of the learning process. The assertion here is that the built environment of the settlement (the relations that determine its form and those that are made possible by it) can be a powerful pedagogical tool. Maps continue to be used as instruments of subjugation, creating and reproducing power hierarchies of knowledge and practice – yet informal settlements have remained notoriously resistant to mapping by outsiders, states and private entities like Google, disrupting formal infrastructural depiction. The act of self-mapping represents simultaneously an act of reclaiming and one of self-empowerment. The unique opportunity that this process allows between situated action and reflection supports Antaki's thesis that '(i)t is informality that makes learning happen.'

Kostourou and Goodship extend the idea of infrastructure to describe how the architectural literature constitutes an infrastructure of knowledge. In the section on the surge of the 'urban trend' for instance, they comment on how the emergence of the internet, an informal infrastructure of linked servers, which in its early years prompted at least in a limited sense a democratisation of information exchange, disrupted the mediation of information by the architectural press, giving rise to new conceptions and influencing new forms of architectural practice. This process of knowledge production and exchange forms an infrastructure that both enables and constrains how practitioners conceive ideas of the informal, which directly influences not just the discourse but accepted practice. They reflect on how the mainstream architectural press has, through a changing narrative, provided a language with which to describe previously unacknowledged (by architects, researchers and other urban practitioners) urban morphologies and forms of social capital, while simultaneously through this process, endangering the very infrastructures and exchanges they attempt to describe.

If 'informality presents an infrastructural condition that resists description' (Chattopadhyay, p. 19), then recognising infrastructure as simultaneously physical, human, non-human, social and optical brings attention to the relational, deepening our understanding of processes that might otherwise be illegible.

Exchange

The notion of exchange has long been at the heart of urban informality. Usually, it takes the form of monetary transactions. Fran Tonkiss highlights the potential for informality to act as an enabler and facilitator of encounters and socio-material and morphological negotiations. The notion of informality that emerges from 'exchange' is one of everyday practice. Tonkiss draws attention to how social relations structure interactions, with trust, social obligation, cultural convention, coercion and power shaping practices of exchange, making them more or less predictable, reliable and/ or binding. In her reconfiguration, law contracts and accounting can be seen as particular modes for ordering exchange, which add to a broader range of elements that structure social life. The latter are, in many cases, more effective in enforcing or ensuring compliance than the former legal mechanisms. Tonkiss identifies three ways of thinking about the informalities of exchange. The first concerns orderings of exchange by custom and convention. The second relates to how economic and social interactions are composed around material architectures. The third addresses the contingent relation between innovation and illegality.

The first of these is present in Chang's account. The processes of assembling, consuming and exchanging of foods that took place on the open ground of the Jian-Cheng Circle market illustrate the complex morphologies of exchanges. Transactions were shaped by culture and conventions, composed around materiality and infrastructure, and the innovative power of the informal. Their transactions surpassed the mere exchange of food for currency and encompassed a myriad of social, cultural and commercial ties. An exciting facet of informal markets is that they promote exchanges between residents and visitors whose lives would otherwise be unlikely to intersect – in the case of Jian-Cheng Circle, Japanese colonisers and political refugees. More broadly, there is a diversity of social classes who frequent informal markets, a diversity that is rarely replicated in formally planned spaces. Certain kinds of informality can offer opportunities to disrupt power relations through configuring the built environment.

The Galician case of Tomiño's *traídas* highlights the role of social norms, behaviours and understandings in shaping interactions and transactions (Cerrada Morato). The view of water as a common good contributes to the reluctance of residents to connect to centralised water infrastructures. The centralised infrastructures require payment, and the residents mistrust water quality as they had no role to play in the governance of the supply system.

The story of the Jian-Cheng Circle can also be viewed through the second of Tonkiss's conceptual lenses, which shifts focus to the material architectures of exchange. Chang identifies specific spatial configurations that contributed to the operational efficiency of businesses – the creation of a shared space for washing of utensils and customer parking, the concentric circles of stalls that allowed for dense occupation. Additionally, Taipei's Jian-Cheng Circle market appropriated a colonial recreational structure. As a range of evening entertainment options began to open in the neighbourhood, the market traders adapted, converting to a night market to cater for business people and tourists. This lens is of particular relevance to the notion of viewing informality through the built environment. Therefore, it is a theme in many of the chapters in this volume.

Accra's visual landscape, which is crowded with signage, advertising billboards, hand-painted signs, spontaneous graffiti, street art and commissioned murals (Tunnacliffe), can also be viewed through the second of Tonkiss's lenses. The built environment provides a canvas for a rich and textured exchange between artistic expression, a homage to tradition, the politics of identity and commercial interests. The concrete walls provide the material surfaces for various kinds of negotiation, social and economic, with, for instance, wall owners sometimes being paid for the use of their wall.

Tonkiss also talks about formal constructions that have been vacated by regular capital or abandoned by the authorities. In her chapter, Gutiérrez describes how these social interactions entail implicit social commitments that need an embodied experience of daily encounters. Space and time and the material resources available in Athens's built environment become agents that elicit specific agreements and obligations. Tonkiss, in her chapter, refers to Gutiérrez's section on the 'Movement of the Squares' – the protests in public spaces in several European cities against an elite politics of austerity in the wake of the post-2008 financial crisis. These protests were extended into many local practices of temporary occupation, improvised use and tactical re-use in creating sites for economic and social provision.

The urban food production sites in Susan Fitzgerald's chapter are seen as adaptable and accessible land resources for supporting food security and social and economic networks. This is despite cultivators often lacking security of tenure, and the sites themselves being abandoned spaces lying between overcrowded and collapsing buildings and lacking civic amenities. Fitzgerald understands these practices as the 'resourcefulness of everyday invention' that contributes to the modification and reinvention of the city. In the absence of top-down order, the phenomenon of *inventar* can be seen to flow and expand through space, fuelled by negotiation. The collapse of buildings, for instance, may provide opportunities for ventilation, space, light and construction materials. This references the third of Tonkiss's lenses, the contingent relationship between illegality and innovation.

Tonkiss draws a parallel between the contrasting dynamic adaptability and stubborn permanence of informal settlements and the fluid resilience of informal economic activity. She highlights how 'just as practices of informal urban settlement range from the highly provisional to the stubbornly permanent, so do spatial infrastructures of informal exchange display a similar temporal contingency.' (Tonkiss, this volume, p. 37)

Image

The cross-cutting theme of image, introduced by Kim Dovey, reflects on the multi-dimensional and multi-scalar nature of aesthetics, visibility, appearance, readability and opacity of urban informality and the built environment. In Dovey's view, the twin aspects of urban informality morphology and meaning cannot be separated. The materiality, morphology and processes of making informality and the cultural and disciplinary background of those who perceive and study it impact the different positions towards informality, its study and the way people and institutions deal with it. Yet a view of aesthetics as a potential tool both used by the powerful and the vulnerable is relevant for the readability of urban informality.

Kostourou and Goodship take the reader from an interrogation of the informal practices to a consideration of the practice of researching informality within the field of architectural studies. It prompts a reflection on how scholars and practitioners have read informality and the forces that shaped these readings. They trace the multiple readings of informality presented in the mainstream architectural press, from the depiction of *barriadas* in Lima in *Architectural Design* (1963) which can be thought of as sparking the first interest in self-build to the peak of references to informality between 1996 and 2010, which they label the urban trend, and beyond. The peaking of interest coincided with a growing awareness of the failures of neoliberal policies that defined the latter two decades of the twentieth century. The chapter documents how descriptions of informal settlements shifted focus from the lack of amenities and poor living conditions to celebrating the informal as 'powerful, inspiring and brutal', and finally to an acknowledgement that informality far from being an exotic phenomenon represents an inherent characteristic of cities.

Particularly problematic to Dovey are those interventions and discourses that romanticise the looks of informally and self-built housing strategies, making opaque the underlying logics, power dynamics and social problems. Elsewhere Dovey and King (2011) refer to the case of Gondolyuin Yogyakarta, Indonesia, to suggest that aesthetic fixation may distract from the goal of making material improvements to the lives of residents. This issue is highlighted in the eventual destruction of Jian-Cheng Circle's night market, where an inorganic imposed architectural vision did not engage with and support the intricate interplay of social relations that attracted customers and allowed businesses to function and flourish (Chang). While as Dovey points out, states have traditionally been embarrassed by images of informality, the growth of so-called 'slum tourism' most notably in the *favelas* of Rio and the *bastis* of Mumbai, creates a complex two-way encounter, highlighting again the role of non-state actors in our changing notions and perceptions of informality.

Fitzgerald's piece on urban agriculture in Havana, Cuba, explores how informality, if viewed from 'above', creates an opaque veil that prevents outsiders from forming a coherent reading of an infrastructure of urban agriculture sites. She suggests that to understand urban informality better the viewer needs to observe the everyday rhythms on the ground, drawing and grasping the changes in morphology and materiality. Fitzgerald's view relates to Dovey's questions about the hidden and the visible and Chattopadhyay's understanding of subaltern infrastructures.

Kim Dovey reflects on 'image' from the perspectives of place, identity and urban character of informal settlements. He focuses on the methodologies of contextual mapping and visual representations to explore power imbalances and transfer knowledge. 'A common view is that this is a superficial approach to the problem – that to focus on image or aesthetics is to ignore the poverty that produces slums or the upgrading challenge that remains. On the contrary, it seems to me that such issues may hold crucial understandings for why upgrading efforts are so often unsuccessful.'(Dovey, p. 44)

Antaki's conception of informality as pedagogy invokes both spatiality and practice. The map-making process includes the fluidity of exploratory mapping undertaken by the students and the skilful crafting of the tapestry by artisans. The final map was a material representation of the settlement and an act of correspondence, embodying the assembled nature of the settlement, and the 'rhizomatic and creative structures of informality in spatial, behavioural but also pedagogical ways'. She draws attention to the situation of Mariamma Nagar, centrally located yet set apart, until recently inaccessible to vehicular traffic, its name indicating a further alienation through the violence of caste hierarchies, physically, visually, materially and morphologically distinct from the surrounding city, yet integrated into the global supply chain and exposed to neoliberal forces.

Tunnacliffe questions current urbanism paradigms, positioning graffiti and street art as a means for the observer to reimagine and relearn the city, with the built environment serving as a canvas, which is more than merely surface, being bound up in social relations. Dovey suggests that a view of aesthetics as a potential means to highlight or opaque underlying issues both by the powerful and the vulnerable must occur if informality's readability is at stake. Tunnacliffe argues that graffiti and street art reposition the power of those living within these settlements to mediate their image by subverting infrastructure and, in turn, negotiating their image to the rest of the city more broadly.

Dino's work departs from conventional understandings of informal urban developments, usually seen as large and poor encroachments onto the formal city in impoverished former colonies. Dino's look at the urban acupuncture interventions in Tirana is telling about the relevance of aesthetics and the need to move on from solely state-centric approaches. Her detailed, micro-scale spatial syntax analysis reveals the complexity, the variety of layers and the multiple actors involved in the urban transformation of Tirana through informal processes. Dino's work highlights the importance of locality, the micro-scale, and the focus on the built environment's morphology, aesthetics and materiality when studying informality processes. The decomposition of the original block through self-build, appropriation, repurposing of existing structures and the generation of new linkages and modes of social and economic exchange resonate with morphogenesis as discussed by Dovey and spatial transactions as expressed by Tonkiss.

The work of Fitzgerald, Antaki and Cerrada Morato lends heft to Dovey's arguments about how mass media, governments and international institutions portray the informal. They support a need to look at the image of the urban areas, their materiality, their aesthetics, their morphogenesis from within. The chapters of Chang, Dino, Gutiérrez and Tunnacliffe show how the place identity of informal urbanism impacts could inform upgrading, demolition and reform of informal areas. All these examples help push our argument forward towards including the voices of those who make and create urban informality. They highlight the need for decolonisation, contextualisation and seeing urban informality through the lens of the built environment.

Urban informality as a relational process

The need to make more legible and transparent, to contextualise urban informality, passes through the need to decolonise the cycles of knowledge creation, to decolonise the field of urban studies and urban informality. Dovey argues that the difficult readability and opacity of informal practices complicate its definition. This difficulty, in our view, is the result of having a state-centric view; as Chattopadhyay suggests, they are the result of seeing not like, but through, the state; of a need for generalisation and a reliance on external views to understand a context.

In sum, this book explores the relationship between an always already politicised built environment and urban informality. Through the contributions, we argue that foregrounding the built environment and decentring the state raises fundamental questions of positionality. Through different positionalities that emerge, we understand different relations and hear different voices, freighted with all their inequalities. From foregrounding the built environment, we conclude with foregrounding questions of positionality and identify new ways to tackle urban injustices.

References

Banks, N., Lombard, M. and Mitlin, D. 2020. 'Urban informality as a site of critical analysis', *Journal of Development Studies*, 56 (2): 223–38. https://doi.org/10.1080/00220388.2019.1577384.
Boudreau, J.A. and Davis, D.E. 2017. 'Introduction: a processual approach to informalization', *Current Sociology*, 65 (2): 151–66. https://doi.org/10.1177/0011392116657286.
Caldeira, T.P.R. 2016. 'Peripheral urbanization: transversal logics, and politics in cities of the Global South', *Society and Space*, 35 (1): 3–20.
Chattopadhyay, S. 2012. 'Conclusion: infrastructure'. In *Unlearning the City: Infrastructure in a new optical field*. Minneapolis: University of Minnesota Press, 243–52.
Dovey, K. and King, R. 2011. 'Forms of informality: morphology and visibility of informal settlements', *Built Environment*, 37 (1): 11–29.
Ghertner, D.A. 2015. *Rule by Aesthetics: World-class city making in Delhi*. New York: Oxford University Press.
Healey, P. (2012) 'The universal and the contingent: some reflections on the transnational flow of planning ideas and practices', *Planning Theory*, 11 (2): 188–207. https://doi.org/10.1177/1473095211419333.
Marx, C. and Kelling, E. 2019. 'Knowing urban informalities', *Urban Studies*, 56 (3): 494–509. https://doi.org/10.1177/0042098018770848.
Roy, A. 2005. 'Urban informality: toward an epistemology of planning', *Journal of the American Planning Association*, 71 (2): 147–58.
Roy, A. 2009. 'Why India cannot plan its cities: informality, insurgence and the idiom of urbanization', *Planning Theory*, 8 (1): 76–87. https://doi.org/10.1177/1473095208099299.
Roy, A. and AlSayyad, N. 2004. *Urban Informality: Transnational perspectives from the Middle East, Latin America, and South Asia*. Oxford: Lexington Books.
Schindler, S. 2017. 'Beyond a state-centric approach to urban informality: interactions between Delhi's middle class and the informal service sector', *Current Sociology*, 65 (2): 248–59. https://doi.org/10.1177/0011392116657296.
Settle, A.C. 2018. 'The informal economy as a site of liquidity: Pakistan's land market', *Development and Change*, 49 (5): 1291–1313. https://doi.org/10.1111/dech.12425.
Simone, A. 2003. 'Reaching the larger world: new forms of social collaboration in Pikine, Senegal', *Africa: Journal of the International African Institute*, 73 (2): 226–50. https://doi.org/10.3366/afr.2003.73.2.226.
Simone, A. 2008. 'People as infrastructure: intersecting fragments in Johannesburg'. In Nuttal, S. and Mbembe, A. (eds.), *Johannesburg: The elusive metropolis*. Durham, NC: Duke University Press, 68–90.
Sindzingre, A. 2004. 'The relevance of the concepts of formality and informality'. In *Unlocking Human Potential: Linking the informal and formal sectors 17–18 September*. Helsinki: EGDI-WIDERr, 2–29.
Yiftachel, O. 2009. 'Theoretical notes on "gray cities": the coming of urban apartheid', *Plan Theory* 8 (1): 88–100. https://doi.org/10.1177/1473095208099300.

2
Informality and infrastructure
Swati Chattopadhyay

Reading informality

The discourse on informality is seemingly caught between the dual problems of hypervisibility and illegibility, of endurance and impermanence. Indexed by images of sprawling urban slums, informality presents an infrastructural condition that resists description. Scholars and policy makers take recourse to satellite views of slums and squatter settlements, hoping to read in their aggregate forms the lineaments of a problem, to visualise what is presumably 'hidden' from the state and the organised sector. But it also evinces an inability to comprehend informality on the ground. Often such aerial views show a sharp contrast between the straggling informal settlement and the capital-intensive high-rise formal urbanscape, reiterating the difference and aberration of informality. The formality of the high-rise urbanscape is used as a frame for understanding the informal.

Such images simulate the kind of visual distancing that Michel de Certeau cited in his observation of Manhattan from the 110th floor of the World Trade Center. The distance from the object of contemplation presents the viewer with a safe analytic space – 'it transforms the bewitching world by which one was "possessed" into a text that lies before one's eyes' (De Certeau 1984: 92). This view of landscape as text constructs parameters that are so removed from the everyday workings in these landscapes that they articulate problems that do not need to be solved. In the process it shrouds the object of investigation – the infrastructural condition – in another layer of opacity. To move beyond this discursive impasse we need to rethink the very idea of infrastructure and our strategies for 'reading' landscapes.

By infrastructure we commonly mean the physical channels of connecting one space with another, enabling the passage of people and goods; we think of roads, railways, canals, airports, gas, water, electricity, sewers, telecommunication lines and digital networks. In its dominant form, infrastructure is synonymous with the institutionalised form of modern infrastructure. In much of the world this version of institutionalised infrastructure – put in place by state or municipal authorities or corporate powers – has come to be understood as an unquestioned good. On the one hand, the term infrastructure has become a catch-all for channeling various forms of subsidies, tax-breaks and land rights to large corporate developers. On the other, the demand for big data and the parallel investment in feeding consumer goods to the middle classes and to those that have slid beyond middle-class hegemony has unleashed a peculiar spatial logic that must confront, and even proliferate, a range of socio-structural inequities on a daily basis. The production of such inequities is fuelled by a desire for international translatability: to become legible in a global grid of economic exchange and to skip scale and territorial limits (Sassen 2007).

The importance of infrastructure to modern nation states resides in the recognition that these systems are not merely channels of economic exchange, but they are by the same token sinews of power, lines of control. They do not merely form the grids that provide urban centres with their physical shape, they are also those links that connect the rural and the urban, they are the means of both exchange and expropriation. Urban forms are not merely products of infrastructural norms, but the physical form of the infrastructure is based on certain understanding and modelling of time and space. These models and the formal vocabulary they produce deserve careful analysis. When infrastructure is appropriated for purposes it was not intended to support, we find a transformation in this formal vocabulary that produces new landscapes. The most ubiquitous type of urban infrastructural transformation is the unauthorised adoption of sidewalks, streets and public space for setting up shops that we see in much of the Global South, a phenomenon that Asef Bayat has described as the 'quiet encroachment of the ordinary' (Bayat 1997: 53–72).

In his book on media and urban infrastructure in Nigeria, Brian Larkin defines infrastructure as the 'technical systems of transport, telecommunications, urban planning, energy, and water that create the skeleton of urban life' and notes that to a large extent these systems dictate the kinds of cultural, religious, social life that are made possible

(Larkin 2008: 5). In Larkin's analysis, the physical infrastructure comes first, and cultural forms are produced either in consonance or dissonance with this infrastructure. In contrast, AbdouMaliq Simone, in his analysis of African cities, has shifted the idea of physical infrastructure to 'people as infrastructure', hoping to understand how city residents make do despite inadequate physical infrastructure (Simone 2008: 71). This shift facilitates rethinking how agency is constituted in the process of building socio-spatial relations, without assuming the priority of physical infrastructure.

If we take infrastructure in its broad definition as the material channels that allow for 'exchange over space' we make it possible to describe not merely how modern infrastructures are appropriated and cannibalised to generate linkages and exchanges that were not intended, we also pry open a vista of other kinds and forms of infrastructure that have a different spatial and temporal imperative. In *Unlearning the City: Infrastructure in a new optical field* (Chattopadhyay 2012), I looked at forms of urban popular culture such as political wall-writing, vehicular art, religious festivals and street cricket to explore the modes through which the existing infrastructure of streets, public spaces and institutions are appropriated and transformed to enable a new set of urban practices by those who find themselves marginalised in the city. Although much of what I was studying constituted the informal, these phenomena were structurally related to the formal economy, party politics and the state. One key aspect of my investigation was tracing the connections between popular culture, subalternity and the state. However, I did not take informality as my key analytic. This is because the notion of informality assumes the form and organisation of the state-supported formal economy as *a priori*. My investigation of infrastructure was going against this train of thought.

Let me present my argument about informality and infrastructure as a series of inferences:

1. Informality is a way of seeing. It only exists in the eyes of those who assume the vantage of the formal economy and the modern state. So, when we see informality, we are seeing it through the eyes of the State – and not from the point of view of those who inhabit the informal. It does not make informality fictitious or spurious but invites reading the statist views as representations.
2. To put it in anthropological terms, much of the scholarship on informality, even when deeply sympathetic, is an etic view. What makes those who partake in the informal economy 'outsiders' is unilaterally dictated by the 'insiders' (see, for example, Marjit and Sarkar 2011).

3. Informality is not outside the State. It is structural to the modern State. And it does not matter whether 90 per cent of the workforce is deemed formal (USA) or 90 per cent is deemed informal (India). Formality and informality are co-constitutive.
4. Informality as a structural condition appears in different fields of investigation as multiple connotations and referents. And here for the sake of analytic clarity we could distinguish among the different aspects of political economy: (a) state and labour, (b) infrastructure and housing, and (c) everyday political relations.

   a   Those dealing with labour are concerned with the State's oversight and regulatory authority over production. The concept of informality was formulated in this domain of study and remains the most prevalent entrée to the problem (Hart 1973: 61–89). The connotations signal the inability of the State to govern and support the labour market. The negative connotations refer to authority (beyond state control, unauthorised); law (extra-legal, quasi-legal, illegal); labour form (non-contractual, ease of entry, low paying); security (risky, unprotected, lacking benefits). In contrast, potentiality (entrepreneurial, solution driven, creative) signals a positive connotation, while scale (micro-operations, micro-credit) carries both positive and negative connotations.

   b   In terms of infrastructure and housing, informality is invoked as the hypervisibility of dwelling practices in slums and squatter settlements. Here the living conditions of workers and marginalised populations are primarily seen in terms of precarity and a series of inadequacies: access to resources (lack of services); body (unhealthy, insanitary); order (danger, threat); futurity (unsustainable); strength (fragile, weak). If some commentators read resilience and creativity in informal housing, they are exceptions to the rule (Neuwirth 2005).

   c   The referents that attempt to describe the discrepancy in power relations, between classes, castes, religious and ethnic groups as a form of disenfranchisement are locational terms (peripheral, marginal); or are cast in terms of visibility (shadow, underground, hidden) and legibility (chaotic, formless). The hypervisibility mentioned above is registered as a form of opacity or illegibility – unyielding to reading, analysis and intervention.

5. The multiple references to invisibility, peripherality and illegibility render informality as subalternity, that is, a phenomenon beyond representation. This is to say there is no avenue to access informality without articulating a method of how one would 'read', that is recognise, a phenomenon that refuses representation.

We do not have any privileged access to the life worlds of the marginalised. In my investigation of popular culture and the cultural production of marginalised populations, I had to articulate a method for reading urban informality as subalternity. This was irrespective of the fact of whether the evidence I was examining had been produced by the State, or through my ethnographic work. The evidence does not come as self-articulatory, transparent facts to be plugged into a narrative. Interspersing an analysis with the utterances of the marginalised does not solve the problem; those utterances need to be *read* – the audible citations of the marginalised cannot serve as unmediated, therefore transparent, evidence of things as they are.

Now, if we accept the proposition that informality is subalternity, how do we understand the life worlds of marginalised populations who have been relegated to the informal without reifying the point of view of the state? Rather than assuming we are able to describe the life worlds of the marginalised, I attempt to understand how they have been constituted as belonging to the world of informality, that is, the process through which the domains of formal and informal have been constructed.

In the balance of the essay, I will focus on one of the above inferences, that informality and formality are co-constitutive. I shall do so by shifting our attention from the urban to the rural and by recourse to a set of historical events in colonial India that came to be called the Santal Rebellion of 1855–6.[1] My interest in the Santal Rebellion as a case study on infrastructure and informality resides in the evidence of the colonial archive that emphasised the importance of infrastructure as a defining condition of the rebellion. The voices and actions of the rebellious Santals here appeared in the form of scripts of interrogation – mediated by Indian translators and colonial authorities – as they were registered in colonial documents before, during and after the insurrection.

Notes on the Santal Rebellion

Between 1780 and 1040 the Santals, a peripatetic people, had been herded into an area called Damin-i-koh, at the borders of present-day West Bengal and Jharkhand. The objective was to use Santal labour for clearing the jungles for cultivation. In 1832–3, the *damin*, an area of approximately 1,366 square miles, was constructed as a bounded space (Datta 1939). This was intended to control the interaction of the Santals with the surrounding indigenous society.

Prathama Banerjee points out that, initially marked by natural features and pillars, the *damin* boundary was strengthened and made absolute by police stations at small intervals: 'it was also argued that the boundary must be made precisely mathematical, and in straight lines wherever possible. Natural features, the government argued, tended to be tampered by the "primitives" and by nature itself' (Banerjee 2006: 127). So, in order to extract labour from the Santals 'the *damin* became a representational space, rather than simply land' (Banerjee 2006: 127). The Santals' bounded space meant they could no longer avoid the colonial state; Santal villages as mobile assemblies became spatially fixed, thus creating new boundary disputes that required the mediation of the state. The *damin* was criss-crossed with roads built by the State in an effort to chase after the Santals who wanted to flee from this bondage. The British administrator in charge of the *damin* made Santals experiment with new cash crops and supervised the various stages of crop production. Forced to extend cultivation beyond the fertile stretch, their crops became vulnerable to natural disasters and this made them completely dependent on the discretionary rights of the colonial state to forego revenue claims (Banerjee 2006: 128).

Having divorced Santal society from freely exchanging goods with outsiders, the colonial state instituted marketplaces for the sale of goods from the outside world, including English long cloth, caps and jackets. Exchanging goods for money – understood to be 'congealed power over the future' – was expected to civilise the Santals who refused to produce a surplus of everything (Banerjee 2006: 132). All transactions with other groups were mediated in and through the colonial marketplace, other locations of trade being prohibited in the *damin*. The only formal economic node became the colonial marketplace and acts of exchange 'became discrete moments of universal time, which the Santals could only participate in, by exiting their "normal" everyday temporality' (Banerjee 2006: 130).

The Santal Rebellion constituted a wholesale challenge to the codes that defined the space and time of the *damin* constructed by colonial authorities. The spatial mode through which the Santals articulated their claims stands out as the key problem of the insurrection in the colonial archive. If we view the records of the colonial administrators with spatiality in mind, we notice the formidable difficulty that the colonial administrators encountered in comprehending the rebellion: the rapid movement of the rebels, their capacity to cover extensive territory, their large gatherings, method of communication and territorial claims took the authorities by surprise.[2]

This is how the rebellion entered the colonial archive. On one fine day, the British administrators and the Bengali landlords and moneylenders suddenly recognised with alarm that the peace-loving, simple Santals had rebelled against colonial authority. The Officiating Magistrate of Bhagalpur hastily penned a note to William Grey, the secretary to the Bengal government in Calcutta in the failing light of 9 July 1855:

My dear Grey,

I write a line in a great hurry to let you know that the Santals of this district [...] have risen to 'take possession of the country'. [...] I have sent for Troops to Bhagaulpore and Murshidabad. [...] I am afraid, however, that on hearing of the arrival of the Troops they may retreat under the hills through Beerbhoom and Bancoorah so to get home. And as they are in considerable force the Police of these districts will not be able to stop them, so I write to ask you if you think fit to get order passed for the sending of Troops per rail as far as they can go to the roads by which the Santals will be most likely to return home. [...] The natives are in a great state of consternation, the railway people are arming and barricading themselves in various places – the Dak is just going so I am in a great hurry.

Yours truly

Mr. R.H. Richardson[3]

Thus, the rebellion was registered as the intention of the Santals to 'take possession of the country'. The sites of colonial authority that marked the landscape: the bungalow, the court, the police station, the railways and the post office, the residences and *cutcherries* (offices) of *zamindars* (landlords) and the marketplace were picked out by Santals as specific targets of insurgency.[4] They disrupted the colonial communication system by destroying the infrastructure of colonial governance – the railways and the post, cutting off the administration in the Damin-i-koh from adjacent jurisdictions and from the presidency town of Calcutta.[5]

The administrators worried that the insurrection would spread to adjacent communities, and that the army/police had no military advantages when fighting the Santals in the forest – their 'native habitat'; the Santals, proficient hunters, knew paths and trails that were unrecognisable to colonial authorities. William Grey reminded Richardson that he needed to provide specific and accurate details of time and space – 'produce maps' he demanded![6]

Switching codes

The colonial archive of the rebellion is marked by a profound problem of legibility. All the signs, marks, practices of the Santals during the rebellion appeared illegible to the colonial state. In contrast, the Santals during the short duration of the rebellion successfully read the spatial network of the state that brought together the power of the government, moneylender and landlord. Based on this reading they took control of the sign-systems that marked the colonial landscape (without access to paper maps), while the colonial state appeared hobbled by its own governing practices and mode of envisioning the landscape. The colonial state could only apprehend the rebellion in terms of its own infrastructure, and the conception of space and representational practices congruent with such infrastructure, practices that were based on a desire for exactitude, certainty, permanence, of objects carrying fixed meaning, and discrete bounded events that could be placed in a narrative of cause and effect.

Most disturbing to authorities was not the pitched battles that the Santals fought with the colonial troops – which after some initial setbacks the colonial armed forces won – but when the Santals were seemingly going about their everyday business. Every gathering, every glance was suspicious; the bows, arrows and axes the Santals carried with them normally had taken on an uncertain valence. When the Santals went about their everyday business of harvesting, mending buildings, hunting and celebrating prior to the insurrection, none of these actions had appeared particularly significant, let alone hostile, to the administrators. These objects and practices of everyday life had remained invisible, so to speak. This everyday was the realm of the informal.

During the rebellion, the colonial authorities suddenly confronted the spectacularism of the Santals' everyday: they were gathering in large numbers, digging tanks and earthworks, building large storehouses, stages and pavilions to conduct the Durga Puja.[7] The problem was that, even if many of these activities were symbolically defiant, these could not be sorted out of the normalcy of everyday life to be described as crime. Arrests were futile, because no colonial court could punish them; there was scarcely any evidence of overturning authority in the normal acts of carrying axes or celebrating a Brahmanical ritual. The everyday entered the colonial archive only when it had exceeded its norms and had taken a particular visible form through magnification of scale.

The Santals self-consciously mimicked the formal conventions of the colonial army in organising their own forces, and chose to partake in high-caste rituals, which they did not ordinarily.[8] The Santals were switching cultural codes to assert the form and formality that would be recognisable to colonial authorities, and in that moment of switching codes their everyday appeared visible. They were speaking in the code of their opponents. They wanted the colonial state to read these acts as insurrectional.

The impossibility of apprehending the Santals in the situation of the 'everyday', resulted in the administrators demanding martial law in the Santal districts, so what passed as 'normality' could be viewed as 'criminality', with no justifications required in a civil court of law.[9] The normality of the informal was to be read as criminality in the formal. But the need for martial law was also articulated as the necessity of dealing with the Santal as a figure of excessive violence that could erupt without notice. This in turn became the rationale for summary executions and burning of Santal villages as a strategy for quelling the rebellion (Datta 1939: 47).[10]

Insurgency as infrastructure

The paradox of space it would seem rests on two contrasting claims: that space is defined by those in power. The stage is set, so to speak, on the peripheries of which marginal groups act out their lives and resistance, and the examples that suggest that intentions of authorities (politicians, architects, planners, police) are but one story of a larger spatial history. At insurrectionary moments, marginal groups exceed their spatial limitations, alter the spatial codes to construct other modes of conceptualising and navigating territory. From what we see as the contours of the rebellion in the colonial archives, we could also surmise that Santals were using insurrectionary tactics to create an infrastructure: to build material channels that would allow exchange over space.

The Santals had for a long time complained to colonial authorities about the unjust dealings of the moneylenders with them, but the state had failed to recognise these as worthy complaints. The Santal term for outsider – *diku* – necessarily also denoted moneylenders (Banerjee 2006: 136). Nothing was done to prevent the moneylenders from extorting ruinous interests, extracting unpaid labour from the Santals, or to protect them from rack-renting. When their petitions failed, the Santals chose to use insurrection as a means of communication.

They not only resorted to symbols of overturning authority, they spatially reconfigured, during the duration of the rebellion, the *damin* and the adjacent countryside. A few examples will suffice. The *dahra* (missive) of *sal* branches sent from village to village and to their enemies as a signal of impending attack was powerfully enigmatic, and struck fear in the ranks of the moneylenders and colonial authorities.[11] Their tactics of dispersal in small groups and gathering in large numbers 'parties of 10,000 men each for the purpose of plundering' at the sounding of the drums, were noted with unaccustomed awe by colonial officers.[12] In terms of territory, they laid claim to lands far beyond the bounds of the *damin*, demanding that the colonial authorities and the landlords and moneylenders retreat beyond the Ganges river.[13] In targeting the bungalows of civil and rail personnel, police stations, marketplaces, residences and offices of moneylenders, they sought to change the geography of colonial occupation.

The Santals enjoyed a remarkable success in inspiring collaboration among a broad swath of low-caste groups beyond their tribal community – 'a large number of non-Santals such as *gowalas* (milkmen), *telis* (oilmen), *lohars* (blacksmiths), and *bhunyas* (*bhuiyas*)' (Datta 1939: 53). The colonial authorities had a difficult time comprehending the participation of non-Santals in the rebellion, and worried about 'connivance' and 'strong sympathy' between Santal prisoners and the Indian jail staff, as prisoners escaped because of the latter's 'carelessness'.[14] Thus the insurgents seemed to have built a new social, spatial and political infrastructure on the wreck of the infrastructure of colonial governance. This elicited further demand to strengthen the very infrastructure that was under attack: colonial officers and European railway staff in the district asked to reinforce the 'gaps' between the military and civil stations, and urged that the railways and telegraph be extended to military stations to the north without further delay.[15]

Coda: beyond regulation

After the rebellion had been quelled, the entire *damin* was reorganised, spatially and administratively, to form a separate district, the Santal Parganas. Twenty years after the rebellion, William Hunter re-introduced the region in his *Statistical Account of Bengal* as a space of protection for the Santals:

> The Rajmahal hills have afforded a retreat to two primitive races – the Paharias and the Santals. In 1832 the tract was marked off by a ring fence of pillars within which Hindus were not allowed to pass. Since that date the protection here afforded to the aboriginal races has led to an extraordinary immigration of Santals. […] With a view to the simple requirements of such tribes, the Santal Parganas have been constituted as a Non-Regulation District, the only one in the province of Bengal-Proper (Hunter 1877: 6).

A Non-Regulation District implied that civil and criminal procedures that governed the rest of the region were held in abeyance in this enclave. Laws and regulations that were applicable to the rest of Bengal were 'found to be unsuited to so uncivilized a race'. Authority over this Non-Regulation District was vested in a deputy commissioner with four assistants, 'all vested with Civil as well as Criminal jurisdiction' (Hunter 1877: 6). The justification suggested that the complex procedural formality of colonial English law was to be abandoned in favour of a more 'informal' paternalistic relation between the district Commissioner and the tribal Santals. The solution then was not to strengthen the formal infrastructure of the colonial judiciary for the benefit of the Santals to enable them to access this system, but to remove them farther from it. The Santal Parganas as a space of exception constituted one more of a series of spatial dislocation for the Santals.

In the decades after the rebellion, colonial authorities resorted to representing the 'Country of the Santals' in picturesque terms and presented the now 'peaceful' Santals as a people in need of protective custody, ignoring the fact that there had been at least three other insurrections in the intervening 20 years. Hunter did not mention these uprisings, confining his comments to the positive retreat of the Santals into primitiveness. Throughout the latter half of the nineteenth century, the Santal Parganas became the prime catchment area for supplying coolie labour to the tea plantations in the north east. It is not a coincidence that the tea plantations in the western Duars and Darjeeling were Non-Regulation Tracts as well, an important condition that allowed the planters to regulate, without the intervention of the judiciary, the mobility and working conditions of the labourers (Bhattacharya 2012: 55–7). That history of collusion between planters, colonial administrators and missionaries that created wretched living conditions for the Santals is well documented.

The power dynamics between the British colonial state and the Santal tribal population was highly asymmetrical, much more so than any condition of urban informality we would encounter now. The Santals were able to construct an insurrectionary infrastructure despite this asymmetry of power. They had recourse to a plethora of social practices that were illegible to the state. The movement between formal and informal that the rebellion entailed, and the historical representations it produced, however, remain useful for understanding how informality is constituted in discourse and practice: informality is not outside the state, it is not outside capital. It is co-constituted by the state and capital.

Notes

1 Prathama Banerjee has made a brilliant argument about the colonial authorities' and the Bengali nationalists' efforts to circumscribe the Santal Rebellion as an event by setting it in a given year – 1855 – and incorporating it within a chronological argument (Banerjee 2006, 160–4).
2 Banerjee's work, as the title of her book suggests, is primarily concerned with the difficulty of constructing the Santal Rebellion as a temporally bound event (Banerjee 2006).
3 Judicial proceedings, memo from Richardson to Grey, 19 July 1855. Richardson first received news of disturbances on 4 July (Ray 1983).
4 See Ranajit Guha's discussion of Santals targeting spatial symbols of colonial authority such as the bungalow (Guha 1983, 68–9).
5 Judicial proceedings, memo from C.F. Brown to W. Grey. 19 July 1855. Extract from the diary of H. Richardson, 20 September 1855, sent to W. Grey (Ray 1983).
6 Judicial proceedings, memo from Grey to Richardson (Ray 1983).
7 Judicial proceedings, report from the magistrate of Beerbhoom to the commissioners of Burdwan division, 24 September 1855. Extract from the diary of H. Richardson, 20 September 1855 (Ray 1983).
8 Judicial proceedings, report from the magistrate of Beerbhoom to the commissioners of Burdwan division, 24 September 1855. Extract from the diary of H. Richardson, 20 September 1855 (Ray 1983).
9 Martial law was proclaimed on 10 November 1855.
10 See Guha's discussion on this point, and how typical it was for the colonial state to systematically burn villages in retribution (Guha 1983, 306–8).

11 Judicial proceedings, report from the magistrate of Beerbhoom to the commissioners of Burdwan division, 24 September 1855. Extract from the diary of H. Richardson, 20 September 1855. H. Richardson to Col. Burney, 21 September 1855 (Ray 1983, 49–51).
12 Letter from the commissioner of Bhagalpur to the Government of Bengal, 11 July 1855.
13 Judicial proceedings, 4 October 1855 (Ray 1983).
14 From R. Thompson, officiating magistrate, to Frances Lowth, esq., session judge of Beerbhoom, 19 December 1855 (Ray 1983).
15 Lt. Governor's minute, dated 12 September 1855 (Datta 1939, 88).

References

Banerjee, P. 2006. *Politics of Time: 'Primitives' and history writing in a colonial society.* New Delhi: Oxford University Press.

Bayat, A. 1997. 'Un-civil society: the politics of the "informal people"', *Third World Quarterly*, 18 (1): 53–72.

Bhattacharya, N. 2012. *Contagion and Enclaves: Tropical medicine in colonial India.* Liverpool: Liverpool University Press.

Chattopadhyay, S. 2012. *Unlearning the City: Infrastructure in a new optical field.* Minneapolis: University of Minnesota Press.

Datta, K. 1939. *The Santal Insurrection of 1855–57.* Calcutta: University of Calcutta.

De Certeau, M. 1984. *The Practice of Everyday Life.* Berkeley: University of California Press.

Guha, R. 1983. *Elementary Aspects of Peasant Insurgency in Colonial India.* New Delhi: Oxford University Press.

Hart, K. 1973. 'Informal income opportunities and urban employment in Ghana', *Journal of Modern African Studies*, 11 (1): 61–89.

Hunter, W. 1877. *A Statistical Account of Bengal.* London: Trubner and Co.

Larkin, B. 2008. *Signal and Noise: Media, infrastructure and urban culture in Nigeria.* Durham, NC: Duke University Press.

Marjit, S. and Sarkar, S. 2011. *The Outsiders: Economic reform and informal labour in a developing economy.* New Delhi: Oxford University Press.

Neuwirth, R. 2005. *Shadow Cities: A billion squatters, a new urban world.* New York: Routledge.

Simone, A. 2008. 'People as infrastructure: intersecting fragments in Johannesburg'. In Nuttal, S. and Mbembe, A. (eds.), *Johannesburg: The elusive metropolis.* Durham, NC: Duke University Press, 68–90.

3
Informalities of exchange
Fran Tonkiss

Urbanists and others concerned with patterns and practices of spatial development for some time have highlighted the primacy of the informal in the production of urban space and the provisioning of everyday urban lives. Much of this analysis centres on the material production of built (and part-built) forms – the provision of housing, infrastructure, commercial and common spaces through informal means, irregular rights and unorthodox plans. Another key strand of this analysis – indeed, the origin of the notion of the 'informal' in this broad area of study (see Hart 1973) – concerns a different sense of the materiality of urban life, focusing on informal economies of employment, income and exchange. Viewed through either lens, informality comes into view as a normal, rather than residual, condition of urban life. While the early impetus for work on informality came from development economics, and from studies of immigrant and ethnic enterprise, unregulated practices have long been recognised as endemic to high-income as well as low-income economies, and as a feature not simply of marginal but of 'advanced' economic sectors (for important earlier accounts, see Portes *et al.* 1989; Sassen 1994; 1997). My interest here is in the *ordering* of these diverse informal exchanges via behavioural norms and spatial forms – the ways in which conventions of conduct and designs on space give shape, in both a practical and a physical sense, to economic activities that fall outside official regulations or authorised planning regimes.

The insistently provisional character of urban settlement and economy sits in some tension with the city as a pre-eminent site of legality; composed, ordered and held together by a complex of planning, local government, environmental, corporate, contract, civil and criminal laws. And yet, so much that takes place in urban settings exceeds or evades the spatial reach of law. This is evidently true in patterns of urban settlement, but is equally the case for urban economic exchange. Just as a significant global share of urban habitation is in the informal sector, so too is a major part of urban economic life – not only in that the **informal economy** accounts for the largest employment or enterprise share in rapidly urbanising contexts in South Asia or Sub-Saharan Africa, but in the fact that a great deal of everyday economic activity *everywhere* is improvised, unregulated or autonomous. Attempts to account for the economic shares of informal trade, labour or production are an important corrective to standard measures of GDP, employment or productivity, even if we are dealing with best guesses as to their extent (see ILO 2013). Economic anthropologists and development economists have played a critical role in making informality visible in this respect, if not always quantifiable. Feminist thinkers have argued even longer for the inclusion of unpaid domestic labour and services in the accounting of economic life.

To put it plainly, informality is what most people are doing much of the time in their economic lives. A great deal of economic activity across different urban environments is spent in practices of 'informal' exchange – preparing food, childminding, sharing rides and offering lifts, working for tips, panhandling, doing favours or giving gifts, buying rounds and chipping in, cadging loans or making them, keeping an eye out, lending a hand, passing on a message – which circulate goods, care, services, money, labour and information in low-key and off-the-record ways. Some of these practices may form the basis of individual livelihoods, but many have to do with the mundane distribution of goods and services in everyday contexts where no contract is entered, no charge is levied and no enforceable terms are agreed. What low-level examples such as these might make us notice is that only a sub-set of everyday exchanges are 'formalised' in any regulatory or institutional sense. They draw attention to the ways in which routine, repetition, social norms and conventions serve to order interactions without fixing them in legal terms. Informal but well-established practices of interaction shape behaviour, reduce uncertainty and ease exchange beyond the constraints of law or contract.

In what follows, I suggest three ways for thinking about informalities of exchange. The first concerns the ordering of informal exchange by custom and convention, familial and social norms, obligations and routines, which vary in their relation to systems of contract or law. Such informal orders of exchange substitute for or circumvent legal measures, and may be more powerful in enforcing the terms of trade than the artifice of any contract or the long arm of the law. The second bears on a further sense in which informal exchanges are given *form*: in terms of how economic interactions are composed around material architectures, such that physical spaces become platforms for informal exchange in more or less visible ways and more or less durable settings. The third frame for considering informal exchange touches on the intersections of different informalities, and the contingent relation between innovation and illegality in this domain. The point of all three is to draw out the ways in which informal exchanges are given social and spatial form, and how they interact with more formal features in making up the economic.

Orders of exchange

The notion that informal exchange denotes economic practices that are somehow 'irregular' or 'unconventional' belies the kinds of order that bring shape and stability to these activities. It also tends to confine economic understanding to a limited set of institutions and interactions, framed by standard conceptions of state and market forms. In a more basic sense, however, the realm of the economic refers to the production and distribution of resources, goods and services to meet people's material and non-material needs and wants. While a significant part of this activity takes place in formal markets or via organised state provision, a greater share is taken by 'informal' or less formal means – through non-monetised or unregulated markets, within household economies, via self-help and mutual aid and in forms of socialised provision that go beyond the remit of the state. Such an anthropological understanding of economic action and interaction assumes that the formal economy – constituted by law, secured by contract, mediated by regular money and legible in accounting terms – represents a certain modality of economic life rather than defining its boundaries.

It follows from such an approach that economic interactions are always forms of social exchange. Some kinds of economic agency – provisioning within the family, for instance – may appear more obviously socialised than impersonal, instrumental (and, increasingly, virtual) market transactions, but this underscores the different kinds of mediation that hold economic exchanges together: from domestic ties to technical devices. Within the family context, furthermore, quite what is to be considered 'formal' and what 'informal'? Stripping away some or all of the legal, accounting and bureaucratic measures that bring certain types of order to exchange offers insights into the various other factors on which actors rely to organise, routinise and bring form to their interactions.

Relations of trust, social obligation, cultural convention, coercion and power give shape to practices of exchange in ways that render the latter fairly predictable, more or less reliable, relatively binding or effectively compulsory.

Law, contract, accounting, in this sense might be seen as particular modes for ordering exchange, but a much wider range of different elements – social norms, conventions of practice, cultural mores, interpersonal bonds, tacit rules, in-group codes or explicit threats – also work to give structure, consistency and force to socio-economic exchange, and the obligations that follow from them. These may be un-codified, unofficial and often unspoken, but this does not make such 'informal' rules of exchange unenforceable or ineffective. Indeed, it may be rather easier for individuals to act in contravention of the law (from not declaring income to non-payment of fines or leaving a restaurant without paying) than to ignore familial obligations to pass on money or provide care, or to violate group norms that require certain kinds of favours or the payment of informal taxes.

Spaces of exchange

This social architecture of informal exchange is shaped by, and in turn helps to compose, material architectures of exchange – from markets and meeting-places to street-corners and sidewalks. Informal economies are quick to colonise the blank or marginal spaces produced by more formal infrastructures of action and interaction: think of the incidental sites of exchange that appear at traffic lights and checkpoints; the cut-price (or premium) trade that takes place outside music venues or sporting arenas; the ambiguous exchanges that occur on the fringes of more regular markets, or the *ad hoc* bargaining that takes place within them; the organisation of day labour exchanges in parking-lots or lay-bys; the small-scale redistributions of cash outside subway stations or adjacent to automated bank machines. Sites of informal exchange take hold, too, in more formal architectures that have been vacated by regular capital or abandoned by the state. Isabel Gutiérrez, meanwhile, describes the 'informal infrastructures of welfare' that emerged in Athens in the wake of financial crisis and shaped an architecture of social care in utilising vacant property and activating open public spaces.

Kim Dovey has written suggestively of the spatial and physical forms taken by informal housing in different urban contexts (see, *inter alia*, Dovey and King 2011, as well as Dovey's essay in this volume). The planning and development of the formal city produces the possibilities, if not exactly the blueprint, for informal gestures of insertion, accretion and extension, always with different levels of visibility, permeability and infiltration. Dovey's primary concern is with morphologies of informal settlement, but such an argument also holds for infrastructures of informal exchange. The types of in-fill, adaptation and occupation described by Gutiérrez work within and around the architecture of the formal city, prising open spaces of commerce, care, shelter, information exchange and social support.

Such spatial continuities between the formal and the informalising city are underlined by Isabel Gutiérrez as she traces the relations between these solidary welfare initiatives in Athens and the 'Movement of the Squares' that saw protests in public spaces in a number of European cities against an elite politics of austerity in the wake of the post-2008 financial crisis. Such a case speaks not only to the spatiality but also to the temporality of the informal. Claims to public space and incursions into private space in the 2011 protests were extended into many local practices of temporary occupation, improvised use and tactical re-use in creating sites for economic and social provision. Just as practices of informal urban settlement range from the highly provisional to the stubbornly permanent, so do spatial infrastructures of informal exchange display a similar temporal contingency – from the quick-footed commerce of rugs spread on pavements to the regularity of long-established marketplaces and the embedded physicality of workplaces and manufactories.

Intersections of informality

The spatial persistence of sites of informal exchange provides a physical infrastructure for very different degrees of prosperity and precarity, for edgy entrepreneurialism and for vulnerable economic lives, for solidary exchanges and often sketchy economic practices. The intersections of different informalities, as well as interactions between the formal and informal, complicate not only the critical analysis of informal economies but the politics of informality. This gets at some of the many contradictions that beset informality as a concept and as a field of economic practice: the conditions that allow for innovation and enterprise also support exploitation and exaction of various kinds and degrees (Tonkiss 2012).

The interplay between informality and illegality – or between what Hart (1973) described in his seminal work on urban employment in Accra as 'legitimate' and 'illegitimate' informal economic opportunities – has been an enduring theme in studies of the informal sector in poor-world contexts. These themes arise in critical ways, however, in an emerging sphere of exchange and employment in high-income economies and advanced service sectors. Exchanges within such marketplaces are often stylised as being peer-to-peer, rather than between buyer and seller, and have a more than passing resemblance to the kinds of informal exchange I have argued characterise an extensive share of everyday economic activities. At the corporate end of such 'collaborative' forms of exchange, though, highly commercial (if not always profitable) enterprises such as Airbnb and Uber have a variable relation to law and regulation – and a fairly tenuous relationship with any commonly understood sense of *sharing*. While the exchange of services and of payment may be regulated, practices around employment, safety, insurance, licensing and taxation tend to be looser. The selective formality of these exchange platforms brings once more into focus the continuities and contradictions between informal and formal economic activities, as well as the place of informality in larger economies of accumulation. A platform such as Airbnb mobilises a kind of petty rentier capitalism in economies that are increasingly geared to the extraction of rents from property; while the company itself generates profit, and has raised substantial capital, on the basis of markets in property that it does not own.

There is nothing new, of course, in suggesting that informality has its uses for conventional kinds of enterprise and extended processes of accumulation. These sorts of high-end platform piracy, moreover, point up the relationship between informality and urban innovation – exploiting the gap, as Saskia Sassen (1994) once put it, 'between new developments and old regulations'. As various jurisdictions race to catch up with players such as Airbnb and Uber, they seek to stabilise categories that have allowed the latter to generate value in fudging distinctions between the formal and informal: insisting on the difference between a home and an unlicensed hotel; between a ride-share and a taxi-service; between an own-account worker and a sub-minimum-wage labourer. The intersections between formality and informality – or, it might better be put, between the more and less formal – are particularly telling sites of urban invention, but legal authorities are not always willing to handle too much innovation.

The association between economic informality and urban legality should not obscure, however, the ordinary character of much informal economic exchange. Working or trading off the books, labouring cash in hand, dealing under-the-counter or off the back of a truck – informal exchanges are imagined as largely unseen, usually un-written and often illicit if not actually illegal. The spectre of illegality dogs the understanding of informal economies, such that the latter comes to be seen as that which takes place outside or in contravention of the law, as the underside of legal economic activity: the black or grey economy of sharp deals, sweated labour, stolen goods and extorted rents. Or, alternatively, the informal economy is seen more benignly as somehow 'pre-legal' – as the self-help practices of the urban poor, existing not simply outside of but prior to legal incorporation, market regulation and other rationalities of economic development. There is something in each of these representations, of course; both black and subsistence economies take major shares of informal economic exchange in different legal and development contexts. But these versions of informality as the economic practices of the criminal, the contrarian or the poor belie the continuities between formal and informal economies, the extent of informality in rich-world and highly regulated economies, and the diverse modes through which informality is regularised even if not always legalised. The essays gathered here are concerned with the resourcefulness of urban informalities, with informal exchange as a spatial practice, and with material geographies of informality in urban environments. Working in quite different contexts – in emergent migrant economies, in urban landscapes of austerity, and in over-heated urban property markets – these contributions point us to the relational norms and spatial forms that underpin practices of informal exchange.

References

Dovey, K. and King, R. 2011. 'Forms of informality', *Built Environment*, 37 (1): 11–29.
Hart, K. 1973. 'Informal income opportunities and urban employment in Ghana', *Journal of Modern African Studies*, 11 (1): 61–89.
ILO. 2013. *Measuring Informality: A statistical manual on the informal sector and informal employment*. Geneva: International Labour Organization.
Portes, A., Castells, M. and Benton, L.A. (eds.). 1989. *The Informal Economy: Studies in advanced and less developed countries*. Baltimore: Johns Hopkins University Press.
Sassen, S. 1994. 'The informal economy: between new developments and old regulations', *Yale Law Journal*, 103 (8): 2289–304.
Sassen, S. 1997. 'Informalization in advanced market economies', *Issues in Development Discussion Paper 20*. Geneva: International Labour Organization.
Tonkiss, F. 2012. 'Informality and its discontents'. In Angélil, M. and Hehl, R. (eds.), *Informalize! Essays on the political economy of urban form*. Berlin: Ruby Press, 55–70.

4
The image of informal settlements
Kim Dovey

The following quotation from Perlman's seminal study of *favelas* in Rio de Janeiro comes as part of a longitudinal social investigation that is otherwise largely bereft of discussion on the spatiality of the *favelas* or their boundaries with the formal city.

> Perhaps the single persistent distinction between *favelas* and the rest of the city is the deeply rooted stigma that adheres to them and to those who reside in them … Even after the extensive … upgrading programs … there is little doubt as to where the *asfalto* (pavement) ends … The visual markers of each are unmistakable, whether viewed from above or on street level. (Perlman 2010: 30)

Perlman's earlier work in *The Myth of Marginality* is notable for establishing the high level of integration of the *favelas* with the formal city, the essential economic roles performed by its residents and the permanence of the informal settlements (Perlman 1976). More than 40 years later these insights are now much reinforced, yet the challenge of understanding and upgrading informal settlements remains hampered by a lack of research in two key areas. First, we know too little of how informal urbanism works in material spatial terms – the complex micro-scale morphologies, typologies and adaptive processes that produce informal settlements. Second, these morphologies construct meanings and identities within the city as places of problematic place-identity. Images of informal settlements violate middle-class visions of the modern city and signify a failure of the state to enforce law and order. These two dimensions of urban informality – morphologies and meanings – cannot be separated. The success of any upgrading strategy relies on a good understanding of informality as both a material mode of production and the ways that the imagery of the 'slum' is constructed in the urban landscape, mediated in turn by a larger assemblage of political and economic interests. My focus here will be on the second of these two dimensions – the image of informal settlements. How do different types of informal encroachment mediate visibility from and interaction with the formal city? How are place-identities of informal neighbourhoods constructed and how does that impact on the politics of eviction, displacement, tenure and upgrading? How do images of informality mediate a larger political economy of urban spectacle, place marketing and slum tourism?

The formal/informal distinction is a framework originally developed in economics for understanding the relationship of informal markets to formal economies. Informality is best defined as a mode of production that emerges beyond state control. Informal settlements are not necessarily unplanned but are characterised by self-organisation rather than formal control. Informality is often conflated with 'squatting' and 'slums', yet tenure is generally ambiguous and contested rather than strictly illegal, and many dwellings in informal settlements are not slums by the UN definition (UN-Habitat 2006: 19). Most typical are the between conditions: slums becoming incrementally upgraded, squatters slowly gaining tenure. A key distinction between the informal settlement and the slum is the material outcome of poverty while informality is best seen as a resource – a means of managing poverty. Nor is there clear distinction between formal and informal parts of the city; rather there is a double movement of informal settlements becoming formalised and formal neighbourhoods becoming informalised through infiltration (Dovey and Kamalipour 2018).

The dominant mode of informal production of architecture is incremental and can be described as room-by-room accretion – buildings are generally constructed one room (or less) at a time in a process driven by the imperatives of poverty and the slow accumulation of scarce resources. There is a very broad range of materials, room types and accretions that vary with culture, climate, density and geography. Locations of informal settlements have highly variable levels of exposure to and visibility from the formal city. They often occupy highly visible waterfronts, escarpments, railway or freeway easements and sidewalks (Dovey and King 2011). Informality also infiltrates the deeper spaces of the city where formal street façades hide informal alleys and dense informal housing. Much urban informality emerges as accretions within and upon formal buildings and infrastructure of the city. While some informal settlements are particularly exposed, many remain deeply invisible even to those who live or pass nearby. Even when visible from a distance, informal settlements are often enclaves as impenetrable to outsiders from a different social class as gated communities.

Governments can be embarrassed by images of informal settlements that signify poverty and a lack of law and order. Informal morphologies are often camouflaged within the formal city for their own protection. Invisibility can protect informal residential and livelihood practices (including crime), and the blurring enables the state to turn a blind eye. Informal settlements can disappear from the cognitive map of those who allocate resources; they generally pay no land tax and are serviced accordingly. Settlements that are exposed can be targeted for eviction, particularly if the city is host to major tourist or political events or there is an excuse for road widening or flood control. Visibility can also attract upgrading schemes but the focus on image can lead to superficial or *ad hoc* approaches.

Informal settlements generally have high levels of social capital due to a shared ethnicity, rural connections or the need for collective defence against eviction (Martin and Mathema 2006). Yet they occupy urban zones with negative symbolic capital – a stigmatised place identity that may also be linked to ethnicity. Invisibility both protects residents and enables the state to abrogate responsibility. Yet visibility puts them on the cognitive map, where they are seen as a blight upon the city and the state. Within this urban field there is considerable political capital available for politicians who can variously gain support for protecting communities from eviction or for cleaning up the city through eviction (Jenkins 2006). The *kampung* improvement programme in Indonesia has often been driven by aesthetic imperatives among others, to create an image of civic order and to win 'beautiful city' awards (Kusno 2000: 129; Guinness 2009).

The issue of visibility and image is complicated further by changes in the global context of urban development. An increase in the flexibility and mobility of capital, increasing flows of tourists and the growth of the information economy have placed new economic importance on the city image as a brand. Cities compete to attract flows of flexible capital and to establish themselves as global cities through the production of urban spectacle (Dovey 2005; Klingman 2007; McNeill 2008). The desire to create conditions attractive to footloose multinational capital leads to increasingly entrepreneurial modes of neoliberal governance (Harvey 2007). Themed and privatised developments proliferate as sites are created for airports, shopping malls, corporate towers, housing enclaves and deregulated development zones (Hannigan 1998; Easterling 2005). This rise of the image in urban development means that informal settlements now emerge in an urban landscape and planning context that has become increasingly unsettled. New middle-class networks of high-rise buildings linked by elevated freeways and railways can rapidly increase the areas of visibility of informal urbanism and many such sites are seen as prime development opportunities (King and Dovey 2013).

The issue of image and visibility is complicated by a burgeoning industry in slum tourism – the *klongs* of Bangkok, *favela* tours in Rio and the slum tours of Dharavi in Mumbai are primary examples. There is a complex mix of attractions here including a quest for authenticity, the shock of the real and an aesthetic of the sublime (Dovey and King 2012). While informal settlements are chaotic, they also have a socio-spatial order that is often highly complex, labyrinthine and picturesque – a vernacular order of urban morphogenesis akin to a traditional village. The gaze of the slum tourist has a double edge in that it can involve an aestheticisation of poverty (Roy 2004) but also exposes the hidden conditions of poverty. This 'taste for slums' often reveals more about the tourist than the settlement but it is a two-way encounter with complex effects (Dovey and King 2012).

The issues outlined above on images of informality are rarely studied in the research literature on informal settlement. A common view is that this is a superficial approach to the problem – that to focus on image or aesthetics is to ignore the poverty that produces slums or the upgrading challenge that remains. On the contrary, it seems to me that such issues may hold crucial understandings for why upgrading efforts are so often unsuccessful. Here we can learn from the work of Bourdieu (1984), who articulates the ways aesthetic distinctions work to stabilise social distinctions between people. Aesthetic judgements operate within a field of power wherein what is at stake is 'symbolic capital': one of a range of forms of capital – symbolic, social, cultural, economic, political – that circulate through fields of power and are convertible to each other in different ways (Dovey 2010: Chapter 3). One way of understanding the informal settlement within the urban field of the developing city is as a place with negative symbolic capital. For local middle classes these are places to avoid; the informal city becomes the 'other' of the formal city and hence essential to its identity. Aside from some recent work on mapping the visibility of informal settlements (Kamalipour and Dovey 2019) this is a field that remains largely unstudied.

There are some important conceptual starting points from the history of social theory and urban studies. First there is Benjamin's work both on the spatial 'porosity' of the slum (with its interpenetrations of public/private space) and the importance of the urban 'dialectic image' where one part deconstructs the meanings informing the other (Benjamin and Lacis 1978; Buck-Morss 1989). Then there is Anderson's (1983) insight about the nation as an 'imagined community' – often constructed and stabilised through urban imagery (informal settlements never appear on stamps, coins or banknotes). Lynch's (1960) seminal work on the *Image of the City* established the importance of urban imagery and cognitive mapping in a manner that has stood the test of time. From this perspective informal settlements are often 'districts' with a character and consistency largely established by their informality. Informality often accrues along the 'edges' or boundaries of the formal city – waterfronts, escarpments, railway and freeway easements. Jameson's (1991) call to pay attention to the political economy of cognitive mapping is also relevant here, together with more recent calls to understand a fragmented or splintered urbanism (Amin and Thrift 2002; Graham and Marvin 2001). Postcolonial approaches have highlighted the legacy of colonialism and the need for subalterns to produce their own narratives (Said 1978; Spivak 2008).

In the book *Framing Places* (Dovey 2008) I argued that research on power in built form requires a multiplicity of approaches – connecting studies of spatial structures (Hillier 2000), spatial practices (De Certeau), discourse analysis (Barthes 1973) and phenomenology (Merleau-Ponty 1962). More recently I have used an assemblage approach (Deleuze and Guattari 1987; DeLanda 2006) as a framework for re-thinking the informal/formal relationship, an approach that treats the settlement and its urban context as an 'assemblage' of interconnected parts where the focus is on connections, flows and dynamic process. Assemblage theory is an approach that links the materiality, spatial structure and everyday life of the city to issues of image and meaning. It is a useful framework for understanding the relationship of formal to informal practices in the city because a range of twofold concepts that resonate with informality/formality are deployed – rhizome/tree, smooth/striated, network/hierarchy (Deleuze and Guattari 1987). Informal practices are rhizomic in contrast to the tree-like structures of urban regulation and planning; they involve minor adaptations and tactics in contrast to the major strategies of master planning; informal network connectivity in contrast to hierarchical control. Assemblage theory is a theory of socio-spatial change that incorporates informality as fundamental to understanding the productivity of cities. Assemblage is a mode of thinking that resists the reduction of the particular to the general, a theory of power that flows both top-down and bottom-up.

While research on the image of the city has burgeoned in the West such studies are rarely focused on developing cities of the Global South. While many scholars have engaged with the issue of informal urbanism (Davis 2006; Neuwirth 2006; Roy and AlSayyad 2004) others have proclaimed the creativity and productivity of informal settlements as a solution rather than a problem (Turner 1976; Brugmann 2009; Brand 2009), yet we have no sophisticated understanding of how informal urbanism works in terms of urban image and place-identity. While slum and squatter settlements have been widely studied within legal, political, anthropological, sociological and economic frameworks, the specifics of form and space are often seen as contextual or irrelevant. Researchers have pointed out the systematic forgetting of informal settlements in the discourses and the maps (Shatkin 2004; Roy 2004; Fernandes 2004) and others have written of 'urban cleansing' (Appadurai 2000), none has studied the issues in detail. While many architects and planners have engaged with planning, design and upgrading projects where the transformation of image is one objective, there is little evaluation of outcomes. The existing research literature remains polarised into the highly technical and the highly social but aspatial.

I want to finish by opening up the range of research questions that might be usefully pursued. In what ways do informal settlements and urban informality become visible or hidden within the urban landscape of the city – particularly as seen from the formal city? To what degree are the spatial structures of informal settlements open or closed to through or passing traffic and how does this mediate visibility from, and interaction with, the formal city? How are informal settlements seen and conceived within the broader socio-spatial field of the formal city with regard to social class and ethnicity? How do the dreams of a modernist city and the middle-class gaze from high-rise towers and elevated toll-roads intersect with the realities of informal everyday life? How are informal settlements portrayed in the mass media? How, if at all, do they impact upon urban branding and tourist literature? How does the place-identity of informal urbanism impact on the politics of upgrading and eviction/demolition? How does it mediate a larger political economy of urban spectacle, place marketing and slum tourism? What are the transformative possibilities of slum-upgrading strategies on the place identity of informal settlements? What are the prospects and implications of such understandings for urban development goals? How does such an understanding link with critical urban theory and political economy? How can urban planning and design strategies be re-thought?

All of these questions are but a means to the larger end of building a more substantial knowledge base for the redevelopment of informal settlements. I began with the distinction between slums and informality because it is crucial that we understand urban informality as a resource, as a mode of production, as a means of managing poverty. Attempts to erase poverty by erasing informality, replacing the informal city with the formal city, rarely stop either the poverty or informality as new housing estates become the new slums and are informalised by accretion. We need to put an end to the notion that image can be ignored in the focus on poverty. Strategies of informal encroachment often engage in copying the image of the formal city in anticipation of formal tenure and political legitimacy. Transformations of the image of informal settlements are already long underway. Many former informal settlements have been incrementally upgraded and are no longer identified as 'slums'. The upgrading of slums is a form of placemaking in which the transformation of image and meaning is an integral part.

References

Amin, A. and Thrift, N. 2002. *Cities: Reimagining the urban*. Cambridge: Polity.
Anderson, B. 1983. *Imagined Community*. London: Verso.
Appadurai, A. 2000. 'Spectral housing and urban cleansing', *Public Culture*, 12: 627–51.
Barthes, R. 1973. *Mythologies*. St Albans: Paladin.
Benjamin, W. and Lacis, A. 1978. 'Naples'. In Benjamin, W., *Reflections*. New York: Harcourt Brace Jovanovich, 163–73.
Bourdieu, P. 1984. *Distinction: A social critique of the judgement of taste*. London: Routledge.
Brand, S. 2009. *Whole Earth Discipline*. London: Atlantic.
Brugmann, J. 2009. *Welcome to the Urban Revolution*. London: Bloomsbury.
Buck-Morss, S. 1989. *The Dialectics of Seeing*. Cambridge, MA: MIT Press.
Davis, M. 2006. *Planet of Slums*. London: Verso.
DeLanda, M. 2006. *A New Philosophy of Society*. New York: Continuum.
Deleuze, G. and Guattari, F. 1987. *A Thousand Plateaus*. London: Athlone.
Dovey, K. 2005. *Fluid City*. London: Routledge.
Dovey, K. 2010. *Becoming Places*. London: Routledge.
Dovey, K. and Kamalipour, H. 2018. 'Mapping informalities'. In Dovey, K., Pafka, E. and Ristic, M. (eds.), *Mapping Urbanities*. New York: Routledge, 223–44.
Dovey, K. and King, R. 2011. 'Forms of informality: morphology and visibility of informal settlements', *Built Environment*, 37 (1): 11–29.
Dovey, K. and King, R. 2012. 'Informal urbanism and the taste for slums', *Tourism Geographies*, 14 (2): 275–93.
Easterling, K. 2005. *Enduring Innocence*. Cambridge, MA: MIT Press.
Fernandes, L. 2004. 'The politics of forgetting', *Urban Studies*, 41 (12): 2415–30.
Graham, S. and Marvin, S. 2001. *Splintering Urbanism*. New York: Routledge.
Guinness, P. 2009. *Kampung, Islam and State in Urban Java*. Singapore: NUS Press.
Hannigan, J. 1998. *Fantasy City*. London: Routledge.
Harvey, D. 2007. *A Brief History of Neoliberalism*. Oxford: Oxford University Press.
Hillier, B., Greene, M. and Desyllas, J. 2000. 'Self-generated neighbourhoods', *Urban Design International*, 5 (2): 61–96.
Jameson, F. 1991. *Postmodernism, or The Cultural Logic of Late Capitalism*. London: Verso.

Jenkins, P. 2006. 'Informal settlements'. In Huchzermeyer, M. and Karam, A. (eds.), *Informal Settlements*. Cape Town: UCT Press, 84–102.

Kamalipour, H. and Dovey, K. 2019. 'Mapping the visibility of informal settlements', *Habitat International*, 85, 63–75.

King, R. and Dovey, K. 2013. 'Interstitial metamorphoses: informal urbanism and the tourist gaze', *Environment and Planning D: Society and Space*, 31 (6): 1022–40.

Kusno, I. 2000. *Behind the Postcolonial*. London: Routledge.

Lynch, K. 1960. *The Image of the City*. Cambridge, MA: MIT Press.

Martin, R. and Mathema, A. 2006. 'Clash of civilizations'. In Huchzermeyer, M. and Karam, A. (eds.), *Informal Settlements*. Cape Town: UCT Press, 126–45.

McNeill, D. 2008. *The Global Architect*. London: Routledge.

Merleau-Ponty, M. 1962. *Phenomenology of Perception*. London: Routledge.

Neuwirth, R. 2006. *Shadow Cities*. New York: Routledge.

Perlman, J. 1976. *The Myth of Marginality*. Berkeley: University of California Press.

Perlman, J. 2010. *Favela*. Oxford: Oxford University Press.

Roy, A. 2004. 'Transnational trespassings'. In Roy, A. and Alsayyad, N. (eds.), *Urban Informality: Transnational perspectives from the Middle East, Latin America, and South Asia*. New York: Lexington Books: 289–318.

Roy, A. and Alsayyad, N. (eds.). 2004. *Urban Informality: Transnational perspectives from the Middle East, Latin America, and South Asia*. New York: Lexington Books.

Said, E.W. 1978. *Orientalism*. New York: Pantheon.

Shatkin, G. 2004. 'Planning to forget', *Urban Studies*, 41 (12): 2469–84.

Spivak, G.C. 2008. 'Can the subaltern speak?'. In Nelson, C. and Grossberg, L. (eds.), *Marxism and the Interpretation of Culture*. Basingstoke: Macmillan: 271–313.

Turner, J. 1976. *Housing by People*. London: Marion Boyars.

UN-Habitat. 2006. *The State of the World's Cities*. London: Earthscan.

5
The role of change maker painters: graffiti and street art in Accra, Ghana

Claire Tunnacliffe

Accra is dominated by signage: from hand-painted 'do not urinate here', businesses advertising their unique selling point, the Ghanaian flag repeated alongside main roads in and out of town, to graffiti and street art outside homes, schools and organisations. To pay attention to the surfaces of Accra is to tap into the many conversations taking place across the city simultaneously. By exploring the use of these surfaces to share services, products, needs and desires, their multifunctional use as sites of exchange is exposed. Graffiti and street art is positioned as an optical

Figure 5.1 Photograph of wall art 'Politics, patriotism and post no bills'.
Source: Tunnacliffe, 2016

infrastructure that emerges within and beyond informal settlements, through which their own image of themselves is mediated to the rest of the city and the possibility of new landscapes is produced.

The chapter begins by exploring the broad spectrum of appropriations[1] on the city's surface and asks how Accra can be 'read' through them, a response to Swati Chattopadhyay's call within this volume, to 'rethink the very idea of infrastructure and our strategies for "reading" landscapes' (Chattopadhyay, p. 20). These 'hybrid surface inscriptions', defined as visual-material sanctioned and unsanctioned urban inscriptions, 'often form qualitatively different parts of the semiotic landscape but their boundaries seem to be increasingly permeable, as graffiti, street art, advertising and street signage recurrently makes less distinct categories' (Andron 2016, 71).

The chapter focuses in particular on graffiti and street art movements that exist in and emerge from Nima, an informal settlement to the north of Accra. These artists play multiple roles within their community in rendering the under-represented visible with their messaging exposing some of the issues, needs and desires experienced by those that make up the community and how these moments of creativity create exchange.[2] Speaking to Chattopadhyay's work on wall writing and urban festivals, optical infrastructures are made visible in the context of informal spaces, whereby these become sites of informal exchange, growth, negotiation, exchanges and dialogues for subaltern populations. These themes will be explored and articulated in response to the following questions:

1. How do we understand Accra from its visual landscape?
2. What is the relationship between creative place making and the informal?
3. How does graffiti and street art engage others in place-led transformation?

The first question explores the wide scope of urban inscriptions that contribute to the city in conversation and asks how Accra can be understood through them. The second addresses the relationship between creative place making as an intrinsic element of place-led transformation, and its contributions to reading landscapes.[3] The last asks how these moments of creativity and encounter act as opportunities for exchange.

Reading informality: infrastructure, exchanges and image

Informality is an intrinsic component of creating new forms of the social and political. The informal is thought of both as the territorial or geographical, and as a domain of the performative social, spatial and political. Informality becomes a catalyst for urban exchanges, 'outside of familiar contexts, protocols and conventions. It provides a meeting point for fluctuating circles of stakeholders and the intersection of economic, cultural and social concerns' (Mörtenböck and Mooshammer 2016, 45). Informal urban activity involves the utilisation, appropriation and alternative use of urban spaces and surfaces, bypassing regulations. Instead, it highlights the 'performative dimension' of urban encounters on different levels (Mörtenböck and Mooshammer 2016, 45).

Informality, both as place and as performance, challenges our global imaginations on the idea and role of the city. As a result, it questions our own paradigms of urbanism, 'within which we have formed habits of imagining, researching and teaching about the city' (Chattopadhyay 2012, ix). Chattopadhyay points to this, through a middle-class desire to become internationally 'legible' or 'translatable' specifically in cities in the so-called Global South. This connects to Kim Dovey's frame of the 'urban brand' arguing that governments are

Figure 5.2 Photograph of wall art 'Don't urinate here'.
Source: Tunnacliffe, 2016

often 'embarrassed' by images of informal settlements within their countries, as they signify 'poverty and a lack of law and order' that does not fit within a desire to 'attract flows of capital and establish themselves as global cities through the production of urban spectacle' (Dovey, p. 43).

Urban informality is conceived here through the lens of the built environment as graffiti and street art repositioning the power of those living within informal settlements. Graffiti and street art allow for the mediation of Nima's own image by subverting infrastructure, negotiating the image of themselves to the rest of city. This posits graffiti and street art as a powerful tool in linking Accra together, positioning informality not as a separate feature of urban life, but as relational.

How do we understand Accra from its visual landscape?

Accra has a rich visual landscape. In looking at the city surface, we begin to understand Accra as a colourful, creative and busy metropolis. Signs stating, 'Do not dump here', 'Post no bills' sit alongside adverts for Indomie and Glo.[4] School walls are decorated with children playing and learning. In the build up to the presidential election in late 2016, political graffiti appeared across the city, '#GHANAGOESGREEN', 'NEW REGISTERS TO VOTE' and 'SAVE GHANA'. Billboards advertise religious services, skin care and weight loss. In and among this, businesses paint the front of their shop with illustrations of their services and products, a traditional form now fading due to the increase in digital advertising. Painted Ghanaian flags rush past taxi windows, displayed along the main arterial roads in and around the city. Cardboard signs strung from light poles advertise 'PLUMBER', 'LANDSCAPE GARDENER' or 'ACCOUNTING' with a simple phone number and no name. Trees become shop windows, colourful clothes hanging low on branches. Once more, hand-painted signs can be spotted at traffic-jammed intersections, herbal medicines offering to help with all bodily ailments, accompanied by illustrations. Taxis and *tro tros*, the local bus service, move around the city and beyond, with messages of faith, love and humour, 'Art can be found in almost every corner in Accra from neighbourhood churches, schools and pubs to street stalls, barber shops and corporate campaigns. Art is serious business. In fact, traditional street art plays an influential part in the advertising history of Ghana' (Kwadwo 2014).

On the wall: urban inscriptions, graffiti and street art

Urban inscriptions are both an all-encompassing term and inexhaustive list. It includes everything that can be found in public spaces and streetscapes that conveys a message – be it commercial, instructive, political, social, religious and the like. While this is broad, the intention is to leave the observer, the city dweller, open to exchanges and interpretation. By exploring the varied forms urban inscriptions can take, this leads to an awareness of the different narratives taking place on surfaces and the power dynamics at play. This includes billboards, adverts and posters, from small stickers to large digital advertising, as well as graffiti and street art,[5] graffiti[6] as well as text-based messages written in chalk, pen or paint. These come in a range of mediums; are illegal or legal, large or small, and can be done by removing, distorting or adding something into the urban environment.

Urban inscriptions therefore are an umbrella term for a range of subsets within the visual landscape of the city, the particularity of graffiti and street art is that it offers a new way of taking ownership of public space:

> … to foster the idea of community in and through art: showing ways of making art in places that might easily be overlooked as derelict or inaccessible, and encouraging creative involvement in our living and dwelling places, so that we can all become artists, performers and spectators of art in city spaces (Young 2016, 77).

These urban inscriptions, both textual and image based, weave themselves into the fabric of the everyday as well as the very subconscious of the city. They have the potential to drive physical changes as, '[they] not only offer insights to help analyse and understand cities but also point to ways of radically altering their futures' (Campkin, Mogilevich and Ross 2016, 148).

While the origins, similarities and differences between graffiti and street art have been discussed historically, this chapter does not have the scope to go further in depth.[7] Defined as a form of visual art that is found in and inspired by the urban environment, as defined by Nicholas Riggle 'an artwork is street art if, and only if, its material use of the street is internal to its meaning' (Riggle 2010, 246). This distinguishes graffiti and street art from advertising, as the same image may be found in a magazine or newspaper with no loss of meaning or impact. Graffiti and street art on the other hand will experience a loss of meaning or value should it be removed from the street (Young 2016, 39). This chapter also adopts these terminologies, because the Ghanaian artists themselves use them. During interviews with artists in Accra, there was no distinction made between both graffiti and street art as separate movements. Additionally, artists explained that there was no equivalent word in a local language that translates directly. Instead, artists spoke openly about their influence of global street art and graffiti movements, while combining their work with more traditional, commercial and spiritual practices in the development of their style:

> The only thing we tell the local people is 'art', it's just 'art'. But then, I can remember from the place that I came from there is this type of painting that they do on the wall. It is called *Sirigu*, which is from the Upper East of Ghana. This is the traditional mural. Only those who live in the rural areas, really know these traditions. *Sirigu*, I do not know the meaning of the word, but I know it is women who do it only.[8]

What is called graffiti and street art in this context pre-dates the movements in New York and Europe from the 1960s onwards, with traditional signage and painting being a long-embedded part of traditional and spiritual life in Ghana. However, in recent years the techniques of graffiti and street art, as well as the gradual increased availability of spray paint, has meant that artists are at an interesting cross section in placing African graffiti and street art on the global scene. Moving between their private studio practices and their work in the street, artists are incorporating elements of traditional signage, social activism and spirituality with elements of graffiti and street art:

> Unlike the classic New York graffiti style, euro-style, and Brazil's *pichação*,[9] African graffiti doesn't have its own easily recognizable style. Most of the artists have drawn inspiration from abroad through books, music videos and the internet. Slowly but surely more African-based artists are exploring their own unique surroundings and incorporating original African designs into their work (Waddacor 2016).

While some argue that an obvious African style of graffiti or street art is yet to emerge, or even to exist, by untangling definitions of graffiti and street art away from Western understandings, it becomes apparent that they have long existed in Ghana (Antwi and Adi-Dako 2014).

Graffiti and street art across Accra

Graffiti and street art exists across multiple sites in the city. The longevity of urban inscriptions generally varies with many seemingly remaining until natural degradation or eventual removal/replacement occurs. With graffiti and street art, their longevity is determined by the wall owner, usually lasting until the surface is repainted for another piece, rather than removed by any official body. Typically, paintings last for many years or fade away naturally due to degradation and the quality of paint. One wall along Kanda Highway, a main road into the city, was painted in 2013 celebrating the 56th year of Ghana's independence. The piece, entitled 'Imagine Accra', aimed to capture the energy of a metropolis buzzing with progress, and during its creation became an attraction for conversation, music and gathering of people moving through the area. In the same year, another wall outside of the Autism School in Kokomlemle, aimed to de-stigmatise disabilities with a piece entitled 'ThisAbility', and had been 'pivotal in enhancing the aesthetic appeal of the school and creating more awareness on autism and the Autism Awareness Care and Training' (Dislabelled 2016). Another piece painted outside of the Canadian Embassy in 2015, invited by the Canadian Ambassador, saw street artists paint a wall on the International Day of the African Child, on the theme of child protection and youth empowerment.[10] The piece aimed to depict the challenges faced by the country's most vulnerable,

Figure 5.3 Photograph of wall art 'The story of Ghana'.
Source: Tunnacliffe, 2016

particularly related to child forced marriages and labour of girls, and the importance of empowering young people through education. The piece was accompanied by, 'A child is not a bride nor a labourer – she is Ghana's future. Empower her!'.[11] During interviews with artists, they revealed that many of the walls are actually commissioned by organisations, such as the Canadian Embassy and the Autism School, but in other cases, artists invest their own savings together to paint.[12]

By observing Accra's visual landscape, four primary sites were identified as having urban inscriptions: commercial (adverts, billboards), miscellaneous 'free for all' space (political graffiti, hand-painted/written business signs, for sale/removal of structures/property ownership signs), festival sites (for example Chale Wote Festival[13]) and the collective (Nima: Muhinmanchi Art and GraffArt Ghana[14]). This chapter focuses here on a collective known as the Nima Muhinmanchi Art Collective (NMA).[15] In 2011, a group of artists living in the community of Nima united with the objective to use art as a call to action. Since then, the NMA has worked to reshape perceptions of the area through cultural programmes, to rethink and beautify public spaces in Accra through graffiti and street art and address a gap in the nation's education system by providing free art workshops for local youth.

What is the relationship between creative place making and the informal?

Using Nicolas Bourriaud's frame that artwork acts as a social interstice, this section addresses the importance of creative appropriations in Accra in creating new awareness and understandings of the urban environment and the people who live their lives within it, tightening relational spaces (Bourriaud 2002, 14). In Ghanaian Law, according to the 1960 Criminal Act, Section 296 (4) permission needs to be sought from the owner or occupier to affix or attempt to affix any placard, paper or thing, or write upon, soil or mark any such building, wall, fence, pillar or post. The legality of painting on surfaces is largely not enforced, instead appropriated by individuals, communities, businesses and politicians alike. These appropriations interject themselves within the visual landscape as social interstices.

However, the notion of permission, particularly within the inner bellies of community, is an important part of the process. While artists could technically paint anywhere without sanctions, permission, often a simple verbal agreement, is sought out of respect.[16] Occasionally, a small

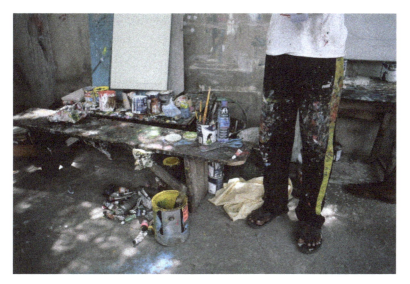

Figure 5.4 Photograph of work bench. Source: Tunnacliffe, 2016

fee is paid to the wall owner but artists are quick to explain that most of the time this payment does not take place, and instead the wall owners are happy for the beautification of their walls. Spirituality and tradition mixes itself into the process through libation, the practice of pouring a drink out in front of the site to appease a deity or god.

Creative place making and place-led transformation

Place making is 'an empowering process in which people represent, improve and maintain their spatial (natural or built) environment' that 'involves the deliberate interventions and actions through which actions, feelings, meanings and fabrics are manipulated and combined to develop a specific identity of place' (Strydom and Puren 2016, 1324). Creative place making more specifically is the act of claiming a space, to communicate and connect, creating a sense of attachment and belonging through creative actions. It can be a means of bringing cities together, particularly in regions of the world where rapidly urbanising cities can create gulfs between challenges and opportunities, 'place making is a powerful tool for democratic change, a means to stitch cities together' (Project for Public Spaces 2016). It does not negate that these places previously had or have one or several identities, communities and functions associated to them. It fundamentally seeks to understand the intricacies of formal and informal, legal and illegal acts of creative place making and place becoming, within a forever shifting sense of place, situated within contemporary discourses on urbanism (Schneekloth and Shirley 1995, 7).

Creative place making is often a collaborative process between public, private, non-profit and communities, however, this presupposes that there is an equal balance between agency, power and impact as well as an end point. Creative place making can mean many different things to different stakeholders. Rather, it is suggested that creative place making is a process without an end point, but the constant defining, re-defining and curating of public spaces, with the local community at the heart of it. This chapter presents graffiti and street art as a grassroots form of creative place making, an approach that empowers and engages people from within their communities. This renders visible the invisible, by harnessing the power of local artists and creatives. It enhances public areas as well as interactions between people, improving community well-being, while fostering conditions to create a sense of identity by defining, drawing attention to and distinguishing them:

> Creative place making is an evolving field of practice that intentionally leverages the power of the arts, culture and creativity to serve a community's interest while driving a broader agenda for change, growth and transformation in a way that also builds character and quality of place (DIY Creative Placemaking 2016).

Accra: the informal city

As of 2020, Ghana's population sits at more than 31 million, with almost 58 per cent of Ghanaians now living in urban areas across the country (Worldometer 2020). With 43 per cent of its urban population living in informal settlements and with 90 per cent of non-agricultural employment being informal, Accra embodies the informal city:

> From public transport to domestic labour to fresh produce, the vast majority of goods and services in this city of 2.3 million are procured informally. Informality is so pervasive, in fact, that it's not unusual to see the homes of millionaires standing adjacent to unfinished informal settlements, or slums occupying some of the most desirable real estate in the city (Benzoni 2016).

Housing in Accra can be grouped into three broad categories: low-, middle- and high-income housing areas. Nima finds itself within a low-income housing area, within which many of Accra's informal businesses are located. To an extent, this chapter looks at informality in terms of settlements, as place, defined by the Organisation for Economic Co-Operation and Development as 'areas where groups of housing units have been constructed on land that the occupants have no legal claim to, or occupy illegally' (OECD 2016). However, it also attempts to go beyond this, to think not only of housing, land and physical infrastructure, but to include social and optical infrastructure. The question of informality belongs as much to the conversations of settlements as they do to belonging and identity, 'Where informality in Cape Town is tied into a history of racial injustice, apartheid, and inequality, in Accra its story is connected much more to questions of belonging and indigeneity' (Myers 2011, 90).

Formality and informality as co-constitutive

These considerations of informality are not as an opposing force to formality, but rather recognise that city-making is in fact a complex relationship between the two. One is entirely reliant on the other, the two working together to produce city forms and urban economies, 'Informal urbanism, from informal settlements to economies and street markets, is integral to cities of the Global South – economically, socially, environmentally and aesthetically' (Dovey 2012, 349). Accra has three cityscapes that sit alongside each other; the formal, globalising city; the informal, indigenous city; and the informal, stranger city (Myers 2011, 92). Life is experienced very differently in each. For those living in the informal, stranger city, life can be difficult. A community like Nima is a neighbourhood that emerged as a hub for West African migrants to Accra in the 1930s, and has become the most densely populated, Muslim, multi-ethnic community in Anglophone West Africa. Rich in music, food, art, fashion and culture, Nima is a place where people converge. Yet it remains a stigmatised area, external perceptions of it being dirty or crime riddled have created prejudice and cultural barriers to the rest of the city:

> Any visitor to the city of Accra is likely to be struck by the appearance of Nima. The congestion that characterizes the community, and the rusted iron sheets of the houses give an immediate impression of a distressed community in West Africa, with deteriorating housing

and social conditions. Most of the houses in the community were built without authorization, resulting in a state of massive congestion that defies rationalization (Owosu, Agyei-Mensah and Lund 2008, 183).

As a result, it has developed its own authorities, rules and policing, undergoing its own development, driven and enforced by its inhabitants. This image of poverty or underdevelopment is also one of entrepreneurial flexibility, creativity and adaptation: 'The challenge is to develop multi-disciplinary, multi-scalar methodologies to explore the ways in which informality is linked to squatting, corruption and poverty on the one hand, and to growth, productivity and creativity on the other' (Dovey 2012, 349).

The role of the artist

The link between the informal complexities of a city and creative place making can be most felt through grassroots environmental activists, writers, musicians and artists. They offer a 'diverse range of fundamentally important cultural voices on urban environments on the continent [of Africa]', breaking normalised negative narratives (Myers 2016, 22). Artists and activists have been inseparable from Africa's contemporary urban history notes Garth Myers, 'and the crucial role of spectacular art/ activism in provoking revolutionary thought. Over and over again, around the cities of the continent, activist artists and writers are challenging the perceived wisdom about urban environments in Africa' (Myers 2016, 138). Instead they advocate how much the environment matters to urban Africans. These artistic expressions empower, both in gaining visibility and acknowledgement, as well as engaging others with the needs, desires, problems and humour of everyday life.

The artists from the NMA explain that their role as artists has different functions. In relation to the rest of this city, their aim is to transform how people perceive and think about Nima. Instead of it being viewed as dirty or poor, to see it as a hub for art and creativity. Part of this is to paint as much of Nima as possible, so that it becomes a reference point for those who are artists, want to become artists or are simply interested in the graffiti and street art scene. It is through graffiti, street art and the artists who form the collective that gradually the perception of Nima is shifting. Interest from national and international newspapers and TV journalists has given the community exposure to the rest of the city and globally, placing the community in the line of sight of other Ghanaians and officials. This not only exposes their creativity, placing Ghanaian graffiti and street art on the map, but also gives an opportunity to share and expose their everyday frustrations and needs. In 2016, a project entitled 'Let's Talk Sh*t' sponsored by UNICEF and launched by Alliance Française Accra tackling open defecation in the city, invited 15 different artists using 15 different mediums to address this issue and to, 'make [it] more public with the support of the media; create a dialogue with the communities using visual arts by exhibiting the pieces of art to people in their communities' (Okertchiri 2016). Moh Awadu, a Nima resident and member of the NMA, said he used his art to change the perception of his community, explaining, 'As an artist you have to make sure you use your artwork to tell stories that change lives. I have taken the role of an ambassador for ending open defecation in my area because when we stop it will create a lot of benefits for us' (Okertchiri 2016).

How does graffiti and street art engage others in place-led transformation?

The social interstices opened up by graffiti and street art suggest other possibilities. However modest the artistic activity, the connections made between artist and urban environment, between artist and community,

Figure 5.5 Photograph of wall art 'African unity'. Source: Tunnacliffe, 2016

between community and wider city, open up pathways, connecting levels of reality kept apart from each other (Bourriaud 2002, 8). Within the triangular relationship between the artist, place and the piece, graffiti and street art interweaves with the unexpected, offering a prism through which the everyday environment can be perceived differently:

> Street art is a powerful tool in reflecting the experience of the urban, provoking an engagement of urbanites with their environment, and in re-socialising public spaces. Exchanges with street art within the everyday create social interstices, opening up ways of seeing and feeling the world differently; allowing for a creative feedback loop between artist, individual spectator and society (Tunnacliffe 2016, 1).

These moments act as retorts, a response or a confrontation. But they also forge lines of connectivity, of empathy and of dialogue.

These creative sites have an important social value – they provide an opportunity to understand how a place feels. Through these exchanges, graffiti and street art repurpose space and in doing so tighten the relational gaps between people and place. Urbanisation can often be an alienating process, particularly for those in informal and subaltern settlements. However, creative place making can create and open up lines of communication and connection:

> People in Africa are curious in general and are not shy to enquire about what you are doing. [...] People are not afraid to engage in your work, trying to interpret the meaning of it. One should be more aware and conscious of what they put up. In Accra, they are doing interesting and exciting work on the walls. There's a large sense of self-awareness and people work with what they have. Africa is full of walls and people with open hearts, and is rising faster than we may see. If they don't break these walls down, then one can cover them with the colour of love, dreams and aspirations (if not our frustrations) (Waddacor 2016).

Through this act of creatively claiming place across the city, the important contribution of the Ghanaian graffiti and street art movements as a form of place-led transformation is highlighted. Place-led transformation is defined as recognising that places are crucial to city-making as well as the role of those who give meaning to these spaces (Project for Public Spaces 2015). These moments of exchanges with graffiti and street art within the everyday open up ways of seeing and feeling the world differently. Pieces with environmental, social, economic, political messages can represent and/or raise awareness of the lived experience. In this way, they disrupt the experience of the urban and the viewer is provided with an alternative vision of the world at play. As a result, at the crossroads between graffiti and street art and everyday life, the viewer evolves from a passive to a potentially active participant.

The relational nature of urban informality is key throughout this volume, and in particular here as graffiti and street art are important in revealing situated knowledges in Accra, as well as a call to look at the city from different perspectives. In doing so, state and Euro-American narratives of informality are decentred, decolonised, and instead graffiti and street art emerges in and from the very contexts they speak to. Nima sits between what Chattopadhyay points to as 'the dual problem of hypervisibility and illegibility' (Chattopadhyay, p. 19). To sit between is to sit on a line, a line may signify a boundary, one which can be extended to the material infrastructure of a place – walls and surfaces – and what constitutes 'in' or 'out', which, borrowing from Chattopadhyay once more, are 'sinews of power, lines of control' (Chattopadhyay, p. 20). In appropriating these infrastructures, graffiti and street artists within Nima repurpose their power and control their own narratives, an argument that connects to postcolonial approaches that 'highlight the legacy of colonialism and the need for subaltern populations to produce their own narratives' (Dovey, p. 41). Chattopadhyay traces the way subaltern groups appropriate, transform, destroy and take over in order to change the authorised use and meaning of infrastructure; through unauthorised adoptions, they create urban infrastructural transformations. By observing the materiality of the urban, the ever-changing human experience can be analysed; by subverting the intended use of infrastructure, new landscapes are produced, 'when infrastructure is appropriated for purposes it was not intended to support we find a transformation in this formal vocabulary that produces new landscapes' (Chattopadhyay, p. 20). Graffiti and street art becomes the scaffolding for this optical infrastructure, rejecting a state-centric view for one where formality and informality are co-constitutive and much like the aim of this volume, read informality from a point of entry not visible from a state-centric position.

This chapter moves across the porous boundaries between the three lenses of exchanges, infrastructure and image framed within this volume, and in this way continues to break out of rigid dualities and silos dominant within Euro-American generalising views. Infrastructure here moves beyond the simply physical to encompass social and optical infrastructures, discussed primarily through the work of Chattopadhyay and understood through the graffiti and street art scene in Nima. Through it, the city's infrastructure – at times the very boundaries and surfaces between what is deemed from a state-centric view as formal and informal – is subverted and harnessed as an infrastructure of expression, a site for community strengthening and further visibility. In this way, the second lens emerges here: exchanges. 'Informality is what most people are doing much of the time in their economic lives' writes Fran Tonkiss. Beyond the more formalised, regulated and institutionalised exchanges she points to the 'off the record ways' such as 'preparing food, childminding, sharing rides and offering lifts, working for tips, pan handling, doing favours or giving gifts, buying rounds and chipping in, cadging loans or making them, keeping an eye out, lending a hand, passing on a message' (Tonkiss 2020). Here too, graffiti and street art become part of the informal exchanges in Accra as part of the hybrid surface inscriptions across the city.

Reading through Tonkiss allows us to focus in on informality economically, with particular emphasis on informality as a space for exchange. Furthermore, Tonkiss notes that there are three ways of thinking through informal exchanges – their ordering, their form and how they intersect – and all three highlight how informal exchanges are given social and spatial form. As forms of informal exchanges, reading the landscapes of graffiti and street art across the city means paying attention to these spaces, as well as how these interventions create an opportunity for conversation. This highlights how informality is both an enabler and facilitator of exchanges, through what Tonkiss calls the material architectures of exchange and how the social architecture of informal exchange is composed around such material architectures. The spaces of informal exchange are inherently social, and thus relational. Taking Tonkiss's second lens, the surfaces upon which graffiti and street artists display their work provides the material site from which various social, economic and political exchanges occur.

The image of informal settlements in relation to the formal city is mediated by an assemblage of political and economic interests. This is an argument made by Kim Dovey within this volume, whose own work uses an assemblage approach as the framework for rethinking the relationship between the formal and informal, 'Assemblage is a mode of thinking that resists the reduction of the particular to the general, a theory of power that flows both top-down and bottom-up' (Dovey, p. 45). This approach links the material, spatial structures and the social exchanges within them

Figure 5.6 Photograph of wall art 'Peaceful election'.
Source: Tunnacliffe, 2016

to issues of meaning and image, revealing the connections. By creating moment for exchange, graffiti and street art provokes a re-engagement of urbanites with the environment, acting as a potential catalyst for transformation at a social and personal level. This chapter highlights the potential of graffiti and street art as opening up a discursive space, revealing the potential power of art to be transformative. Doing so means thinking differently about the ways urban life is created, planned and experienced:

> By 2050, almost 70 per cent of people in the world will live in urban areas. How will we thrive in these communities? Around the world, urbanists, planners, activists and artists have been experimenting with new ways of using city spaces to promote social cohesion and increase well-being for the people who live in them (Bland 2016, 5).

The 'change maker painters'

Ras Aminu Larry, co-founder of the NMA, explains how graffiti and street art is an opportunity to transform everyday spaces, empowering local communities. He sees art as a powerful tool to changing the perception of

Figure 5.7 Photograph of wall art 'After the floods'. Source: Tunnacliffe, 2016

Nima. Larry is passionate about the power of art as transformative, calling the artists in the NMA the 'change maker painters' – because through their craft they create change as artists and activists. Engagement with the local community threads itself throughout the painting process, beginning during a feasibility study. A wall is first identified, in relation to how much footfall it has, followed by a conversation with the community, including chiefs, the wall owner and households in the immediate vicinity. The artists then present what has been noticed about the area or what other people have raised with them – the graffiti and street art acts as a vehicle to talk about issues, while the artists become the tool through which people can do so, whether the topic is unity, underdevelopment or waste management. For example, the exterior walls of a public latrine were painted with local residents with three purposes: to beautify the building, to generate ownership and to talk about upcoming elections.

The graffiti and street art becomes a subject of conversation before, during and after their production; people stop to talk and ask questions, sharing their own experiences. For example, in 2015 after Accra was devastated by a flood and an explosion that saw the loss of 150 lives, the NMA decided to paint a wall along Kanda Highway (Figure 5.7). They wanted to stress the importance of proper waste management, one of the main causes identified for the catastrophe. As a result, the artists explain that people are attentive to cleaning their drains outside their homes and in their community more frequently, creating preventative methods of avoiding another flood, and changing some of their daily habits. Rufai Zakari explains:

> We choose places that have no life, to bring them back to life. That's my aim as a street artist, to be painting back to life. People see a real change in their areas. Some people even call me to do something on their walls, to bring life to those walls, now most of my work in the community is through people asking me. Ever since we finish with a mural, the space around is kept tidy and neat. By having the art there, value is there, and people respect the spaces around it.[17]

Conclusion

Accra is a creative and dynamic city, its visual landscape a thick tapestry of politics, social, environmental and economic messages. This tapestry ranges from the religious billboards that dominate much of the main roads to the political graffiti that flicker past moving vehicles to the Ghanaian flag that is bold and colourful, the graffiti and street art in communities and the streets of Accra more widely. These situate themselves within traditional understandings of signwriting, blurring the lines between commercial, traditional and spiritual. There are many ways in which urban inscriptions are communicated to the city and its inhabitants, orchestrated by individuals, communities, businesses, artists and politicians. While their intent and agency may vary, the wall is a space for appropriation, discussion and transformation, and as a result gives way for the informal to represent itself.

Ghanaian graffiti and street art not only makes visible the communities of informal settlements through the practice of creative place making, but these movements also expose the issues, needs and desires experienced by those that make up the community. These artists play an important role in making visible the otherwise stigmatised and ignored community of Nima to the wider city, by enhancing public facing areas as well as interactions between people. The NMA has worked to reshape perceptions of the area through cultural programmes, to rethink and beautify public spaces in Accra through graffiti and street art and have addressed a gap in the nation's education system by providing free art workshops for local youth. Their role as artists has multiple functions: to beautify, to generate ownership and to talk about social, political, environmental and economic issues. The NMA's mission is to transform how people perceive and think about Nima by painting as much of the area as possible, so that it becomes a reference point for those who are artists, want to become artists or are simply interested in the graffiti and street art scene. It is through graffiti, street art and the artists who form the collective that gradually the perception of Nima is shifting. Interest from national and international newspapers and TV journalists has exposed the community to the city and the world. The change maker painters point to the value of graffiti and street art before, during and after they are produced, engaging with the local community throughout the process, with people stopping to talk and ask questions, sharing their own experiences.

Graffiti and street art renegotiates a relationship between the informal and the formal, by mediating its own image. In subverting the infrastructural, the power dynamics played out on the city surface are revealed. By fostering conditions to create a sense of identity, these artists gain visibility for their community as well as engagement. Infrastructure here moves beyond the simply physical to encompass social and optical infrastructures, discussed primarily through the work of Chattopadhyay and understood through the graffiti and street art scene in Nima. Through it the city's infrastructure is subverted and harnessed as an infrastructure of expression, a site for community strengthening and further visibility. As a result, this chapter has highlighted the potential of graffiti and street art as opening up a discursive space, revealing the potential power of graffiti and street art to be transformative.

Informality is also relational, with the built environment comprising overlapping social and physical spaces and relations. In using the built environment as an entry point, exchanges, infrastructure and image have been the lenses through which new understandings of urban informality have been argued. In particular, this chapter has asserted that graffiti and street art reposition the power of those living within informal settlements to mediate their own image by subverting infrastructure, and in turn mediating the image of themselves to the rest of city more broadly. Place-led transformation is not only the result of creative place making, but also a key part of engaging others. The change maker painters expose a city in conversation, uncovering the under-represented and highlighting the vibrant, creative voice of those living in informal settlements. These artists play a crucial role in challenging the perceived notions of current urban environments in Accra, with artists and activists at the forefront in creating revolutionary thought.

Ghanaian graffiti and street art movements in this context are less about the individual than they are about the collective, the community. These change maker painters see themselves occupying two roles, one within their own communities, painting the inner bellies of their communal courtyards to address very localised problems, but also more widely in the streets of Accra, drawing attention to who the community is, to changing its perception, and to showing Ghanaians and the world their art. Ghanaian graffiti and street art counter monolithic images of global cities through the sharing of contextual messaging unique to the places they emerge from, while rendering visible a community often left out of these visions. Additionally, from a purely aesthetic point of view, graffiti and street art is often argued as a tool for beautification, and in turn subverting these often-unchallenged assumptions that informal settlements are anything but. The appropriation of the informal on the infrastructural reveals power dynamics played out on the surface of the city, ones that expose new ways of imagining, researching and teaching about the city. Thinking through urban informality challenges our global imaginations on the idea and role of the city. As a result, it questions our own paradigms of urbanism, while graffiti and street art teach us to reimagine and relearn the city. Ghanaian graffiti and street art are important transformative tools in revealing situated knowledges in Accra, as well as a call to look at the city from different perspectives, moving away from a state-centric view, and revealing how graffiti and street art create space for potential new social and political forms.

Notes

1   The data used within this chapter was collected through a series of transect walks and semi-structured interviews with street artists during two fieldwork trips that took place in 2016.
2   The emphasis on 'some of the issues' is important to stress, as the artists cannot speak for everyone's lived experience and an awareness of who is invisible is intrinsic to bear in mind throughout. Particularly as most of the artists are straight, able-bodied men. However, the themes of the art often speak to issues felt from the broad spectrum of community members.
3   There are several ways to spell this term, however, the preferred spelling is by separating the three words to stress the relationship between each other. This idea was developed during a workshop on 25 September 2015 as part of an Academy of Urbanism grant.
4   Indomie is a brand of instant noodle by Indofood, the largest company in Indonesia, with a plant in Nigeria since 1995. Glo is a telecommunications company providing service in Ghana, Nigeria and Benin.
5   Quite simply as art in various mediums created or placed in the streets.
6   Graffiti first started to appear in the 1960s/70s on New York City subway trains and involves mostly illegible letter-based inscriptions.
7   For a more complete discussion see *Street Art World* (2016) by Alison Young.
8   Interview with Rufai Zakari in August 2016 (Tunnacliffe 2016).

9   Pichação is the name given to graffiti in the South Eastern metropolises of São Paulo and Rio de Janeiro, Brazil.
10 16 June annually.
11 The piece is part of a global initiative by 'Canadian embassies and high commissions around the world [who] have also undertaken a wide range of other advocacy initiatives to build greater awareness and action around ending child, early and forced marriage through engagement with a broad spectrum of actors' (Government of Canada 2016, 5).
12 Many of these pieces were first identified through transect walks, before meeting the artists themselves. Authorship is identified by the listing of artist names, an email and often a phone number alongside the painting that facilitates the proliferation of artists' work.
13 Chale Wote Street Art Festival began in 2011 as a platform bringing together art, music, dance and performance into the streets of James Town, Accra.
14 GraffArt Ghana movement is a group of young artists from Ghana with the aim of using art to address issues facing the continent and also to promote Ghanaian art and culture to the rest of the world.
15 Nima Muhinmanchi Art means 'importance of art' in the Hausa language.
16 Countries like the UK include hefty fines and sentences. Section 6 of the Criminal Damage Act 1971 stipulates offences in relation to graffiti. If a person is caught doing graffiti they will be found guilty of a criminal act, and liable to pay up to £5,000 in fines if the damage they have caused is less than £5,000. If the cost of damage is more than £5,000, then the case will be referred to the Crown Court for tougher sentence. Alternatively, for young offenders they will be given a community service order rather than a fine.
17 Interview with Rufai Zakari in August 2016 (Tunnacliffe 2016).

References

Andron, S. 2016. 'Interviewing walls: towards a method of reading hybrid surface inscriptions'. In Avradmisi, K. and Tsilimpounidi, M. (eds.), *Graffiti and Street Art: Reading, writing and representing the city*. London: Routledge, 71–88.

Antwi, E. and Adi-Dako, M. 2014. 'Painting: is it indigenous to Ghanaian culture?', *Journal of Art and Humanities*, September. http://www.theartsjournal.org/index.php/site/article/viewFile/552/316.

Benzoni, S. n.d. 'Accra, Ghana', Nextcity.org, https://nextcity.org/informalcity/city/accra.

Bland, J. 2016. 'Creative construction: a new kind of innovation for your city: an evaluation of Playable City Lagos', September, British Council and NESTA Report. http://creativeconomy.britishcouncil.org/media/uploads/files/Playable_City_Lagos_e valution_sept_16.pdf.

Bourriaud, N. 2002. *Relational Aesthetics*. Dijon: Les Presses du Réel.

Campkin, B., Mogilevich, M. and Ross, R. 2016. 'The agency of urban images in urban change'. In Campkin, B. and Duijzings, G., *Engaged Urbanism: Cities and methodologies*. London: I. B. Tauris, 147–54.

Dislabelled. n.d. 'ThisAbility', Dislabelled.org, http://www.dislabelled.org/thisability/.

DIY Creative Placemaking. n.d. 'Approaches to creative placemaking', artscapdediy.org, http://www.artscapediy.org/Creative-Placemaking/Approaches-to-Creative-Placema king.aspx#approaches_introduction.

Dovey, K. 2012. 'Informal urbanism and complex adaptive assemblage', *International Development Planning Review*, 34 (4): 349–67.

Government of Canada. 2016. 'Canadian efforts to address child, early and forced marriages'. In *Report for the Office of the High Commissioner for Human Rights on progress towards ending child, early and forced marriage worldwide, pursuant to General Assembly Resolution 69/156 adopted on 18 December 2014*.

Kwadwo, N.O. 2014. 'Going digital: is Ghana's street art obsolete?' ACCRA [dot] ALT Radio, 24 March. https://accradotalttours.wordpress.com/2014/03/24/going-digital-is-ghanas-street-art-going-obsolete/.

Mörtenböck, P. and Mooshammer, H. 2016. 'From urban talent to commodity city: encountering marketplaces in the informal economy'. In Darling, J. and Wilson, H.F. (eds.), *Encountering the City: Urban encounters from Accra to New York*. London: Routledge, 45–62.

Myers, G. 2011. *African Cities: Alternative vision of urban theory and practice.* London: Zed Books.

Myers, G. 2016. *Urban Environments in Africa: A critical analysis of environmental politics.* Bristol: Policy Press.

OECD. n.d. 'Glossary of Statistical Terms', stats.oecd.org, https://stats.oecd.org/glossary/detail.asp?ID=1351.

Okertchiri, J.A. 2016. 'Ghanaian artists talk sh*t', dailyguideafrica.com, 10 September. http://dailyguideafrica.com/ghanaian-artists-talk-sht/.

Owosu, G., Agyei-Mensah, S. and Lund, R. 2008. 'Slums of hope and slums of despair: mobility and livelihoods in Nima, Accra', *Norsk Geografisk Tidsskrift/Norwegian Journal of Geography*, 62 (3): 180–90.

Project for Public Spaces. 2015. 'Placemaking and place-led development: a new paradigm for cities of the future', https://www.pps.org/reference/placemaking-and-place-led-development-a-new-paradigm-for-cities-of-the-future/.

Project for Public Spaces. 2016. 'Placemaking is a powerful tool for democratic change, a means to stitch cities together', twitter.com, 23 December. https://twitter.com/PPS_Placemaking/status/812264163951177730/photo/1.

Riggle, N. 2010. 'Street art: the transfiguration of the commonplaces', *Journal of Aesthetics and Art Criticism*, 68 (3): 244–57.

Schneekloth, L.H. and Shirley, R.G. 1995. *Placemaking: The art and practice of building communities.* New York: John Wiley and Sons.

Strydom, W.J. and Puren, K. 2016. 'An exploration of the dimensions of place-making: a South African case study', *International Scholarly and Scientific Research and Innovation*, 10 (10): 1324–32.

Tonkiss, F. 2020. 'City government and urban inequalities', *City*, 24 (1–2): 286–301.

Tunnacliffe, C. 2016. 'Interview with Rufai Zakari', inthestreets.city, 8 September. http://inthestreets.city/interview-with-rufai.

Waddacor, C. 2016. 'Urban renaissance: the African graffiti movement', 10and5.com, 26 May. http://10and5.com/2016/05/26/urban-renaissance-the-african-graffiti-movement/.

Worldometer. 2020. Ghana population. https://www.worldometers.info/world-population/ghana-population/.

Young, A. 2016. *Street Art World.* London: Reaktion Books.

6
Informal everyday water infrastructures in the in-between territories of Galicia

Lucia Cerrada Morato

In this chapter I will explore the relationships between different models of water delivery in a hybrid scenario of service provision – in particular the relationship between the municipal and market-led network and community-led water supply systems – and the role urban informality plays in this supply. I will analyse these relationships and the conflicts among actors in this hybrid water supply scenario, in the urbanised periphery known as the in-between territories (Sieverts, 2003) in a region in the north of Spain. These tensions result from the forced displacement of pre-existing community-based water supply infrastructures, called *traídas*,[1] for the benefit of corporation-led centralised modes of water access. *Traídas* are water supply networks built by communities in the 1960s and 1970s in areas outside cities for household consumption, which continue to be managed and maintained by residents. Most *traídas* in the in-between territories still exist today. Here, I understand informality as a process of negotiation and resistance to the commodification of water resources and the privatisation of infrastructures. This chapter will contribute to the literature by first exploring informal infrastructures as a tool to transform the governance paradigm; second, by using the concept of informality as a lens through which to reimagine the transition of the in-between territories.

> Summer 2016. 'Water is not arriving as usual to households and public fountains in Pedrouzos, a village that forms part of the metropolitan area of Santiago de Compostela. Residents meet to discuss and organise a visit to the water tanks up in the mountain;

> they need to check why the supply is poor. Maybe it has been the lack of rain this summer or tree roots have blocked the tanks. Every year tanks have to be cleaned; maybe today is that day.' Ethnographic notes, diary August 2016.

In Pedrouzo's community, residents of all ages and backgrounds manage one of the many *traídas* that still survive in Galicia. This community inspects the water quality in the mains once a year, maintains and repairs the network when required, and cleans the tank twice a year.

> In Pedrouzos, there is news: centralised water from the municipality will arrive to the village in a couple of months. Reactions vary: some residents are willing to connect and forget about handling things on their own. However, most of them assure they will not connect to the municipal lines, 'our water is better, and water as a public resource should be free!' (Resident #1). They will not pay to consume water and fear the municipality will somehow ask them to pay to consume water or force them to shift to the municipal service. Ethnographic notes, diary August 2016.

Galician residents in the in-between territories value this form of provision highly. According to a survey I developed in the metropolitan area of Santiago de Compostela, almost 70 per cent of households with water supplied with a *traída* that were offered to connect to the municipal service did not connect.[2] And most of the 30 per cent who did continued using the water from the *traída* or individual private wells as their primary source for drinking. However, according to the law, a dual connection for household consumption is illegal. Nevertheless, as data indicates, these pre-existing infrastructures are prevalent in the municipal service. Residents resist their abandonment and lack compliance with current regulations.

This is the reality in many villages and in the in-between territories in the northern Spanish region of Galicia. These communal-managed infrastructures, with historical roots in the more archaic and traditional rural communities, were built as metropolitan areas became more urbanised and infrastructure demand increased in the urbanised periphery, while municipal governments failed to deliver infrastructures outside the core city. While institutions and political discourses initially acknowledged and supported communities in delivering and self-building infrastructures, they now consider them outside their preferred water provision mode. This shift follows the construction, in the last 10 years, of

Figure 6.1 Photograph of a household water deposit connected to the *traída* in Pedrouzos, Galicia, Spain. Source: Cerrada Morato, 2020

large and centralised networks currently covering most peripheral areas. As the ethnographic notes illustrate above, this threatens the existence of *traídas* despite communities' preference and active resistance.

Galicia, a dispersed region

Galicia is a region in northern Spain characterised by a diffuse and dispersed urbanised landscape. Agricultural and cattle-raising activities have historically sustained the region's economy. Minifundia and the territorial structure of the region hindered large modern agricultural holdings and promoted subsistence farming. Processes of industrialisation were limited to maritime activities and only of local importance until the 1960s (Badía 2004) when they diversified and started to attract population to cities on a larger scale. Furthermore, and due to its geographical position, Galicia was very isolated and poorly connected with the rest of the peninsula until the twenty-first century, reinforcing a very basic and self-sufficient economy. The latest census still presents Galicia as one of the less developed regions in Spain with high levels

Figure 6.2 Photograph of one of the *traída* collective water deposits in Pedrouzos, Galicia, Spain. Source: Cerrada Morato, 2020

of emigration and strongly dependent on importation. Consequently, Galician society didn't fully enter the capitalist economy until the late twentieth century. Numerous examples of natural resources – such as water or mountains – managed by communities as common goods still survive nowadays.

The increase in car ownership in the 1960s, the economic growth in the final stages of Franco's dictatorship and the return of immigrants and their income resulted in the intense urbanisation of the periphery of cities across Galicia. This growth primarily clustered around rural settlements. It continued, supported on the historical network of roads and paths, which made the territory highly accessible. This carpet of settlements and different urban fabrics, which are not rural and/or urban but a combination of both, is what I call the in-between territories. Since the beginning of the explosive growth of cities and their peripheral urbanisation, various planning laws have been approved by the regional government (the most significant in 1956, 1976, 1985 and 2016) in an attempt to control and plan this growth. In spite of this, a continuous, low-density dispersed urbanisation along the Atlantic Axis highway has

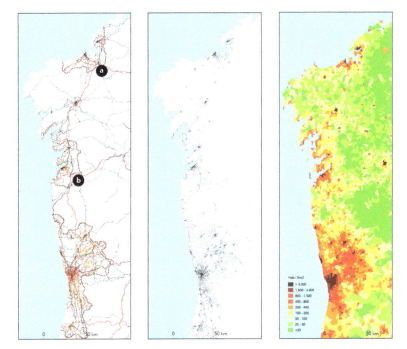

Figure 6.3 Map of the Atlantic axis of Galicia-north Portugal. Legend: a) Abegondo b) Tomiño 1) Territorial structure 2) Built density 3) Population density at the parish scale. Source: adapted from Dalda *et al.* 2002 and Dalda *et al.* 2005

consolidated in what is now called the Atlantic Arc. This infrastructure and urbanised corridor connect A Coruña, in the north of Galicia, with Lisbon in Portugal, stretching for more than 600 km.

Metropolitan areas in this region belong to a dual world. On the one hand, they are conveniently located within or close to cities that provide jobs and access to urban and modern services. On the other, they are rural, holding primary activities belonging to or near rural settlements and rural communities. Access to rural infrastructures is key to their culture and values outside capitalist and market-led logics. However, since the 1980s with the incorporation of Spain into the EU, the in-between territories have started to modernise. By becoming a European member, Galicia received enormous economic subsidies and funds to support the modernisation of peripheral regions across Europe, fundamentally through the construction of infrastructures. So for the last 20 years in Galicia networks of all types have been built – transport, train, water, energy – changing the landscape and the culture and lifestyle of residents in these areas. In this context, various laws, including the Water Act (LAG 9/2010), have framed some of these traditional rural practices and infrastructures as less formal or informal.

In this modernisation process, peripheral municipal governments, which are small but manage enormous and complex territories, failed to engage with traditional and community-led infrastructures. They also struggled to maintain and operate these new large municipal water networks and as a result they generally externalised to private companies their day-to-day management. In consequence, private companies' interests and the market logics lead the planning and development of water services. Indeed, these companies, which belong to international corporate conglomerates, have been very influential in policymaking, which has promoted the continuous growth of centralised, networked infrastructures and continues to do so. In expanding monopolised and private services, legislative action threatens pre-existing forms of provision for household consumption.

Traídas, which are small in scale and lack legal representation, could not dispute or challenge these processes. However, in 1996 an organisation of *traídas* in the south of Galicia – called Coxapo – became very vocal and influential in opposing new legislation. This group has been active in improving these forms of water infrastructure and lobbying for their recognition by the regional and local governments as a legitimate and sustainable form of water supply and embodying valuable cultural heritage.

Coxapo, changing the governance framework

In this chapter I focus on the peripheral municipalities of Tomiño and Abegondo (see Figure 6.3, previous page), using data collected through fieldwork carried out in 2016. Both municipalities have partnered and are supported by Coxapo. They are transforming the role of *traídas* and their relationship to formal institutions and the local and regional government.

Tomiño is a small municipality in the south of Galicia, situated in the Atlantic Arc and bordering with Portugal. Its population is distributed across various rural settlements and two small urban centres. In between these units there is extensive and dispersed urbanisation. Despite the lack of big urban centres, the population density is higher than the average in the region. The municipality's economy is supported by agriculture and industry, given the proximity to industrial areas. Similarly to the rest of the region, *traídas* are very popular here and provide water to various communities in the municipality. In 2016 there were 4,860 households in Tomiño, of which almost 4,000 received their water supply from a *traída*.

The constitution of Coxapo was the outcome of a conflict in Estas, a parish in the municipality of Tomiño, between two communities disputing the same water source for each of their networks. One of the groups had to look for a new water main, and as a result they created a larger infrastructure. Then the group looked for more *traídas* in the area and were surprised to discover they were widespread not only in Tomiño but in the province and wider region. Some individuals of the *traídas* then promoted an association. The group's initial aim was to build alliances with other *traídas*, creating a network to share information and look for support and resources from the public sector.

The organisation soon realised the need to support *traídas* to improve performance both from an environmental and economic perspective and a health and safety perspective. During the early years of the organisation, Coxapo's activities focused firstly on helping *traídas* understand current regulation; secondly, supporting *traídas* in scaling and rationalising their size through merging existing *traídas* into larger networks; thirdly, providing good quality infrastructure to increase efficiency; fourthly, supporting communities with everyday maintenance; and finally, helping communities to handle the billing and management of the service. The result is that *traídas* belonging to the association significantly improved the sanitary controls over their consumption, as well as control over consumption levels. This form of provision now delivers good quality water that is continuously monitored (and information is available online to consumers), at a reasonable cost and contributes to the strengthening of relationships between residents, building social capital in the municipality.

While this innovative form of service provision was being implemented in Tomiño, at a national, regional and local level in the rest of Galicia, *traídas* for household consumption were not incorporated into official documents; neither users nor community leaders were present at any board or discussion group, and therefore made invisible and framed as informal.

However, between 2007 and 2010, two events took place, signalling a move from a governmental *laissez-faire* approach to the gradual pressure and prohibition of this form of provision. In 2007 the regional government presented a draft law in which all forms of consumption, including *traídas*, had first to meet the same standards of municipal networks – sanitary and quality – and second, pay a water canon to

Figure 6.4 Photograph of an upgraded catchment point at the *traída* A Malata, Abegondo, Galicia, Spain. Source: Abegondo municipal government, 2018

the regional government. This canon was designed to contribute to the general regional cost of water treatment and provision. Coxapo and other users of *traídas* opposed both. On the one hand, they were being asked to meet the same standards of municipal networks of highly treated waters, which did not recognise the diversity of water sources with different chemical compositions, and posed huge challenges to the communities managing *traídas*.

On the other, communities had paid for the construction of infrastructures and their everyday maintenance, and therefore having to contribute to the cost of state-led infrastructures seemed unfair. The second event in 2013 was caused by the regulation passed by the Water Confederation Miño-Sil[3] – where Tomiño is located – which obliged residents to connect to municipal networks if these were at a certain distance from their homes and to abandon *traídas*. On top of that, the regional government announced that if a municipal network was close to a *traída*, they wouldn't renew its licence. This dual move effectively meant gradual eradication.

Under this new context of pressure from the regional government and other institutions to abandon *traídas*, the role of Coxapo changed. It stepped from being a local actor organising and improving *traídas* performance to becoming a key regional, national and international stakeholder lobbying for this form of community-led infrastructure. In partnership with Abegondo's municipal government they were awarded a LIFE grant, a European subsidy, to investigate and implement the upgrade of *traídas* in Abegondo. In doing so they were seeking to improve the capabilities of the local population in the provision of non-centralised water supply services. This initiative has been pioneering in Europe, and organisations in Ireland and Austria[4] have partnered with Coxapo to lobby and raise awareness at the European level. They demand the transformation of European regulations concerning the quality of water intended for human consumption (Directive 98/83/EC) and the protection and management of water (Directive 2000/60/EC), both of which challenge the future of *traídas*.

A new governance framework: informal infrastructures as a tool to transform the governance paradigm

Traditional *traídas* are organised through informal agreements among users. Those agreements generally set maximum quantities to be consumed by each user as well as shifts to clean and maintain the network and tanks. The spatial and social characteristics of each community and *traída* define each different agreement. Some communities would check the quality of the water more regularly while others undertake maintenance and clean more frequently, and so on. In general, decisions are made primarily according to the availability and quality of the physical resource. Users of *traídas* do not pay for water consumption. Economic contributions and payments take place when repairs and extensions are needed. *Traídas* rarely have those agreements recorded on paper and rely on verbal accords. As Fran Tonkiss argues in this volume, these water infrastructures and the social relations they create are informal exchanges.

In the 1980s and 1990s, there are records of subsidies from provincial and local governments to communities managing these infrastructures, either for repairs or extensions, what Teresa Caldeira (2017) calls transversal logics. However, from the 2000s onward, this symbiotic relationship between local and regional authorities and community-led infrastructures disappeared. From that point forward, the authorities began to consider the *traídas* outdated, informal and necessitating change. This change was mainly due to two factors. Firstly, the *traídas* were not mapped or registered. They didn't exist in official records and surveys. This invisibility resulted in their disregard in regional and local plans and water provision assessments, obviating their contribution to the wider water and sanitation system and metabolic flows. Consequently, there was a total disregard for this form of provision as a valuable asset in future plans for the region. Secondly, this institutional informalisation became more confrontational. As described above, *traídas* were cornered through active regulation, limiting their presence and prioritising municipal and networked forms of water provision for household consumption.

Despite the above, communities that use *traídas* tend to continue exactly as before and either ignore regulations or deliberately hide their activities. Both attitudes imply a deep distrust of the local and regional authorities. Users of the *traídas* perceive these authorities as a threat to their infrastructures, and more generally to their way of life. Indeed, the communities I interviewed saw these new policies – quality standards and water canon payment – as processes of commodification of a previously public and free resource. Furthermore, as municipal networks are generally maintained and operationalised by private companies, the communities here interviewed see these policies as a protection of private interest in detriment of the public interest.

Coxapo organised resistance to those processes of erasure and forced commodification, as opposed to other examples in which informal infrastructures are tolerated and deliberately overlooked by institutions or substituted by formal services (Allen, Davila and Hoffman 2006). Coxapo pursued a different approach and relationship. Through bottom-up organisations and lobbying at different government tiers, including European levels, Coxapo demanded the transformation of the legislative framework to recognise this form of provision as a valid service for household consumption. They pressed for a new relationship between the regional and local governments and civil society groups. Coxapo's actions have resulted in the transformation of the governance of the water service. This transformation is on the one hand a slow and still ongoing process at the regional level, but on the other hand a radical and comprehensive transformation at the local level in Tomiño.

From a regional perspective, Coxapo has built a strong relationship with *Aguas de Galicia* – the regional water institute – and other institutions such as FEGAMP – the municipal governments association – and *Confederaciones de Aguas*. Through engagement and lobbying their main achievement has been the governmental recognition of the existence of these networks in the region, highlighting their current role – *traídas* serve 580,000 households in Galicia. To do so, new data gathering and mapping methods that better capture the diverse systems and infrastructures outside the municipal and regional network were incorporated. This is seen as a first step to render visible non-municipal, non-networked and non-standardised forms of provision. Another important transformation

Figure 6.5 Photograph of the new technologies to monitor water quality in a catchment point, Galicia, Spain. Source: Coxapo, 2020

in Galicia is the incorporation of bottom-up participatory processes in policymaking. For example, the design guides produced by Coxapo and Abegondo municipal government – the main outcome of the LIFE project – have been supported and adopted by the regional government, hence acknowledging the role of *traídas* and communities more generally in the production and transformation of the water and sanitation systems. These design guides seek to provide support and information to other communities and officers and politicians at the local level to either build or upgrade their own *traídas*. Finally, Coxapo has achieved the flexibilisation and broadening of acceptable standards of water provision.

At a local level in Tomiño, the communities that manage *traídas* and the municipal government have built an innovative public–public partnership. Tomiño's local plan now recognises the important role of *traídas* to provide water to rural and more dispersed areas and does not intend to invest in extending the municipal network. This is rarely found in any other local plan in the region. Furthermore, Tomiño's municipal government has not disengaged with or ignored these organisations. On the contrary, it has built new relationships. The municipal government shares machinery at different scales and provides subsidies to support the communities of the *traídas* to help them maintain and repair the network when needed. This has radically changed the relationship between the communities and the local government. As Tomiño's Mayor argues:

> It [*traídas*] is a model of public resources managed by the public, not by civil servants or bureaucratic processes, but by neighbours. (…) But we do not only advise them [*traídas*], we provide funding to those that need to be upgraded. The fact is water and sanitation is by law a municipal obligation, so we need to support them.

In a way, Coxapo has resisted the current dichotomy of public vs private, to move beyond it and reclaim the right of communities to self-manage their own resources with the support of the public sector.

Looking at the water supply infrastructure of the *traídas* through the lens of urban informality provides a layer of richness, contextualisation and empowerment. Informality unveils a series of exchanges. It allows the processes of contestation, of rendering visible and of transforming relationships and governance. In the case of Galicia, these processes have resulted in new governance frameworks that shift the debate from formal vs informal to a broader consideration of progressive, participatory and democratic bottom-up infrastructure provision and consumption. As argued by Cumbers (2012), progressive movements need to challenge the current private–private or public–private framework to reclaim the role of communities and 'construct alternatives based around more collective ethics and values' (Cumbers 2012, 4).

An opportunity for a suburban renascence: reimagining the transition of the in-between territories through informal infrastructures

Informal infrastructures are often assumed to exist in places outside core cities and formally planned urban areas (Roy 2005; McFarlane 2012). However, Tomiño, and other places in Galicia where *traídas* can be found, are urbanised areas and settlements that escape conceptualisations of the informal as outside of the formal. These areas have a strong place in formal planning documents; they escape state-centric attempts at defining informality. However, their traditional infrastructure and resource consumption and management practices are described and perceived by 'formal' parties (policymakers, the regional and local authorities) as archaic and not suiting modern demand. The formal spectrum dismissed these infrastructures as unsuitable or needing radical transformation or eradication. They began to make the *traídas* opaque, erasing them from maps, planning and legal documents, quietly forcing *traídas* into the 'informal' realm, what I call an institutional informalisation.

Literature and policymaking have described these areas outside dense cities as unsustainable (European Environment Agency 2006). Car dependency, high levels of land consumption and energy demand are some of the key arguments used to match this form of urbanisation with negative outcomes (Galster *et al.* 2001). Networked infrastructures in particular have been described as challenging both in terms of cost for its implementation and its long-term maintenance (Hortas-Rico and Solé-Ollé 2010). This narrative is rooted in widely accepted Anglo-Saxon perspectives and history that see areas outside city centres as suburban and sprawling. However, the nature of the in-between territories outside cities in most of Europe is quite different: denser, more heterogeneous and less car-dependent. Despite the diverse contexts and realities, the Anglo-Saxon perspective persists. It is rarely challenged in academia and political terms. The main policy strategy dominating urban and regional planning in Spain is the densification of cities' hinterlands and implementing new technologies to achieve sustainable outcomes. In this debate, little attention has been paid to the transformation of pre-existing practices and lifestyles that could improve the in-between territories' sustainability.

However, a recent body of scholarship suggests that consumption practices in the in-between territories have the greatest capacity to transition to a more environmental, economic and socially sustainable future (Alexander and Gleeson, 2019), reducing consumption and waste. These studies propose alternative production and consumption practices outside the standardised forms primarily created to suit the needs and capacity of urban infrastructures. These alternative forms of provision, usually antagonistic to what is described as 'modern' or 'urban', challenge current consumption levels. They advocate for circular and off-grid infrastructures and propose the decommodification of resources. Under current governance and legislative frameworks, some of these practices can be described as informal (Barraqué 2004; Barraqué and Zandaryaa 2011). There is no legislation against them in many instances, but because of their innovative nature and the slowness of bureaucracy, they are not incorporated into policy. They become opaque infrastructures, difficult to classify. That is why a non-state-centric approach to their study might be revealing. As Tonkiss proposes, this case shows a relationship between informality and (sub)urban innovation.

In the context of Galicia's in-between territories, informality doesn't match the description of physical infrastructure or practice outside of the formal. Instead, it is the ongoing reimagination of a service provision from the bottom-up, disrupting widespread and well-known practices of standardised infrastructure planned for consumption and production in dense urban areas. As a propositional production and consumption process outside the dense urban and modern paradigm, informal infrastructures are positive and necessary disruptions to the system in the in-between territories. However, as demonstrated with *traídas* in Galicia, the disruptions do not always emerge as pure innovations – as literature has pointed out (Coutard and Rutherford 2012) – but also as a resistance of long-established forms that have survived the rollout of modern services.

Conclusion

After more than five decades of intense urbanisation along the Atlantic Axis, alternative forms of infrastructure provision are under threat. Intense urbanisation has implied the dispersed construction of households along this north–south highway and the extension of municipal and networked water and sanitation infrastructures. The result is not a new and unproblematic hybrid infrastructure landscape but a scenario of multiple processes of conflict and tensions. In this context, urban and rural lifestyles and cultures try to co-exist. One example is the *traídas*. The economic interests of private companies have influenced policymaking and preconceptions of policymakers and civil servants, which have erased these traditional infrastructures from maps and policy documents. They have quietly tried to informalise them in a bid to make them illegal, opaque and difficult to manage, in what I call an institutional informalisation.

Traídas and other forms of community-led and non-commodified infrastructures are characterised by participatory processes where informal interactions and non-monetary exchanges – outside capitalist and market-led principles – guide relations. These infrastructures adapt to the needs and material characteristics of the community in each area. Arguments against this form of water service provision include uncontrolled consumption levels, sanitary risk and insecure access to future tenants. However, this form of provision has also demonstrated a strong capacity to deliver a cost-effective service. *Traída* users know the availability of resources and plan consumption accordingly, making this a more sustainable and conscious service delivery. They constitute flexible and resilient structures that can easily accommodate change. In the context of climate crises, some of these values are very important. However, current consumption levels and water waste disposed of in the environment increasingly compromise the status of the resource. To minimise water consumption, both *traídas* and the centralised infrastructure systems need to improve their efficiency. In particular, communities need to improve the performance of *traídas*, reducing leaks along with the network, metering and increasing awareness among users and ensuring the monitoring of the resource to avoid contamination and its resulting drought.

This chapter argues that informality is better understood in context. It cannot be solely understood as an abstract generalist concept, as a geographical place, or a practice outside the control of the state. As this case study demonstrates, informality is also an active and transformative form of resistance to 'modern', commodified, market-led and consumerist models. Informal infrastructures made up of relationships between humans, history, culture and needs therefore constitute an opportunity and desirable process for a reimagined governance of community and public–public collaboration in the in-between territories.

Notes

1   *Traída* is a decentralised water communal network that connects a source, typically in the mountains, with a series of households in a community.
2   Based on a recent survey developed in this municipality for my PhD research.
3   A public entity responsible for tasks such as hydrological planning, resource management and exploitation, protection of the public hydraulic domain, concessions of rights of private use of water, water quality control and the design and execution of new hydraulic infrastructures.
4   Such as the National Federation of Group Water Schemes in Ireland.

References

Alexander, S. and Gleeson, B. 2019. *Degrowth in the Suburbs: A radical urban imaginary*. Singapore: Palgrave Macmillan.
Allen, A., Dávila, J.D. and Hofmann, P. 2006. 'The peri-urban water poor: citizens or consumers?', *Environment and Urbanization*, 18 (2): 333–51.
Badía, X. 2004. *La industria en Galicia: Un repaso historiográfico*. Padua: University of Padua Press.
Barraqué, B. 2004. 'Not too much but not too little: the sustainability of urban water services in New York, Paris and New Dehli'. In Coutard, O., Hanley, R. and Zimmerman, R. (eds.), *Sustaining Urban Networks: The social diffusion of large technical systems*. London: Routledge, 188–202.

Barraqué, B. and Zandaryaa, S. 2011. 'Urban water conflicts: background and conceptual framework'. In Barraqué, B. (ed.), *Urban Water Conflicts*. Boca Raton, FL: CRC Press, 1–13.

Caldeira, T. 2017. 'Peripheral urbanization: autoconstruction, transversal logics, and politics in cities of the global south'. *Environment and Planning D: Society and Space*, 35 (1): 3–20.

Council Directive 98/83/EC of 3 November 1998 on the quality of water intended for human consumption. Accessed 26 May 2021. https://eur-lex.europa.eu/.

Coutard, O. and Rutherford, J. 2015. 'Beyond the networked city: an introduction'. In Coutard, O. and Rutherford, J. (eds.), *Beyond the Networked City: Infrastructure reconfigurations and urban change in the North and South*. London: Routledge, 19–43.

Cumbers, A. 2012. *Reclaiming Public Ownership: Making space for economic democracy*. London: Zed Publishing.

Directive 2000/60/EC of the European Parliament and of the Council establishing a framework for community action in the field of water policy. Accessed 21 September 2021. https://www.eea.europa.eu/policy-documents/directive-2000-60-ec-of.

European Environment Agency. 2006. 'Urban sprawl in Europe: the ignored challenge'. EEA Report No. 10/2006. Copenhagen: EEA.

Galster, G., Hanson, R., Ratcliffe, M.R., Wolman, H., Coleman, S. and Freihage, J. 2001. 'Wrestling sprawl to the ground: defining and measuring an elusive concept', *Housing Policy Debate*, 12 (4): 681–717.

Hortas-Rico, M. and Solé-Ollé, A. 2010. 'Does urban sprawl increase the costs of providing local public services? Evidence from Spanish municipalities', *Urban Studies*, 47 (7): 1513–40.

LAG 9/2010, de 4 de noviembre, de aguas de Galicia, 2010. Boletin Oficial del Estado 292, 100597–656.

McFarlane, C. 2012. 'Rethinking informality: politics, crisis, and the city', *Planning Theory and Practice*, 13 (1): 89–108.

Roy, A. 2005. 'Urban informality: toward an epistemology of planning', *Journal of the American Planning Association*, 71 (2): 147–58.

Sieverts, T. 2003. *Cities Without Cities: An interpretation of the Zwischenstadt*. London: Routledge.

7
A morphogenetic approach to informality: the case of post-socialist Tirana

Blerta Dino

Informal growth makes up most of global urban development over the past half-century. A third of the world's urban dwellers live in 'informal' housing, and this share is growing incrementally. As a term, informality was imported into urban studies from economics, understood as part of the economy not regarded in official national accounts (Dovey and King 2011, 11–29). In this light, urban informality is perceived in opposition to formal urban development. It has for decades been associated with poorer countries and societies, represented by impoverished *slum* development or *squatted* lands on the periphery of rapidly growing cities. Informality is seen as an unregulated, chaotic and often inefficient settlement or use of land. In this sense it is positioned as fundamentally different from the ordered, regulated, efficient notions of planned land use and settlement (Porter *et al*. 2011, 115–53).

    This understanding of informality as the opposite of formal, as on the margins of state regulations, does not seem to be sufficient to represent and study urban informal processes. In this chapter, informality will be studied from the perspective of a bottom-up urban development motivated by a fundamental need to adapt to socio-economic transformations caused by a rapid shift in political ruling regimes. As Kamalipour and Dovey (2020, 102–33) suggest, informality is a resource and process of adaptation and survival rather than outcome of poverty. In contrast to instances where informality is associated with high levels of poverty and deplorable living conditions, in Albania informality is almost entirely associated with the population taking over the production of the city.

Tirana: a historical perspective

Tirana is the capital and the largest city in Albania. Its origins date back to antiquity, and its existence is first recorded during Ottoman rule in the seventeenth century. Until the beginning of the twentieth century, Tirana's organically grown urban fabric was characterised by narrow, curving streets and low-rise buildings. It had two main areas with specific functions: the centre was the socio-economic hub with the main mosque and bazaar, while the rest of the built form consisted of purely residential units (detached houses) (Kera 2004; Aliaj et al. 2004). Tirana became the administrative capital of the country in 1920. The first attempt to modernise Tirana was made during the rule of King Zog in 1923 when Austrian and Italian architects were contracted to design a masterplan with wide boulevards and streets lined with buildings of contemporary architecture, a new square in the centre of the city, an orthogonal road and neighbourhood system, and a ring road network (Aliaj et al. 2004).

After the Second World War, in 1945 the Albanian communist party (PPSH-Party of Labour of Albania) began a tenure that was to last nearly five decades. With regard to urban development, the totalitarian government exerted highly centralised control of the cities' development. The government exhaustively planned to the last detail in order to fit the communist party ideology and reflect its propaganda. This urban planning found its expression in Social Realism: besides rigorous dictation of architectural style, the city's population was strictly controlled, and free internal migration was banned. Planning and restrictions were exerted on the built environment on basic human needs: food consumption, mobility, religion and freedom of thought. The utilised model has been described by Tosics et al. (2002, 12–149) as an 'original Stalinist model extended with harsh controls over mobility'. By the end of the 1960s, religion was entirely banned in Albania, which was officially declared the world's first atheist country. The country grew increasingly isolated; from the late 1960s, Albania suffered from unstable diplomatic relations even with other Soviet Union countries and the People's Republic of China.

In the process of developing the country to its standards, the communist party discarded the past and tried to assert that the creation of Tirana corresponded to the communist government taking the lead.

They redrew the regulatory plan of Tirana in 1957, and all previous plans were dismissed (Aliaj 2003). Prevailing city planning models included the abolishment of private ownership at all levels, introduction of zoning, provision of mainly standardised mass production, social housing and a mono-centric city model (Aliaj 2004). As the central issue of Albania's urbanisation was the provision of housing, large housing units were built, with most apartments sharing similar layouts and amenities. The mandated parity of the amount of space and essential public services allocated to each family unit was supposed to clear inequalities, and the population of the new housing complexes was socially mixed. The layout of the new housing estates consisted of semi-perimeter or free-standing prefabricated blocks with access (points) from the internal block's courtyard.

By the end of the 1980s, Tirana's urbanised area covered 12 km^2, and its population counted about 250,000 inhabitants. Despite the increasing urban population, three out of every four Albanians still lived in rural areas (Aliaj 2004).

Conceptualising post-socialist transformations in south-east Europe

The communist regimes collapsed in a domino-wave effect across central, eastern and south-east European countries between 1989 and 1992. The immediate effects of the communist fall were significant political and economic crises, and in some countries, bloody ethnic wars and national breakdown (Hirt 2015).

The paths of urban development and change in former central and eastern European countries diverged significantly from those in south-eastern European ones (Hamilton *et al*. 2005). Numerous publications have identified that in south-eastern Europe a distinctive form of post-socialist urbanisation has taken place. Scholars have used various terms to refer to this process, 'Balkanisation' (Hirt 2012), 'Turbo-urbanism', and 'Turbo-architecture' (Weiss 2006). These terms reflect cultural dispositions expressed through their spatial outcome; such terms are strongly associated with the geographical context and cultural characteristics of the Balkan region. Thus, a substantial characteristic of spatial evolution since the early 1990s across the post-socialist Balkan Peninsula is related to informal development (Tosics 2005, 44–78).

Studies into the informal process of urban adaptation in building are scarce, and those concerning post-communist development in Europe and Albania are non-existent. Dovey and King's detailed studies of informal settlements highlight how cities are built from informal processes as much as formal ones (Dovey and King 2011, 11–29). If informality is understood as a process of survival and adaptation as Kamalipour and Dovey suggest (Kamalipour and Dovey 2020, 102–33), the medieval fragments of many European cities can also be understood as being among the oldest of informal settlements.

However, often informal constructions are referred to as parts of cities that develop and operate almost entirely outside the formal control of the state. Regardless of where they belong to geographically, all urban informality processes stem from the residents' speculative initiatives based on their needs and are dictated by their circumstances. As Tonkiss points out, urban informality is the result of human–human and human–environment exchanges (Tonkiss 2020, 286–301). In my case studies, these types of market exchanges appear when affordability accrues in the interstices left by formal planning and regulation (Baross 1990, 57–82).

It should be noted that independent to their geographical location, informal housing and land markets are not just relevant to the poor. They are frequently encountered in the middle-class and the elite neighbourhoods of specific regions. For instance, in the Balkans, (after the fall of the socialist regimes) entire middle-class neighbourhoods, which had not been legally approved, established themselves across cities. In more general terms, this phenomenon is evident in lower income countries (Roy and AlSayyad 2004). Albanian cities faced a rapid transition from the top-down socialist mode of planning to an unregulated city-development model (Hamilton *et al.* 2005). Mainly during the first decade of post-socialist transition, there have been limited formal capital investments, which reverted into significant investments by the Albanian population in the construction of commercial and residential properties (Tsenkova 2010, 73–84).

Tirana and its post-socialist urbanisation

This study focuses on the forces that have shaped post-socialist urban development in Tirana and its contribution to life in the city. Such forces include the elimination of national government control over land and housing, the privatisation and restitution of property to individuals and private organisations, the empowerment of residents with their increase of freedoms, and the decentralisation of decision making towards municipalities (Hirt 2015). Regime changes instigated the emergence of new private-sector actors, such as real-estate developers

Figure 7.1 Photograph of former public space converted informally into parking space. Tirana, Albania, 2016. Source: author.

and private banks. Throughout the 1990s, Albanian cities followed an unregulated model of development characterised by limited official capital investments, significant investments by the local population in the informal economy, differentiated incomes and weak public control over land, planning and the construction sector (Tosics 2005, 44–78). After the ceasing of administrative restrictions in early 1991, rural–urban migration started taking place at a faster pace. The result was the creation of self-built settlements and buildings within and around Tirana (Tsenkova 2010, 123–49).

The 2001 Population and Housing Census showed that during the first decade of post-socialism, 65 per cent of the total migrants shifted towards the capital from all around the country (INSTAT 2001). As a consequence, Tirana's metropolitan area almost tripled its population from 225,000 to 600,000 inhabitants (Felstehausen 1999). During this period an estimated 8,000 to 9,000 new households moved to Tirana each year from different parts of the country. Approximately 70 per cent of the housing supply accommodating this population was self-built (Tosics 2005, 44–78).

Under these conditions, the pre-existing city neighbourhoods witnessed significant densification while its boundaries grew outward, tripling the geographical footprint of Tirana. Even essential planning functions were clouded by ambiguity; it was unclear which regulatory plans were to be followed, and who was issuing planning permissions

Figure 7.2 Photograph of an extension to an early 1990s apartment block showing an appropriation of public space by cafés. Source: author.

(Hirt and Stanilov 2009). Lack of expertise in economic analyses, combined with an absence of infrastructure standards, and significant problems with the legal status of the urban land contributed to the authorities' inability to develop a masterplan (Aliaj 2003). Besides, there was a stark scarcity of professionals and deficiency in state funding for development (Hirt and Stanilov 2009).

Albania's development towards a free-market economy led to the dissolution of all previous types of public control, without the introduction of any new type of formal control over the private land market, planning and building process. As Tonkiss (2020, 286–301) expresses in her chapter in this volume, urban informality takes advantage of the in-between of old and new/yet-to-be regulations. This absence of regulation led to densification in central areas and sprawl outside the centres.

Methodological approach

The study of urban form, often referred to as urban morphology, comprises several different perspectives. One methodology that has triggered interest since the early 1980s (though it has a much longer genealogy) is Conzenian plan analysis and its three morphological levels (Whitehand 2007, 12–15). The three morphological levels of Conzenian analysis are: the town plan, or ground plan (comprising the site, streets, plots and block plans of the buildings); building fabric (the three-dimensional form); land and building utilisation (Conzen 1960). I use this methodology to understand Tirana's urban block evolution.

Another methodology is space syntax analysis. Hillier and Hanson (1984) developed it, defining network properties of street systems and relating these to patterns of use, social activity and cultural meaning. Space syntax argues that all morphological arrangements contain social information (Hillier *et al.* 1976, 147–85). An interesting notion from their *Social Logic of Space* is the 'beady ring', a spatio-temporal unfolding of a simple local rule (Hillier and Hanson 1984). The 'beady ring' concept helps to understand how local processes encode social rules. I apply this concept to the analysis of Tirana in differing ideological periods. The local rule is consistent with prevailing social and cultural norms, here understood as informal, and can be regarded as phenotypical and as settlements grow global genotypes emerge at the global scale.

This research endeavours to understand how and to what extent the range of informal phenotypical (local) rules in Tirana emerge as genotypical forms of relation at the global and urban scale. It endorses a combined approach of these two methodologies. On the one hand, it notes the Conzenian concern for the historicity and materiality of urban form. On the other, it highlights the emphasis of space syntax on how emergent and informal spatial arrangements are also patterns of social information (Griffiths *et al.* 2010, 85–99).

Changes in human circulation, land use, and built form can give accurate insights about how and why the urban block is altered over time. Several morphological studies have acknowledged (Hillier 1999, 107–27) the importance of the urban block as a fundamental element of the physical structure of urban areas – in both planned and unplanned settlements. Siksna's (1997, 19–33) findings suggest that initial block forms and sizes lead to predictable outcomes in successive development. For instance, his research claims that incompatibilities between plot size and building form can be resolved either by developing new building forms in response to constraints posed by plots, or by creating plots through subdivision or merging in response to the required building form. Siksna's (1997) research findings can be applied to the Albanian context where informal post-socialist development transformed existing block structures and at the same time led to the creation of new blocks with a wide range of sizes and form.

I also introduced the most recent aerial map of Tirana in a Geographical Information System (GIS) software platform and superimposed it with the geo referenced built form and road network. I adopted the 'cartographic redrawing', a GIS-based modelling methodology pioneered by Pinho and Oliveira (2009, 107), to systematically study Tirana's morphogenesis to analyse its informal growth over time. I worked backwards to remove non-existent elements and to readjust urban fabric where needed. I acquired the 'rough' data for the contemporary period (2007) from the institutions that produced it as three separate layers. I then revised and added detail to this base-line by double-checking visible paths, routes and buildings digitally and adding information collected through fieldwork conducted in Tirana during late May 2016. Once I had created the underlying dataset, I was able to enter all the collected qualitative information on the same platform. The collected information layers include land use at the ground floor level, access points to buildings, and building period.

Urban growth is a challenge to traditional analytical methods due to its complex nature and requires an interdisciplinary approach in terms of methodology in order to derive a coherent description of patterns and trends of urbanisation (Besussi *et al*. 2010, 13–31).

Evidence from the ground

The two case studies presented in this chapter – Kombinati and Shallvaret – capture and illustrate all the attributes of post-socialist urban life and help illustrate how posterior informal urban development processes contributed to shaping contemporary Tirana. They illustrate differences at the socio-morphological level between two contrasting political, social and economic models. During the period of this study, one of the case study neighbourhoods, Kombinati, consisted almost entirely of residential units (except when they were institutions). Residents have, through negotiations and informal exchanges, converted the area into a mixed-use neighbourhood, which has directly contributed to the dynamic and character of the built fabric. This move has helped the people cater to local needs and adapt to the demand for services and goods.

Case Study 1: Kombinati

Before the regime change, Kombinati was an industrial 'satellite' town of Tirana. The national government built all the residential units that could be found in Kombinati for the workers of the most significant textile

Figure 7.3 Diagrams showing the change from 1989 (left) to 2016 (right) in pedestrian and vehicle circulation as well as access points to buildings in the Kombinati case study, Tirana, Albania. Source: author.

Figure 7.4 Diagrams showing land use distribution (left) and morphological evolution (right) up to 2016 in the Kombinati case study, Tirana, Albania. Source: author.

industry of the country. The buildings of the former textile industry are still part of the urban landscape; however, now they are serving mainly as industrial warehouses.

The case study area is situated along the eastern edge of the pre-1991 Kombinati industrial town. Nevertheless, since the regime change, Kombinati has become part of the city of Tirana with a significant addition of residential units. In the case study area, 70 per cent of the units were constructed after 1991 from which 58.3 per cent are informal extensions to buildings (mainly socialist era units) and only 14.6 per cent are new constructions. The majority of the buildings are between two and three storeys high, with the tallest buildings being five storeys high, which are mainly located alongside the central and eastern parts of the study area.

The primary non-residential land use consists of retail, which accounts for 35.6 per cent, with 24.8 per cent comprising bars and betting amenities, located mainly along the busiest streets. The extent of vacant commercial units in this case study is noteworthy, adding up to 20.8 per cent. These are mostly units located along inner streets, those having less pedestrian and vehicular movement.

Case Study 2: Shallvaret

The Shallvaret area is situated centrally and is currently one of the most expensive parts of Tirana in which to buy or rent properties. Tirana's central authorities built nearly 30 per cent of the units before 1991, of which only one building had commercial activity at that time. As regards the number of new buildings constructed after the fall of the regime, about the same number of residential units has been added to the built form within the boundaries of this study area.

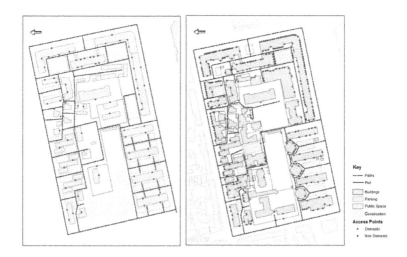

Figure 7.5 Diagrams showing the change from 1989 (left) to 2016 (right) in pedestrian and vehicle circulation as well as access points to buildings in the Shallvaret case study, Tirana, Albania. Source: author.

Figure 7.5 reflects the informal densification of the built fabric from 1989 to 2016. The blue (domestic) and red (non-domestic) dots highlight the increase in access points to the buildings whereas the dotted lines lay out the transformation of the circulation routes within the block. Open spaces as shown in Figure 7.5 have been either persistently built up or transformed into permanent parking space by residents and business owners.

If we consider the number of extensions that residents, mainly informally, have added to the units (40 per cent of the entire units), there is a substantial increase of built fabric, which in total adds up to about 70 per cent of total units of the area (see Figure 7.6). Also significant is the increase in façade activity, which has contributed to a considerable number of services, and retail, that residents and private developers have informally created progressively since 1991.

Land use analyses (see Figure 7.6) show that retail has the highest distribution among non-domestic activities, with 45.3 per cent of the units, followed by services, 22 per cent, and third spaces (cafés and restaurants), 20.8 per cent. Retail activity is again mainly located along the busiest streets, those with higher integrated segments within the network system. Third spaces, which are made up of restaurants, cafés, bars, betting bars and patisseries, are mainly located just off the high street; this is different from the other case study area where third spaces are mainly on the high street with more prominent exposure

Figure 7.6 Diagrams showing land use distribution (left) and morphological evolution (right) up to 2016 in the Shallvaret case study, Tirana, Albania. Source: author.

and visibility. 'Other' land use refers to vacant, under construction or garage spaces. Mostly, these spaces are along inner neighbourhood routes, which possibly influence their status of not being able to operate as businesses when vacant or with no necessity to be along main routes when designated for garages.

Discussion: emergent processes and historically resilient structures

Post-socialist cities are transforming into multi-nodal metropolitan areas characterised by high levels of housing, services, public spaces and privatised transportation, similarly to other western European cities (Stanilov 2007). However, what is significant about the Balkan patterns of urban transformation is the rapidity of urban development. Urbanisation in Western Europe has been taking place gradually for half a century whereas in Eastern Europe it has happened within a decade (Szelenyi 1996).

Hillier (1999, 107–27) argues that, historically, city centres not only grow and shrink but also shift and diversify. With the growth of a large town or city level, a whole hierarchy of centres and sub-centres usually appears diffused throughout the foreground network. Consistent with this argument, my analysis shows that Tirana now has a structure of centres and sub-centres. This decentralisation is mainly the result of informal exchanges and urban informality in the creation and modification of the built environment. These exchanges include changes in land use, new constructions and morphologies that have fragmented the socialist urban block. Residents, private developers and sometimes the city authorities have created new streets and alley roads that have opened up the pre-1991 blocks in order to integrate new buildings and facilitate new land uses – especially in parts that formerly were considered as quiet inner residential areas.

Numbers reveal that in Kombinati residents and private developers have built about 6,836 m² of new units since 1992, constituting 37 per cent of the total built form. Whereas in Shallvaret a total area of 12,070 m² has been built since 1992, making up nearly 46 per cent of the total built form. Overall, across the 45,355 m² of the two case study areas, 42 per cent of the buildings were built after 1992. The ratio of pre- and post-socialist built form is consistent throughout the metropolitan scale of Tirana when referring to areas that have had any built form at block level

Figure 7.7 Map of overlaid urban growth in 1989 and 2016, Tirana, Albania. Source: author.

until 1991. Morphological research sheds light on how changes in form, density and land use of individual buildings contribute to fragmentation, even leading to the creation of new blocks.

According to Batty and Xie (1999, 109–24), the change of location for an activity within the urban fabric sets off a chain reaction so that other activities are motivated to move. Ultimately, such activities readjust their locations to the changed circumstances. Focusing on the built environment as an analytical lens for social and urban change in Tirana, one can appreciate how informal growth has transformed whole blocks that pre-1992 had single residential use and are now mixed-use – especially on the ground floor of the residential units – pushing material adaptation of the buildings to be accessible from street level. As part of a self-regulating process, individual residents and private developers added multiple entrances to buildings, which previously only had one access point, enhancing the number of connections of buildings with streets. In order to facilitate these new entries, they also added new alleyways along the other façades of the buildings.

Figure 7.8 Photograph of an extension to an early 1990s apartment block showing conversions to non-domestic land use on the ground floor in Tirana, Albania. Source: author.

Figure 7.9 Photograph highlighting high demand for commercial units in Tirana, Albania. Source: author.

Sztompka (1991, 295–311) and also Hirt and Stanilov (2009) theorise that the economic crisis of late socialism and early post-socialism has led to the growth of the informal sector as a 'coping strategy' – something that both Dovey and King (2011) and Tonkiss (2020) mention. Potentially, after being abused by the authoritarian governments for decades, 'people no longer perceive[d] it as morally wrong to exploit any system (communist, capitalist or "transitional")' (Hirt and Stanilov 2009). For instance, building in public space was not perceived as something inappropriate to do, confirmed by continuous appropriation from the public realm. Across post-socialist Europe, there was an overnight emergence of new entrepreneurs who needed to find space for their newly established businesses (Stanilov 2007). The need for space for new activities triggered a wave of acute urban public space appropriation and the gradual conversion of residential ground floor apartments to permanent business activities. Currently, the socialist and post-socialist patterns coexist as layers of new development that are superimposed over the old urban fabric where space and society have changed concurrently (Hillier and Netto 2002, 181–203).

Conclusion

Tirana was initially designed under rigid planning concepts supported by politics. With the transition to a capitalist model, public spaces gave rise to private initiatives throughout the urban fabric. Interestingly, it seems that in the contemporary city residents and entrepreneurs are informally 'undoing' the rigid structure, and intuitively they are adopting a mixed-use orientated development close to what Alexander calls the semi-lattice (Alexander 1965, 344–8).

Figure 7.10 Photograph of Tirana, Albania. Source: author.

Informal growth has erased the sharp separations between activities or land uses. Empirical evidence shows that in both case study areas, there has been a 167.5 per cent increase in residential activity along façades and a 248 per cent increase of commercial activity. Besides, before the regime change, 88.4 per cent of total active façades were used for residential purposes and only 11.6 per cent for commercial purposes. In 2016 the ratio of façade activity was 34 per cent residential and 66 per cent commercial.

The rise of new urban patterns created mainly through informal processes has had significant implications for pedestrian and vehicular circulation. Informal urban growth has increased building density and mixed use, and has contributed to the emergence of a new identity of contemporary Tirana. Current development trends are in line with Jane Jacobs's (1961) argument that cities work best at a higher density, with mostly mixed rather than segregated uses.

In the last 25 years of pluralism there have been several local scale 'acupuncture' interventions in Tirana mostly outside of city-scale strategic plans. Looked at through an urban lens, contemporary Tirana is an organically evolved 'self-made' city (Tsenkova 2009), which has through informal exchanges invariably written its own rules of growing and reinventing itself.

References

Alexander, C. 1965. 'A city is not a tree', *Ekistics*, 139: 344–8.
Aliaj, B. 2003. 'Albania: a short history of housing and urban development models during 1945–1990' In Aliaj, B. (ed.) *Making Cities Work: Official final publication of the International Conference of ENHR, Tirana-Albania, 26-28 May 2003*. Tirana: Co-Plan Publications, 24–45.
Aliaj, B., Lulo, K., Myftiu, G., Pone, S., Shqarri, E. and Kenuti, P. 2004. *Tirana: The challenge of urban development*. Škofja Loka, Slovenia: Sloalba.
Baross, P. 1990. 'Sequencing land development: the price implications of legal and illegal settlement growth'. In Baross, P. and Van der Linden, J. J. (eds) *The Transformation of Land Supply Systems in Third World Cities*. London: Avebury, 64–5.
Batty, M. and Xie, Y. 1999. 'Self-organised criticality and urban development', *Discrete Dynamics in Nature and Society*, 3: 109–24.
Besussi, E., Chin, N., Batty, M. and Longley, P. 2010. 'The structure and form of urban settlements'. In Rashed, T. and Jürgens, C. (eds.), *Remote Sensing of Urban and Suburban Areas*. Dordrecht: Springer, 13–31.
Conzen, M.R.G. 1960. 'Alnwick, Northumberland: a study in town-plan analysis', *Transactions and Papers (Institute of British Geographers)*, 27: iii–122.
Dovey, K. and King, R. 2011. 'Forms of informality: morphology and visibility of informal settlements', *Built Environment*, 37 (1): 11–29.
Felstehausen, H. 1999. 'Urban growth and land use changes in Tirana, Albania, with cases describing urban land claims'. Working Papers, University of Wisconsin-Madison, 12806.
Griffiths, S., Jones, C.E., Vaughan, L. and Haklay, M. 2010. 'The persistence of suburban centres in Greater London: combining Conzenian and space syntax approaches', *Urban Morphology*, 14 (2): 85–99.

Hamilton, F.E.I., Andrews, K.D. and Pichler-Milanovic, N. (eds.). 2005. *Transformation of Cities in Central and Eastern Europe: Towards globalization*. New York: United Nations University.

Hillier, B. 1999. 'Centrality as a process: accounting for attraction inequalities in deformed grids', *Urban Design International*, 4 (3): 107–27.

Hillier, B. and Hanson, J. 1984. *The Social Logic of Space*. Cambridge: Cambridge University Press.

Hillier, B., Leaman, A., Stansall, P. and Bedford, M. 1976. 'Space syntax', *Environment and Planning B: Planning and Design*, 3 (2): 147–85.

Hillier, B. and Netto, V. 2002. 'Society seen through the prism of space: outline of a theory of society and space', *Urban Design International*, 7 (3): 181–203.

Hirt, S. 2012. *Iron Curtains: Gates, suburbs and privatization of space in the post-socialist city*. Chichester: Wiley.

Hirt, S. 2015. 'Planning during post-socialism'. In *International Encyclopedia of the Social & Behavioral Sciences, 2nd Edition*, Vol. 18. Amsterdam: Elsevier.

Hirt, S. and Stanilov, K. 2009. 'Revisiting urban planning in the transitional countries'. Unpublished regional study prepared for the Global Report on Human Settlements.

INSTAT. 2001. *Population and Housing Census of Albania*. Tirana: INSTAT.

Jacobs, J. 1961. *The Death and Life of Great American Cities*. New York: Modern Library Edition.

Kamalipour, H. and Dovey, K. 2020. 'Incremental production of urban space: a typology of informal design', *Habitat International,* 98: 102133.

Kera, G. 2004. 'Aspects of the urban development of Tirana: 1820–1939'. Paper given at *European City in Comparative Perspective*, Seventh International Conference on Urban History, Athens. https://tinyurl.com/2m8kwc4z.

Pinho, P. and Oliveira, V. 2009a. 'Cartographic analysis in urban morphology', *Environment and Planning B: Planning and Design*, 36 (1): 107–27.

Porter, L., Lombard, M., Huxley, M., Ingin, A.K., Islam, T., Briggs, J., Rukmana, D., Devlin, R. and Watson, V. 2011. 'Informality, the commons and the paradoxes for planning: Concepts and debates for informality and planning self-made cities: Ordinary informality? The reordering of a Romany neighbourhood: The Land Formalisation Process and the Peri-Urban Zone of Dar es Salaam: Tanzania street vendors and planning in Indonesian cities: Informal urbanism in the USA: new challenges for theory and practice engaging with citizenship and urban struggle through an informality lens', *Planning Theory and Practice*, 12 (1): 115–53. https://doi.org/10.1080/14649357.2011.545626.

Roy, A. and Alsayyad, N. (eds.). 2003. *Urban Informality: Transnational perspectives from the Middle East, Latin America, and South Asia*. Lanham, MD: Lexington Books.

Siksna, A. 1997. 'The effects of block size and form in North American and Australian city centres', *Urban Morphology*, 1 (1): 19–33.

Stanilov, K. (ed.). 2007. *The Post-socialist City: Urban form and space transformations in Central and Eastern Europe after socialism*. Cham: Springer Science and Business Media.

Szelenyi, I. 1996. 'Cities under socialism – and after'. In Andrusz, G., Harloe, M. and Szelenyi, I. (eds.), *Cities after Socialism: Urban and regional change and conflict in post-socialist societies*. Oxford: Blackwell, 286–317.

Sztompka, P. 1991. 'The intangibles and imponderables of the transition to democracy', *Studies in Comparative Communism*, 24 (3): 295–311.

Tonkiss, F. 2020. 'City government and urban inequalities', *City: Analysis of Urban Change, Theory, Action*, 24: 286–301.

Tosics, I. 2005. 'City development in Central and Eastern Europe since 1990: the impacts of internal forces'. In Hamilton, F.E.I., Andrews, K.D. and Pichler-Milanovic, N. (eds.), *Transformation of Cities in Central and Eastern Europe: Towards globalization*. New York: UN University Press, 44–78.

Tosics, I., Hegedüs, J. and Remmert, M. 2002. 'Housing in south-eastern Europe: between state and market', *SEER: Journal for Labour and Social Affairs in Eastern Europe*, 4 (4): 123–49.

Tsenkova, S. 2009. *Self-made Cities: In search of sustainable solutions for informal settlements in the United Nations Economic Commission for Europe region*. Geneva: United Nations Publications.

Tsenkova, S. 2010. 'Informal settlements in post-communist cities: diversity factors and patterns', *Urbani izziv*, 21 (2): 73–84.

Weiss, S.J. 2006. *Almost Architecture*. Stuttgart: Akademie Schloss Solitude.

Whitehand, J.W.R. 2007. 'Conzenian urban morphology and urban landscapes'. In *6th International Space Syntax Symposium*, 12–15. http://spacesyntaxistanbul.itu.edu.tr/papers/invitedpapers/Jeremy_whitehand.pdf.

8
Informal structures of welfare: emerging spaces of social reproduction in Athens

Isabel Gutiérrez Sánchez

Informality: a critical lens for emerging citizen-led initiatives in times of crisis

In times of crisis it is common to see the emergence of self-organised networks of mutual help in response to economic and social distress. People hit and deprived by the crisis build new support structures by organising around everyday matters of *social reproduction*. These emerging circuits of self-reproduction develop outside or alongside the official institutions of welfare provision, instituting what the anthropologist Theodoros Rakopoulos[1] (2015: 86) has referred to as a 'hidden welfare system'. In his ethnographic work he defines the informality that shapes this system as a form of social interaction based on agreed codes of behaviour that entail implicit social commitments.

This chapter focuses on contemporary Athens, a crisis-ridden city. Informality will be used as a critical lens that first and foremost draws attention to the increasing number of people who have been displaced to the margins of society. The chapter draws on anthropological fieldwork in three *solidarity initiatives*,[2] which were set up upon the enforced implementation of austerity programmes in Greece. The three studied initiatives are *O Allos Anthropos Social Kitchen*, the *Athens Community Polyclinic and Pharmacy (ACP&P)*, and *City Plaza Refugee Accommodation Centre*. Of the three only *City Plaza* is no longer active at present. The chapter will present and reflect on how – at the time of fieldwork in 2016 – informality yielded a specific form of doing and conceiving politics within these citizen-led initiatives. Furthermore, it will seek to show that this mode of organising and ruling was strongly dependent on the informal re-use, re-appropriation and transformation of urban spaces and buildings, as well as on the production of new informal spatial arrangements that would subvert established urban boundaries. It will be argued that informality, in conjunction with a vocation to care, actually sustained and nourished the studied solidarity initiatives.

Importantly, the definition of informality here elaborated is explicitly site-specific. The concept will be problematised by analysing the specific features of this logic of social interplay, what it elicits, allows and fosters, as well as the tensions and contradictions to which it gives rise in the three studied urban instances. Underpinning this stance is the belief that by avoiding the use of the concept as a pre-defining and blind attribute, informality can become a powerful analytical tool to engage critically with emerging practices of mutual help at the local level. I also explore the role of urban space in/for these practices and the imprint of these on the urban environment. In other words, informality can help question the diverse mechanisms by which citizen-led projects develop in and transform a city in crisis, and how they may expand beyond this context.

A crisis of social and urban reproduction

Seven years after the outset of the crisis that started in the international financial sector, by 2015 Greece still remained in recession.[3] Despite European institutions' promises and successive changes of national governments, the country had no prospects of rapid recovery. Bailout agreements and austerity policies implemented from the first Memorandum of Understanding[4] in 2010 until 2018 transformed the country into a site of radical neoliberal experimentation, ultimately worsening the national economy and seriously harming Greek society. Such experiment – perpetrated from above by political and economic elites – in fact came to continue and intensify a general trend in Europe towards widespread economic liberalisation[5] in order to strengthen the private sector.

The first austerity packages did not bring about any economic recovery. The country's GDP growth dropped, unemployment rate increased and public debt grew.[6] Greek households lost more than one third of their incomes.[7] Paradoxically, the cost of living remained high as the prices of basic products, power and water continued rising due to further taxation[8] and privatisation of public companies. The severe economic stress together with the great cuts in public spending and social benefits for unemployment, disease and pregnancy left a great share of the population in debt. Cases of extreme poverty increased dramatically, with more than a third of the population[9] under the poverty line.

The attack on people's livelihoods enabled by the crisis directly affected their everyday life and the processes of *social reproduction*.[10] Deriving from Marxist and feminist theories, social reproduction refers to the material and social maintenance of a group of people and their social bonds on a daily basis as well as to their generational regeneration. Social reproduction therefore encompasses material and social aspects, namely the bodies and livelihoods of the group as well as the structuring of the social relationships and identities derived from these specific ways of subsistence. Throughout the contemporary capitalist world, increasing numbers of people are facing growing difficulties in securing their means of living, as the main institutions bearing and organising the set of reproductive functions are currently crumbling.

In Greece, the state and the family – fundamental pillars of the country's social welfare – have been especially hit by the crisis. As such, the long-established and acknowledged social safety net of Greek society has been severely damaged. Yet, the collapse of the welfare system – in Greece and other European countries – is not an exclusive consequence of the latest economic downturn. It is part of a crisis of social reproduction at a global scale that reflects a long-running systemic trend towards structural unemployment, impoverishment and dismantling of welfare structures. The series of cuts in Greece's public expenditure, taxation increases, privatisation of public goods and welfare infrastructures have aggravated this crisis of reproduction of people's livelihoods in the country. Additionally, the long-term state of emergency has legitimised the restriction and sometimes the violation of fundamental socio-economic and democratic rights, like the right to healthcare, housing, electricity and water supply, or the right to pacific protest. The Greek capital has been a major witness to all these enforced measures and processes. Urban lands and public assets have been sold off or privatised, a large segment of its population has been excluded from social welfare and urban services, and police presence and operations especially targeting migrants, activists and marginalised urban dwellers have notably increased (Vaiou 2014; Kalandides and Vaiou 2015; Boano and Gyftopoulou 2016; Koutrolikou 2016).

In response to the violent changes in their lives and welfare, the people in Greece mobilised to fight back against the devastating impacts of the austerity regime. Since the beginning of the crisis, a myriad of struggles and citizen-led initiatives emerged across the country, mainly in the big cities. Many of these self-organised initiatives were established following the social uprisings of the so-called *Movement of the Squares*. In 2011, this series of social mobilisations packed the squares of hundreds of European cities with protests against the political class and their austerity politics. Interestingly, the movement linked the protests with the claim of public space. In Athens, open-air assemblies and an informal encampment were set up in Syntagma Square in front of the Greek parliament. The informal occupation, which for several weeks radically subverted the established rhythms of everyday life at the core of the Greek capital, would become a site of experimentation of forms of organising, politically and socially. After the encampment was violently evicted, the movement spread across the city taking root in some neighbourhoods in the form of solidarity initiatives, many of which informally occupied spaces as a conscious political action of confrontation or resistance. Ever since, these collectives of organised urban dwellers have practised public acts of claiming rights, open-air assemblies, installation of self-constructions or temporary settings, creation of gardens and playgrounds and refurbishment of unused or abandoned buildings. In this way, many sites and resources neglected, abandoned or actually closed off and privatised as a result of the economic crisis have been brought back to common use by informal means in imaginative and innovative ways.

The emergence of soup kitchens, social groceries, exchange-networks without intermediaries, social clinics and pharmacies, cultural and social spaces, mobile laundries and accommodation centres for/with immigrants and refugees brought about a grassroots movement popularly referred to as *the Solidarity Movement*.[11] The solidarity initiatives, many of which have continued into the present, have largely engaged people hit by the crisis and thus excluded from many of the social realms – the labour market, the public services and some public spaces. Since their respective onsets, these different groups have strived to provide practical solutions to meet basic daily needs, as well as local strategies to safeguard the means of living (Rübner Hansen and Zechner 2015a; 2015b). In so doing, they have built new infrastructures of collective care and mutual aid. Over time, they have eventually created an architecture of social care composed by operative – albeit unsettled – networks and circuits of self-reproduction across the metropolitan territories, instituting thereby a sort of 'hidden welfare system', as noted by Rakopoulos (2015). This system is characterised by a remarkable informal character.

Informality in this context refers to a form of reciprocity that stems from face-to-face communication processes rather than from pre-fixed universal rules or protocols. In this mode of personal interaction and exchange, the awareness of a web of interconnected relationships gives rise to a tacit acknowledgment of accountability to others. This recognition of interconnection that develops from the embodied experience of daily encounters is what actually sustains the web. In this light, informality is a logic of social interplay that is relational and contingent on the context rather than absolute and abstract. Alongside informality there is another aspect that also permeates the everyday practice of the solidarity initiatives. It is a personal disposition to help and share. As has been mentioned, people in these initiatives interact and organise around everyday matters of social reproduction on a volunteering and collective basis. This, on the one hand, intensifies the awareness of interconnection and expands the sense of implicit obligation to be accountable to others, towards an acknowledgment of shared responsibility and willingness to take care of each other. On the other hand, it also reinforces the need to embrace the contingency of the material conditions of the context. In these daily arrangements space and material resources play a fundamental role. In turn, the urban environment also experiences transformation – or counter-transformation.

The solidarity movement: three urban instances

This chapter draws on anthropological fieldwork carried out in 2016 and 2017 in three solidarity initiatives in Athens, namely *O Allos Anthropos Social Kitchen*, the *Athens Community Polyclinic and Pharmacy (ACP&P)*, and *City Plaza Refugee Accommodation Centre*.[12]

O Allos Anthropos Social Kitchen

O Allos Anthropos Social Kitchen (*O Allos Anthropos* translates as *The Other Person*) launched in 2012 driven by Konstantinos Polychronopoulos, who at that time had been jobless for more than two years. The primary aim was quite focused: to provide anyone in need with free meals. The project started growing as friends and new volunteers became involved. Eventually, they began installing a makeshift kitchen daily in squares and other urban open spaces. They would cook at the chosen site and then they would enjoy the meal together with the rest of the people. At the time of my fieldwork, they used to hand out around 70 daily portions on average, reaching 300 on busy days. The initiative centred on a rented building in the neighbourhood of Metaxourgeio in central Athens that was used as the headquarters. The space comprised a kitchen, a warehouse and a space for school support activities, and also offered night accommodation and free baths for homeless people. In 2019 the headquarters were relocated in the Keramikos area, quite close to the former one.

Opposed as they are to any institutional engagement, the people of *O Allos Anthropos* have managed to partnership with independent food suppliers and stall-holders in the municipal markets. Besides, the initiative is part of a network of other social kitchens across Greece and beyond. Food distribution has actually been the most prominent solidarity activity since the start of the crisis. Strikingly, by 2013, a fifth of the Greek population was unable to cover their food needs. The plethora of social kitchens that has emerged across the country varies in organisation and scope. Notably, they constitute the underpinning infrastructure of many other solidarity initiatives, such as the distribution of clothing or medicines.

Athens Community Polyclinic and Pharmacy

The *Athens Community Polyclinic and Pharmacy (ACP&P)* is one of the multiple self-organised medical centres – popularly known as 'social clinics' – that emerged in the city in the wake of the implementation of the first austerity packages. The institution of social clinics was primarily a response to the breakdown of the Greek National Health System and the privatisation of part of the healthcare sector. Thus, at the beginning, the *ACP&P* provided free of charge health services, prescriptions and pharmaceuticals to Greek citizens and migrants excluded from the NHS. The clinic functions on the basis of donations and volunteer work by doctors with different medical expertise, pharmacists, social workers and other volunteers responsible for administrative tasks. The medical treatments include among others pathology, paediatrics, neurology, cardiology and dental care as well as minor surgical procedures. It also counts on psychologists and social workers. The clinic is part of a network of other social clinics across Athens, and has agreements with some public and private hospitals where patients with special needs are referred. The *ACP&P* has been running since 2013 in premises near Omonoia Square – an area with a high migrant population in central Athens.

Figure 8.1 Diagrammatic depiction of *O Allos Anthropos Social Kitchen*, Athens, Greece. Source: Gutiérrez, 2016.

Figure 8.2 Diagrammatic depiction of *Athens Community Polyclinic and Pharmacy*, Athens, Greece. Source: Gutiérrez, 2016.

City Plaza Refugee Accommodation Centre

In April 2016 several groups of activists from the political left and a group of refugees came together under the initiative *Solidarity Initiative to Economic and Political Refugees*, and occupied an abandoned seven-storey hotel in the area of Victoria in central Athens. Throughout its life, the squat or the 'house' – as residents used to refer to it – operated as a self-managed and self-funded housing community. Different working groups covered all the daily housekeeping chores – cooking, cleaning, security, storage and logistics – as well as additional tasks and specific activities such as reception, the women's space, the clinic, the bar, media communication, children's activities, language lessons, art workshops and other entertainment activities such as cinema and dancing. Periodically, they also organised parties and political actions to protest and demand migrant and refugee rights, as well as talks and events with invited international intellectuals and activists. The project was sustained by economic and in-kind donations of food, hygiene and cleaning products, clothing, toys and other equipment for children. Until July 2019, when the residents eventually left the building voluntarily, *City Plaza* provided safe and dignified accommodation for 2,500 refugees in total, as well as dozens of so-called international 'solidarians'.

At the time of my fieldwork, alongside *City Plaza*, there were around another dozen buildings in Athens that had been occupied to shelter displaced people. Some of these spaces remain active at the time of writing. They constitute a bold response from the grassroots to repressive EU border policies, to the great deficiencies of successive programmes for refugees' relocation across Europe, and to the failed reception system established by the Greek state in the wake of the large-scale arrival of migrants and asylum seekers in 2015, all of which has entailed multiple exclusions and human rights violations.

Politics of informality

The organisation of solidarity initiatives has been rooted from the beginning in relations of mutuality stemming from face-to-face interactions and tacitly recognised social obligations. Namely, informal interactions and exchanges have constituted the principal mode of operation of the majority of these grassroots projects. This informal logic has prevailed over a system of prescribed normative procedures. As Rakopoulos (2015) points out, in everyday life these casual social

Figure 8.3 Diagrammatic depiction of *City Plaza Refugee Accommodation Centre*, Athens, Greece. Source: Gutiérrez, 2016.

agreements often tend to be more binding than many formalised contractual relations established with officially recognised institutions. An awareness of interconnection and the embracement of interdependence, which is very specific to the solidarity initiatives, feed a sense of mutual responsibility and engagement that keeps most of the initiatives running. In the light of this, for instance, it was usual to see people who had been previously helped by the *O Allos Anthropos* collective approaching the makeshift kitchen in Monastiraki Square with homemade spinach pies and biscuits. They would usually say that they came just for the good time and the conversations they had during food preparation and the common meal that followed. With time, some would eventually engage with the kitchen offering voluntary work on a regular basis. Similarly, in *City Plaza*, it was common practice to look after the neighbours' children and the elderly when someone needed to be absent for a while. The favour would then be returned either in the same way or through an invitation to tea and pastries in the room. In addition, there were volunteers who would visit former resident families with babies or elderly people in their new homes – which for a period were provided on a temporary basis by the state for certain asylum seekers. They would assist the elderly in their daily shower and also look after the medicines they needed. As for the

ACP&P, at a certain point, the social clinic started receiving monetary and in-kind donations from former patients – migrants in their majority – who had eventually settled in the neighbourhood and set up small businesses.

The flexible organisation around day-to-day matters of social reproduction in these studied initiatives came to yield a form of doing politics characterised by a rather instinctive accommodation of the contingency and multiplicity of everyday life. Space took on an active role, eliciting the informal emergence of common codes, pacts and commitments. Decisions were made according to the specificity of each situation, giving room for affection and prioritising personal relationships over absolute rules. The way the working groups functioned in *City Plaza* exemplifies this point. In parallel to the general assembly – the so-called 'house assembly' – the different working groups had their own regular meetings where more specific issues concerning the organisation and management of activities, resources and spaces were addressed. The logic on which they operated often clashed with the rationale of the house assembly, which sought general norms of mandatory compliance as the basis to rule and manage the squat. In everyday practice, those pre-established rules became subject to constant re-negotiations. One of these rules, for instance, established that anyone skipping a mandatory shift more than twice would be expelled from the squat. In practice, the implementation of this rule was rather vague, for on the one hand, it was unclear whether a group had the actual power to enforce it, and on the other, membership in the groups was usually quite blurred. Even the expulsion of someone could turn revocable depending on each case and individual.

Reservation towards formalised procedures is in fact a commonplace across the spectrum of solidarity initiatives, albeit in varying degrees. During my fieldwork time, this was visible, for instance, in the opposition of the *ACP&P* to set formal or paid training courses for the volunteers at the clinic. The same approach was observed by the anthropologist Heath Cabot[13] (2016) in her fieldwork at another social clinic in Athens. For its part, in *City Plaza,* there was a time when the house assembly argued for a long time the convenience of establishing a sort of ID card for any resident, visitor or volunteer at the squat, to finally decide against the proposal on the premise that they were not an 'organisation'. The standardisation of procedures was widely seen as rigid, inefficient and discriminatory by most of the people in the squat. In contrast, their informal way of organising did actually facilitate the incorporation of particular suggestions and the accommodation of unexpected situations.

Their form of decentralised and flexible organisation did in fact make possible continuous readjustments in the daily routine in response to the concrete material and affective needs of the residents.

The rejection of bureaucratic procedures that most solidarity initiatives shared goes beyond the preference for a specific mode of interaction in managerial terms. It usually comes from a rather widespread distrust in formal institutions, especially the state. In this respect, the non-formalised status of most of the solidarity initiatives and their ambivalent organising structure has been used in many cases as a defence mechanism against legal action from third parties as well as potential police raids. At the time of my fieldwork, this was most evident in the case of *City Plaza* and other squats housing refugees. The aforementioned discussion about the potential establishment of ID cards in *City Plaza* also attests to this political attitude. Nevertheless, it must be recalled that informality is also common in practices at institutional level, especially in times of crisis when extraordinary measures are allowed under a state of emergency. Unlike informal practices of coping, which are quite often discredited, informality within institutional frameworks is rarely seen as illegal. In fact, many solidarity initiatives have faced different sorts of accusations and attempts at illegalisation at some point. Given the case, the lack of a legal and defined body has hindered the possible accusation or charge of specific individuals. As such, in these instances, informality becomes more a collective strategy based on opacity that is used against external threats or attacks to the group.

Nevertheless, as noted already, the stance against legal or formalised organisations varies depending on the case. The three studied initiatives actually had some sort of relation with public institutions or NGOs, yet was not exempt from controversy within each of the collectives. In the social clinic this relation was more open, as it had agreements with certain hospitals as well as with non-profit organisations from which they openly received pharmaceuticals. For their part, both the social kitchen and *City Plaza* did accept some donations from NGOs at some point. Furthermore, as their activities consolidated in time, a kind of semi-bureaucratisation was eventually established for practical reasons. Particularly in *City Plaza*, discussions about the extent to which rules and a set of fixed procedures ought to be established came up on a daily basis. Not everyone embraced informality equally. This created frequent friction among those who were more used to this way of functioning, and those who needed and reclaimed a more formalised system. The latter denounced the lack of more fixed rules as creating confusion among newcomers, and allowed the emergence of injustices or discrimination.

In fact, significant problems of power imbalance did emerge at times when for example personal communications failed or no agreement was reached, or when equal access to participate in the management of the space was not guaranteed, for example when the rota system – intended to provide everyone with the chance to participate interchangeably in all of the working groups – stagnated. In such situations certain individuals accumulated the power to decide and execute to the detriment of others, who assumed a subordinate position. Indeed, when informality was played out internally as a mechanism to hide, it jeopardised the sense of responsiveness and responsibility that sustained the group. Thus, used as an opaque resource for individual purposes, informality no longer works as a mode of interaction that builds on the recognition of interconnection and interdependence among people. It is no longer a form of reciprocity but rather a form of accumulation of power; in this way informality actually becomes an internal threat for the initiatives, which need transparency, trust and openness to keep running.

These accounts attest to the significant vulnerability of the solidarity initiatives, which paradoxically does not deny their value, strength and potentiality especially for those deprived and excluded in a city in crisis. Most solidarity initiatives – some of which are no longer active at present, as with *City Plaza* – constitute in reality quite unsettled structures. As spaces in constant flux and permanent reconfiguration, most of them do have a precarious presence. Ambivalent and unstable, they often become vulnerable to internal disagreements on the one hand, as well as to external attempts at criminalisation or co-opting by public authorities or private – usually commercial – interests on the other. In most cases their survival is subject to external support, as in the case of the three examples presented in this chapter, which at the time of my fieldwork were all sustained thanks to donations from external agents.

Nevertheless, despite the internal tensions and contradictions within the solidarity initiatives, at a broader level, their politics of informality proved quite successful in creating cohesive and active political communities. The frameworks and mechanisms of collective participation in common matters that have been created in these spaces do reinstate actual citizenship rights by which migrants, refugees and those deprived of many rights in the crisis recuperate a political self (Cabot 2016). Importantly, as the architect Stavros Stavrides (2016) has contended, there are no homogeneous communities resulting from experience in the solidarity initiatives, but rather communities permanently in the making. As has been noted, the political character of these initiatives develops from the everyday economy of resources and space, from the collective practice of constructing the space. This fosters processes of subjectivation that do not produce specific collective identities. This characteristic displaces the focus on identity towards narratives and imaginaries around notions of home, solidarity and mutual care, which take on renewed meanings.

Spatial imprint: considerations on informality in space-making practices

The institution of solidarity initiatives has been linked to the creation of what Stavrides (2014; 2016) has theorised as *common spaces*,[14] which have been set up through spatial occupations, re-arrangements and re-definitions of existing spaces in the city. The three studied initiatives are examples of this. For instance, the occupied hotel *City Plaza* was turned into a centre that integrated accommodation with healthcare facilities and common areas, which alternately served as playgrounds, classrooms, workshops, spaces for collective celebrations, assemblies, film screenings or just casual gatherings. Similarly, the *ACP&P* was set up in the premises of a building in the city centre with most of its floors in disuse. An extensive refurbishment was carried out prior to the opening so as to accommodate different areas, the pharmacy, a number of medical rooms and equipment. For its part, *O Allos Anthropos* social kitchen, which at the time of my fieldwork used to change location on a daily basis, would take over squares and open spaces for a few hours reactivating them with new activities and rhythms. Since their inception, solidarity initiatives have been proof of the fact that cities constitute grounds of relentless struggle, which in times of crisis even become amplified by emerging forms of resistance through which urban space is reclaimed and transformed. Certainly, urban space has acted as a fundamental constituent of solidarity initiatives, not merely as the setting for their practices, but also as their very means of conformation and development (Stavrides 2014; 2016).

Solidarity initiatives began introducing new uses into the city from the early months of the aftermath of the Movement of the Squares. The reorganisation and re-arrangement of social reproduction services in the urban space outside – or parallel to – official institutions has created new *spatialities* and dynamics in the city's everyday life. In Athens, kitchens and dining rooms re-emerged on the streets and squares, while the latter moved to the living rooms and common spaces in the squatted accommodation spaces across the city. For example, when the people partaking in *O Allos Anthropos* initiative arranged the makeshift kitchen in the square, for a period they blurred the established demarcations between public and private, creating what Stavrides (2016) has called a *threshold*.[15] In such a temporary setting, a kitchen migrated from its traditional domestic sphere onto the street, while in turn the street – its life, varying dynamics and materiality – became part of the action of cooking and eating together. These subversions brought about spatio-temporal scenarios where encounters, exchanges and collective deliberations flourished, reinstating a space of conviviality in many public spaces where collective life had actually been lost either to big commercial real estate speculative interests or to direct neglect and disinvestment by the authorities. In those sites enlivened by the social kitchen, social interactions and face-to-face communications were indeed intensified and expanded in time. Participation was thereby encouraged and the chosen site became more dynamic, porous and resilient. In a similar fashion, the intimate spaces of *City Plaza*'s bedrooms quite often transformed into temporary living and dining rooms bringing together residents, neighbours and friends around home-made meals and tea.

As these brief accounts show, the resulting spatiality of the everyday practices of the solidarity initiatives reflected – and in those still active still does – the underlying informality in their mode of interacting, organising and ruling. Space was produced by continuous negotiation among the members of the groups themselves, newcomers and external agents, following the logic of non-predetermined norms or plans. Thus, the space that came forth was never finished or completed. Rather it was a space always in-the-making, as happened with the communities that were created (Stavrides 2016). Certainly, the spatial contours of the studied initiatives were always in permanent fluctuation, creating a form of fluid and ever-changing spatiality. Their boundaries did not finish at the physical borders imposed by the materiality of the buildings. On the contrary, they challenged those, expanding and contracting according to the constant negotiations and the varying plethora of activities that were performed. *City Plaza* exemplified this well. In the mornings, the reception hall of the former hotel became a barbershop. In the afternoon, the staircase connecting the different residential floors turned into a playground when children arrived from school. At night, either the living room or the rooftop transformed into an open cinema. The result was a rather formless space that had no defined boundaries, for these limits were always changing. Clearly, space in the initiatives was a key collective asset to reclaim, protect and care for. As such, participants in the social kitchen would for example clean up the place carefully after each common meal. Likewise in *City Plaza* rotary cleaning teams would sweep and mop the floor daily, with eventual common 'deep-cleaning-days'.

Despite some solidarity initiatives being short-lived, at present the imprint of the practices of those remaining in the city space keeps producing a non-planned spatiality, which remains permanently incomplete, open to newcomers and unforeseen situations, unstable, diffuse, ambivalent and liminal. Importantly, by reinstating negotiation and decision-making practices as well as self-keeping and maintenance of an extended public space, solidarity initiatives have informally expanded the space of politics and reactivated the social function of the public space (Vaiou 2014; Kalandides and Vaiou 2015). Arguably, this mode of informally producing urban space, which challenges enclosures imposed from above as well as long-fixed demarcations and brings back collective life to the streets and neighbourhoods by means of new rearrangements of everyday urban social reproduction, stands in opposition to the neoliberal drive that has guided urban development in many cities of Southern Europe since the 1990s. Such a drive has seen fragmenting, segregating and polarising of the urban geography as well as the prolongation and intensification of these processes with new privatisations and enclosures during the crisis.

Conclusion

A decade after the introduction of the first structural adjustment package, Greece remains in crisis, with significant numbers of people still unable to meet daily needs. The drastic cuts in state welfare provision and the dissolution of the long-held social safety net procured by the family stand out among the dramatic changes brought about by the crisis and the austerity regime. In this context of hardship, however, the emergence of informal solidarity initiatives has posed a challenge to the social and urban exclusions generated – or amplified – during this enduring crisis. These grassroots initiatives, most of them set up in urban areas as is the case in the three presented in this chapter, have actually created an insurgent social movement that has enabled the construction – or reconstruction – of interconnected protective networks against exclusion and isolation. The wide diversity of solidarity projects has come to compose a kaleidoscopic landscape of self-organised groups striving to provide alternatives to an ever-deepening crisis of social reproduction especially patent in everyday life. In many cases, their endeavour has included the informal recuperation of abandoned or neglected spaces and buildings and the reintegration of these into the public urban circuit. In others, it has seen the temporary reactivation of squares and open spaces across the city.

As has been expounded, solidarity initiatives are informal in nature. Namely, the sense of responsibility and caring for each other that underpins the daily function of these groups is largely channelled through informal interactions and exchanges in the everyday. This makes possible and sustains the web of relations that each initiative comprises. Interestingly, informality in the initiatives derives from a form of doing and conceiving politics based on the organic adaptation to people's material and affective needs. In this way, organising and ruling become site-specific practices that respond to the material contingency of everyday situations. In turn, space – its use, management and maintenance – becomes a central political constituent. That is, the political praxis of these self-organised collectives is also a spatial practice, which manifests and translates the logic of informality and mutual care into a specific spatiality. This spatial outcome is characterised by diffuse and ever-changing borders. It is dynamic, unfinished, resilient, polyvalent and liminal. As such, it brings forth in-between moments that subvert established spatial demarcations. However, and importantly, it is also unstable, conflictual and vulnerable.

As has been noted, tensions and contradictions are also part of everyday life in the solidarity initiatives, as sometimes the scarcity of fixed norms lays the ground for some individuals to take advantage of others. However, and despite the fact that some solidarity initiatives are no longer operative due to different circumstances, as a movement they have certainly managed to thrive in the gaps left by the state and those that the family can no longer cover. The politics of informality of the solidarity initiatives, inherently associated with practices of space reclaiming and transformation, has otherwise been quite successful in creating well-functioning platforms of organisation of social reproduction, that is, they have many times, and in various ways, in overt opposition to the official institutions of the state or large non-governmental organisations. As a matter of fact, in the management of the Greek crisis, public institutions and many NGOs have failed in creating the type of social bonds that can foster collective engagement, partly because their formal operating mode actually precludes the capability to reciprocate. In contrast, the indefiniteness and indeterminacy of the solidarity initiatives have proved a fertile ground for people to learn to be, to work and to struggle together. Furthermore, as Kalandides and Vaiou (2015) have highlighted, in experimenting with different frameworks of participation and decision-making in and through the urban space, solidarity initiatives reconfigure the public as it has been defined – and constrained – under austerity. Through their multiple activities, these groups – albeit to different degrees depending on the case – certainly challenge the processes of segregation and polarisation as well as the spatial degradation yielded by the crisis. More so, amid and despite a context of deprivation and shortage, they generate new imaginaries of alternative forms of living together, and in so doing, they pave the way towards a potential new political and urban horizon in which social reproduction would be placed at the centre of social and urban life. In this light, informality in conjunction with the vocation of caring may arguably become a desirable move in politics and the spatial production of the city beyond the crisis.

Notes

1   Theodoros Rakopoulos is a Greek anthropologist who has researched food co-ops and alternative food distribution networks during the crisis in Greece (2013–16).
2   The emergence and expansion of citizen-led initiatives during the crisis in Greece came to be widely referred to as the 'Solidarity Movement' (or 'solidarity initiatives'), first in everyday discourse and later in the media, academia and the government.
3   The Real GDP growth in 2015 was -1.4 per cent. Source: *European Commission Annual Macroeconomic Database, November 2015*.
4   The first Memorandum of Understanding (MoU) was agreed in May 2010 between the Greek government (PASOK) and the IMF (International Monetary Fund), the European Commission and the ECB (European Central Bank).
5   The liberalisation of the economy encouraged in Europe over the last three decades includes polices of deregulation and free trade, privatisation of public goods and infrastructures and reductions in public expenditure.
6   By 2015 Greece's GDP growth had dropped to -1.4 per cent. The national unemployment rate increased from 9.5 per cent in 2009 to 24.6 per cent in 2015, with 49.5 per cent youth unemployment. Source: *European Commission Annual Macroeconomic Database, November 2015*.
7   In five years, the average wage dwindled by 38 per cent, while pensions were reduced by 45 per cent. Source: *Hellenic Statistical Authority (EL.STAT)*.
8   VAT increased to 23 per cent, and special tax on real estate property was enforced.
9   In 2015, the percentage of population under the poverty line (that is, under the 60 per cent of the national average of available income) was 34.6 per cent. Source: *Hellenic Statistical Authority (EL.STAT)*.
10 As the feminist scholar Silvia Federici (2012) explains, the concept of social reproduction was used in the 1970s mainly in terms of domestic work. Later, the notion was expanded stressing the fact that the reproduction of life (and the workforce) happens also outside the home, and encompasses the care of the environment too.
11 See note 2.
12 The three examples of solidarity initiatives presented in this chapter are part of my PhD research project. They have been introduced in other chapters of edited books to discuss topics and aspects related to my research, but different from the elaborations presented here.
13 Heath Cabot is an anthropologist from the United States who has done extensive research on Greece, and more particularly, on social clinics during the crisis.
14 Term coined by the architect Stavros Stavrides in Stavrides (2016).
15 See note 14.

References

Boano, C. and Gyftopoulou, S. 2016. 'Crisis, hidden spaces, politics, and the social imaginary: the case of Athens', *Critical Planning*, 22: 67–97.
Cabot, H. 2016. '"Contagious" solidarity: reconfiguring care and citizenship in Greece's social clinics', *Social Anthropology*, 24 (2): 152–66.
Federici, S. 2012. *Revolution at Point Zero: Housework, reproduction, and feminist struggle*. Oakland, CA: PM Press/Common Notions/Autonomedia.
Kalandides, A. and Vaiou, D. 2015. 'Practices of collective action and solidarity: reconfigurations of the public space in crisis-ridden Athens, Greece', *Journal of Housing and the Built Environment*, 31: 457–70.
Koutrolikou, P. 2016. 'Governmentalities of urban crises in inner-city Athens, Greece', *Antipode*, 48 (1): 179–92.
Rakopoulos, T. 2015. 'Solidarity's tensions: informality, sociality, and the Greek crisis', *Social Analysis*, 59 (3): 104–85.
Rübner Hansen, B. and Zechner, M. 2015a. 'Building power in a crisis of social reproduction', *Roar Magazine*, 0, 1–11.
Rübner Hansen, B. and Zechner, M. 2015b. 'Social reproduction and collective care', *The Occupied Times of London*, 20 August. http://theoccupiedtimes.org/?p=14000.
Stavrides, S. 2014. 'Emerging common spaces as a challenge to the city of crisis', *City*, 18 (4–5): 546–50.
Stavrides, S. 2016. *Common Space: The city as commons*. London: Zed Books.
Vaiou, D. 2014. 'Is the crisis in Athens (also) gendered? Facets of access and (in)visibility in everyday public spaces', *City*, 18 (4–5): 533–7.

9
Rhythmanalysis as exploration of urban informality in Havana, Cuba

Susan Fitzgerald

Originally published in a different format in: Fitzgerald, S.A.M. 2022. *Havana: Mapping lived experiences of urban agriculture*. New York: Routledge.

Sites of urban agriculture in Havana, Cuba, present an interesting case study in urban informality. The definition of informality applied to these gardens is not solely because they meet the United Nations's definitions and tenuously occupy abandoned spaces in between overcrowded and collapsing buildings with limited access to water and sanitation. But rather it is because these spaces exhibit entrepreneurialism in a country where such practices have, until recently, transgressed the values of the Revolution. These sites echo James Holston's observations of the 'autoconstruction' in the *favelas* of São Paulo as these gardens 'turn the neighbourhood into a space of alternative futures', so that the 'lived experiences' become both the 'context and the substance' of the evolving city (Holston 2008: 8–9). These sites are perhaps the vanguard of an evolving revolution, and that somehow makes them *other* (Gold 2015: 74) in their use of creative strategies to meet daily needs for provisioning that can no longer be met by the Cuban state. Amid the ruin of the city, they also provide a place for spontaneous exchanges to occur – a space where things are cultivated, mixed, taught, discussed and sold. The boundaries adjacent to the gardens are shared and transgressed and across their thresholds work, knowledge, goods and conviviality are exchanged.

While there has been much written about the creativity of informality, there has been little work on qualifying or quantifying it (Dovey and King 2011: 26). Such spaces emerge from quotidian life, so finding a method to understand and record the daily interactions and their materiality is difficult as it depends on serendipity and trust as much as methodology. In addition, as Swati Chattopadhyay observes in this volume, informality is all about point of view and does not exist at all to those living among it. The lived experiences of informality are attuned to the everyday and evolving life of the city, the seasons, and the weather. These rhythms shape sites of urban agriculture and their activities, at times structurally transforming the surrounding neighbourhood and then, just as quickly, returning it to a new normal. While it might be seen as impossible to create a coherent quantified reading of such places, perhaps it is possible to record these rhythms at a specific moment at a site. Measuring the polyrhythmic nature of a site over time could help generate robust knowledge about the qualities of the urban experience and the materiality of these gardens.

Henri Lefebvre's rhythmanalysis serves as a valuable tool to understand this relationship as it captures the everyday and evolving urban narratives of a place. Rather than hovering over the city it involves getting close to a site to understand how it is made and re-made. Rather than comparing it to something *other*, it relies upon recording a specific place over time and understanding the performative and sensorial qualities of everyday urban life within it. It moves away from prevalent discourses that concentrate on the formal, static and visual, which tells us little about the daily lived experience. This suggests that this methodology may hold promise as a tool to understand the less tangible characteristics of informality within the city. Over time, understanding these rhythmic attributes may also be useful for the future design of a more inclusive city – rather than relying solely on the visual, economic, and political indicators that we typically use to measure success (Lefebvre 2004).

This chapter focuses on the rhythms surrounding a specific site of urban agriculture in San Isidro in the municipality of La Habana Vieja in Havana, Cuba. This site provides neighbourhood access to food, green medicine and religious plants while also serving as an educational and social hub in the community. The products cultivated are dependent upon the resourcefulness of the producers, the demands of the local consumers and access to insecure state infrastructures such as water and electricity. The daily operations are influenced by seasonal, climatic and political rhythms. These gardens are common in Cuba and represent a paradigm shift in the country from the state supply of food through neighbourhood rationing stores and price-controlled markets to local self-sufficient provisioning, within an emerging entrepreneurial economic model.

How should one unpack the tangle of people and places interacting together surrounding these sites within the city? As an architect, I question if recording such a site in a city through drawings can help serve as both an analytical and explanatory tool. The illustrations operate as an instrument for comparing how space is iteratively produced and re-produced over time. This involves drawing and mapping the atmospheres, activities, materiality and patterns of the neighbourhood rather than just the formal characteristics. This type of drawing does not homogenise the city but rather detects its changing rhythms. Urban experience has always been inextricably linked to various scales of drawing, revealing and reconstructing the multiple layers including the social, political and ecological to expose the lived experience of urban space (Brook 2011: 11–12).

The rhythms of San Isidro

Walking along Habana Street in San Isidro in the intense heat and humidity is a visceral experience including olfactory, somatic, auditory and haptic sensations within a city that is in constant motion. Against the milieu of scarcity, the slow decay of infrastructure and the sudden collapse of buildings is the resourcefulness of everyday invention in a city that continually 'modifies and reinvents itself' (Hernández, Kellett and Allen 2010: xi) through everyday life. Trying to construct an intelligible, rational city from this disorder seems impossible. Still, it is easy to identify specific urban patterns encompassing beats of 'particularities and similarities, repetition and difference, rupture and continuities' (Smith and Hetherington 2013: 6). The act of walking entails encountering these patterns and rhythms by negotiating the unevenness of the decayed streets and the narrowness between sidewalk and pavement. It involves avoiding the strewn garbage and stagnant puddles of water; dodging between people, vegetable carts, bicycle-taxis and dogs; ducking when water drips from air conditioners and laundry. And the whole time it allows views into everyday life through the doorway grilles that separate the street from the home. De Certeau linked meaningful study of space in the city to the practice of walking, and it was through walking that I first encountered sites of urban agriculture within the city of Havana (De Certeau 1998).

The garden in San Isidro is in the south of La Habana Vieja. La Habana Vieja occupies an area of four square kilometres. Merced Street bounds San Isidro to the north, while Egido Street forms the west boundary and the diagonal Desamparados Street is located to the south and east. Despite very few vegetated spaces, this community was ironically named after a protector of market gardens and cultivated fields and became the part of the city where the dock and railway workers lived in *solares* – the Cuban word for rooming houses (Taylor 2009: 149). *Solares* still comprise much of the housing stock that since the Revolution of 1959 have had to accommodate whole families within a single room. Due to lack of space in the houses, the narrow streets in this dense eighteenth-century neighbourhood form the public spaces of the community with '11,385 residents living in about 1,384 dwelling units' (Taylor 2009: 150). The morphology of La Habana Vieja consists of connected houses with high ceilings and courtyards for ventilation within these narrow streets. It was a Spanish design solution for hot dry climates but not so favourable for the hot, humid conditions found in the tropical climate of Havana (Tablada et al. 2009: 1943) (Díaz et al. 2006: 1–5). The problem has been exacerbated since occupants have encroached into the courtyard ventilation shafts and in-filled the tall floors with mezzanines in a desperate struggle to gain extra space for dwelling. To make matters worse, the ratio of green space in this part of the city is incredibly low. At 1.1 metre per inhabitant, vegetated spaces are so few that a heat-island effect takes place, where the district is always warmer than the surrounding city (Scarpaci, Segre and Coyula 2002: 105).

For this reason, the site of interest to this study is particularly important within this area as it is a garden, an oasis of vegetation within the density. Given the right to use this land, by usufruct, Julio tends this 13 by 34-metre plot. It occupies the space where a house collapsed in about 1990. During the Special Period of the 1990s, the land was used for food cultivation within the community. However, one day in 2011, while the municipality was undertaking repair work in the street, the city inadvertently disconnected the domestic water supply to the site, making the lack of infrastructure impossible for the water-intensive plants. Immediately, Julio had to transition to crops requiring less irrigation. The plants that are currently cultivated are used in Santería religious ceremonies, whose rituals involve the use of herbs, roots and flowers. Such plants are also used in homoeopathic remedies, or what is called green medicine, for their healing properties and include moringa tree, basil, chija, oregano, garlic, cotton, ginger, hibiscus, avocado and aloe vera. According to the producers, the site's shady, dry conditions support these plants. Customers now come from all over the city to this cultivated area to purchase the products and seek medical advice.

Figure 9.1 Photograph of street view outside Julio's garden in La Habana Vieja, Cuba. Source: Fitzgerald, 2015.

A lockable gate separates the site from the street. The hours posted for consultations are between 10am and 2pm from Monday to Friday. Green medicine is endorsed by the medical community and used in conjunction with conventional treatments. While there is ample access to doctors in Cuba, drugs are very scarce and to fill the void physicians encourage their patients to use herbal remedies. The head producer, Julio, gives his medical advice on the plants from behind a mobile counter he wheels into place at the front of the garden during hours of operation. He also sells products from other producers at his point-of-sale counter, connecting the site to the extended local economy. His three part-time assistants help collect the leaves, flowers and roots from the various plants and Julio carefully mixes or wraps the medicine in front of his waiting clients. The mixtures are handed to the customers in jars, newspaper and bottles recycled from the surrounding neighbourhood with verbal instructions for their use. The counter, shelves, milk crates, canopy and a selection of chairs are all found objects that collectively make up his consulting room and pharmacy. From behind his counter, he talks at great length with each group, often oblivious to the growing queue of eager customers developing around his site. The nature of an

Figure 9.2 Photograph of harvested plants in Julio's garden in La Habana Vieja, Cuba. Source: Fitzgerald, 2018.

individual's medical issue does not appear to be sensitive or private as other customers often sympathetically share the same health concern and decide to purchase, for their own well-being, the remedy recommended to the previous patient. Julio informed me that, in 2015, he consulted with 1,460 people, recording each of their names in a handwritten log kept under his counter, along with the remedies and plants he prescribed.

The financial exchanges for these products often occur through the bartering of goods and services in return for the remedies. This fluid and informal economy is typical of this network that involves recycling, inventing, sharing and creating to extend the 'margins of the [...] system' (Hernández, Kellett and Allen 2010: xiii) to find space in it for all citizens. *Trabajadores por cuenta propia* is the name given to self-employed workers that operate outside of the state-controlled centralised economy. It has been legal in Cuba since 1993 but is limited to a list of 201 legal occupations, and it is a controversial sector within the Cuban economy as it signifies the emergence of individuals working for private

Figure 9.3 Photograph of customers on the street outside Julio's garden waiting to buy plants in La Habana Vieja, Cuba. Source: Fitzgerald, 2017.

gain (United States International Trade Commission 2016: 32). Sites of urban agriculture straddle between this market sector. When asked about their work on this site and the forms of financial compensation, the workers highlight that their commercial endeavours are linked to altruistic activities such as providing produce and homeopathic remedies to the elderly and pregnant within the community. They do this to stress their deep connections to the core values of socialism and the revolution through their daily activities.

Such participation in the life of the community shapes the daily goings-on for Julio and his assistants. In addition to donating food and medicine, four local primary schools come to his site in the afternoons to learn about cultivation, production and green medicine. Each school is named after famous revolutionaries including Sergio Luis Ferriol, Carlos Manuel de Céspedes, Don Mariano Martí Navarro and Oscar Lucero Moya. The groups consist of 15 to 20 students. They come without a teacher and sit in the part of the site Julio calls the classroom, outside a small structure referred to as his office. This little clearing prevents the children from damaging any of the plants as they are briefed on the lessons and activities for the afternoon, which typically include path

Figure 9.4 Photograph showing views from above of Julio's garden in La Habana Vieja, Cuba. Source: Fitzgerald, 2015.

clearing, weeding and watering. Handwritten signs at the end of all the beds encourage them to learn the plant names. This garden works well as a classroom and there have been several modifications to facilitate learning opportunities with spaces and paths cleared for students to gather around the compost area and cistern so that the children can understand about the necessary inputs for growing plants. Eager to share his knowledge, he invites other curious visitors into his garden, ensuring they rub powdered chlorine disinfectant on their shoes and hands before entering to not contaminate his plants. Besides Julio discussing these charitable activities, he also clearly enjoys being part of them. However, these opportunities are largely unofficial and evolve with the interests of the teachers and students at the local schools.

Julio revealed that all his knowledge in green medicine and religious plants has been gained from the newspaper, television and radio. So great is his knowledge that he is now a contributor to the sources from which he originally received his education, and he regularly appears on the local radio station. He frequently consults resources he keeps in a scrapbook of clippings and stores under the counter to validate his recommendations. His clientele respects his advice and, with little access to the internet or books, they have no better sources. Clearly, Julio is well liked within the community. Passers-by on foot and in bicycle taxis continually shout out greetings to him and often stop to chat or drop off bottles for his use as containers for medicines, or even plants with which to build future credit. Over the years, the neighbours across the street have invited me up onto their roofs to see the aerial view of the garden. It was apparent that Julio's garden was a source of pride for the neighbourhood as it was repeatedly stressed, by different people, Julio's professionalism and knowledge of plant medicine. The neighbour's roofscape environment was also made more comfortable by the shade and fragrances from the vegetation across the street.

The block's public telephones and garbage dumpsters are located adjacent to the site. As many people still do not have phones in their home, they shout up to friends and family to receive calls. The calls often last for more than an hour, and at times, when they become heated or emotional, the garbage bins provide some privacy and a place to lean. People are also frequently dropping off refuse including emptying buckets of organic waste and nylon sacks of dry goods. Anything that might be of value to others is placed alongside the dumpsters, and people rifle through it for useful materials (Del Real and Pertierra 2008: 78).

From the garden, Julio has an excellent view of these dumpsters and collects items he determines to be valuable, such as wood and steel that he observes being discarded. Anything that can be used to contain or package his remedies is particularly useful to his daily operations. He also stockpiles at the rear of his property anything suitable for ongoing repairs to his site or trading with the community. The government promotes the practice of invention or *inventar*. The book *Con nuestros propios esfuerzos: Algunas experiencias para enfrentar el período especial en tiempo de paz* (With Our Efforts: Some experiences to confront the Special Period) was released in 1992 by Editora Verde Olivo, the publishing house of the Cuban Revolutionary Armed Forces (Verde Olivo 1992). The book documented production and consumption survival strategies employed during the Special Period that involved cultivation practices, recipes and everyday devices to help alleviate scarcity. While the state circulated it, the resourcefulness came collectively from the citizens and communities. This exchange between state control and individual ingenuity signified an evolving departure in Cuba as the government relinquished entrepreneurial power to the citizens (Mackie 2017). Using reclaimed and recycled materials has become the norm. *Inventar* has very different patterns with its daily social interactions, the sourcing of materials and products within the community, reimagining uses for materials so that everything is reused, and negotiating with people within the neighbourhood to make necessary acquisitions (Del Real and Pertierra 2008: 89). Julio's garden is both a product of *inventar* and a hub for transactions. All the 10 beds, each approximately 0.75 m wide, are constructed from corrugated metal siding recycled from collapsed roofs. The canopy for the transaction counter and the storage shed are also created from found materials in the neighbourhood including wood members repurposed from a collapsed floor, and steel posts and siding material from the old ice factory. The wrought iron gates and grilles were retained from when the house on the site collapsed.

Valuing 'use value' as opposed to 'exchange value' with its associated protection of personal property means that projects are no longer fixed. *Inventar* flows and expands across space, throughout the community, fuelled by negotiation and invention. In fact, at the rear of the property, an adjacent neighbour has carved out a small portion of Julio's land for hanging up laundry in an outdoor space. As part of a single room within a *solar*, this neighbour's acquired exterior space doubles their dwelling area. A flimsy wire mesh fence defines this boundary. This negotiation of space does not appear to bother Julio as he reorganised his recycling storage area to accommodate this newly formed patio area.

Buildings continually collapse in this city and become part of this rhythm of re-creation. In fact, in the 'spring of 2008, there were between one and three partial or complete collapses a day. Partial building collapses range from part of a balcony breaking off to a roof or wall falling' (Birkenmaier and Whitfield 2011: 78). Once a building is destroyed, the land that the house once occupied reverts to the government. The timeline of collapse involves repeated warnings by authorities to vacate dangerous buildings and people desperately trying to prop up structures at risk of collapse. People are often given multiple warnings to vacate decaying residences from the government, but they resist relocation primarily because they will lose ownership of their property. If the building partially collapses families often work around the debris and contract their living arrangements. However, the collapse of a building also provides serendipitous opportunities for the adjacent spaces for ventilation air, space and light. This has happened to the north of Julio's site with the addition of louvres and windows to the building that increases cross-ventilation for the occupants. Materials from the collapse are also scavenged as part of the *inventar* economy for immediate use or to put into inventory. However, collapse also challenges the integrity of the neighbouring structures. The rooming house, to the south of the garden, has been very compromised. Heavy rain, hurricanes and salt air have also taken their toll. Julio collects the rainwater from this adjacent roof through a web of gutters and pipes directing it into barrels and a cistern along the edge of his property. This symbiotic relationship helps prevent the stormwater pooling on the compromised roof, while the access to irrigation water is essential to Julio's operation. Before the threat of Hurricane Matthew in October 2016, Julio and his neighbours cleared debris and leaves from the gutters and pipes in preparation for the onslaught.

Along with water and sunlight, compost is the other input required for the garden. Cuttings and household organic matter are used by Julio to produce soil additives in three wooden containers consisting of biological material, a worm bed and bat guano that act as a natural fungicide and compost activator. Compost is created by the decomposition of organic matter 'accompanied by physical, biological and chemical changes' brought about by the high temperatures attained in the process. The end product is a 'stable fertiliser free of harmful bacteria' and parasite eggs (Koont 2011: 92). Source separation is not officially practised in Cuban cities. 'On average, the composition of waste from the city of Havana is as follows: paper and cardboard (13.3 per cent); metals (1.8 per cent); plastics (11.0 per cent); glass (2.5 per cent); textiles (2.9 per cent); wood (3.5 per cent); food waste (62.4 per cent); rubber (0.3 per cent); leather (0.5 per cent) and other (2.0 per cent)' (Lloréns *et al.* 2008: 2014). Sites of urban agriculture typically act as the location for neighbourhood garbage containers, as residents within the community do not want to live adjacent to the odorous bins. They are meant to be emptied daily, but this rarely happens. With the average household producing approximately 65 per cent organic matter much of this could be composted at unofficial 'decentralised composting units […] located at urban agricultural farms' as these 'farms […] have a high demand for organic fertiliser' (Körner,

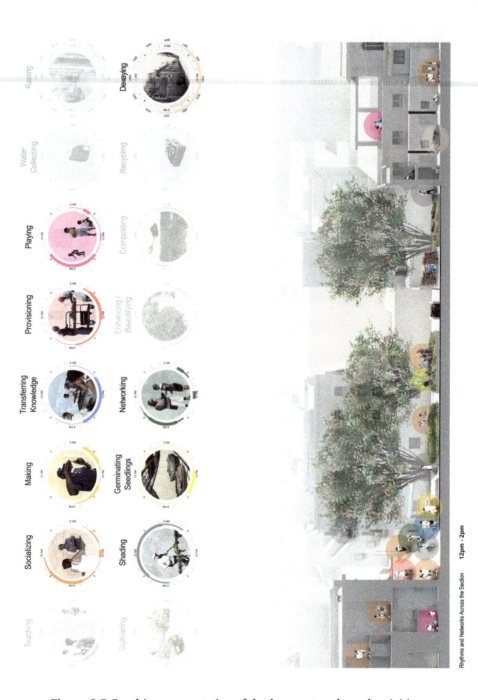

Figure 9.5 Graphic representation of rhythms, networks and activities from 12 to 2pm on any given day in a specific section of La Habana Vieja, Cuba. Graphic assistance from Alicia McDowell (Gilmore) and Lucas McDowell. Source: Fitzgerald, 2021.

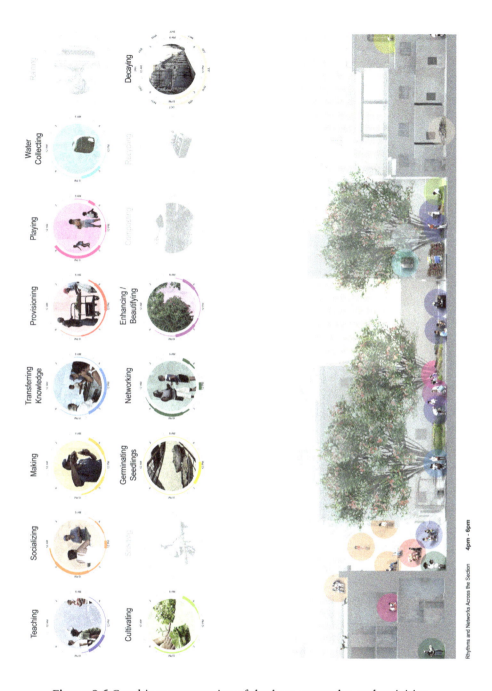

Figure 9.6 Graphic representation of rhythms, networks, and activities from 4 to 6pm on any given day in a specific section of La Habana Vieja, Cuba. Graphic assistance from Alicia McDowell (Gilmore) and Lucas McDowell. Source: Fitzgerald, 2021.

RHYTHMANALYSIS AS EXPLORATION OF URBAN INFORMALITY

Saborit-Sánchez and Aguilera-Corrales 2008: 64–72). This already happens informally within Julio's garden, and the high quality compost is shared with neighbours and other local producers.

In the early evening the street is full of children of every age playing in large groups outside of Julio's site. The vegetation in the garden moderates the torrid temperatures making it more comfortable than the neighbouring streets. Chalk, string and articles of clothing define the limits of the court or pitch that is continually produced and re-produced. The games that evening include soccer, target practice at cans along Julio's fence, tag and marbles. Observed by adults enjoying the evening on decks, roofs, patios and front steps ensures that these activities never become too boisterous. As twilight falls, the atmosphere of the street resembles a living room. The doorsteps serve as sofas as the community socialises. The voices are quieter as darkness envelops the street. Children are sent to bed, but the adults remain and talk in hushed tones about everyday issues including baseball, boxing, work, politics, money, love and family. One of the most common conversations involves house sales as Cubans can now legally sell their homes and handwritten 'for sale' signs are starting to appear throughout the neighbourhood. While foreigners are unable to purchase property within Cuba legally, there are whispered discussions within the community about precarious deals taking shape through intermediaries. As one of the only sites for urban agriculture in the colonial city, there may be people clamouring for the space.

Conclusion

The usufruct access to the vacant land that Julio enjoys is assessed through the Committee for the Defence of the Revolution and the People's Power, the neighbourhood organisations in charge of surplus land distribution. While Julio currently has the use of this land, the community controls the future of the site. To preserve this ownership status requires that the garden must contribute positively to the neighbourhood. Whether the community feels this has been adequately accomplished on this land impacts his continuing tenure. But far from being just a site of production, Julio appears to be highly motivated by altruism, and the landscape he has constructed does not focus solely on providing food or green medicine for economic return, but fulfils more pressing needs within the neighbourhood (Gold 2011: 33). The space has been modified to encourage knowledge transfer with the local primary schools and among customers. Constructed infrastructure on the site forms part of a storm water mitigation plan and community composting and recycling programmes. A portion of the property has also been donated to his neighbour for their use and enjoyment as a patio. But when I comment to my Cuban colleagues how much material change has come about over the years, they look perplexed, as they do not see any modifications. When these rhythms of informality are studied and mapped over time, they reveal the subtle changes in the materiality of everyday life and over time the findings are profound. Many authors, such as De Soto (2000) in *The Mystery of Capital* and Robert Neuwirth (2006) in *Shadow Cities*, have recognised the resourcefulness of the informal. However, their research has mainly focused on the economics and politics of informality rather than the everyday rhythms of life exposing the material, social and cultural qualities.

Much can be learned from going into these neighbourhoods and listening carefully to their rhythms. Rhythmanalysis does not concentrate on the spectacular or extraordinary but rather the quotidian to understand daily life. Julio's site and the surrounding neighbourhood display co-operation, conviviality and creativity as they adapt to everyday struggles. These interactions stitch the fragile environment together as resources including land, water, shade, waste, ventilation, medicine and crops are shared and redistributed in a type of community sustainability and symbiosis. Julio's site is an evolving space for education, culture, material waste recycling, harvesting of natural resources, social engagement, knowledge transfer and innovation. The vegetation on his site shades the street and brings beauty, fragrance and respite to the community to help improve uncomfortable climatic conditions. The site is Julio's livelihood, and his continued access to the land is not dependent solely upon its financial success but upon the social contribution of the enterprise to the neighbourhood. The site and its materiality demonstrate a deep commitment to the community and the environment that is only identifiable by studying the place over multiple visits throughout the day and across seasons. Change within cities, as with everything, is inevitable. Havana will collapse if it does not evolve (Hamberg 2012: 74). However, from carefully studying the everyday city rhythms surrounding this site, it seems as though many of the answers already exist within the community in the everyday practices that are continually evolving to construct a spatiality that is robust, flexible, entrepreneurial and sustainable. These polyrhythmic layers include the natural, cultural and social in a resilient ecology that provides for people and their everyday activities within a transformative future view of Havana (Fitzgerald 2022).

References

Birkenmaier, A. and Whitfield, E.K. 2011. *Havana Beyond the Ruins: Cultural mappings after 1989.* Durham, NC: Duke University Press.

Brook, R. and Dunn, N. 2011. *Urban Maps: Instruments of narrative and interpretation in the city.* Farnham: Ashgate.

De Certeau, M. 1998. *The Practice of Everyday Life.* Minneapolis: University of Minnesota Press.

Del Real, P. and Pertierra, A.C. 2008. 'Inventar: recent struggles and inventions in housing in two Cuban cities', *Buildings and Landscapes: Journal of the Vernacular Architecture Forum,* 15: 78–92.

Díaz, G., De la Peña, A.M. and Alfonso, A. 2006. 'Learning from the past: the traditional compact city in hot-humid climates', PLEA 2006: The 23rd Conference on Passive and Low Energy Architecture. Geneva.

Dovey, K. and King, R. 2011. 'Forms of informality: morphology and visibility of informal settlements', *Built Environment,* 37 (1): 11–29.

Fitzgerald, S.A.M. 2022. *Havana: Lived experiences of urban agriculture.* New York: Routledge.

Gold, M. 2011. 'Urban gardens: private property or the ultimate socialist experience?'. In Riobó, C. (ed.), *Cuban Intersections of Literary and Urban Spaces.* Albany: State University of New York Press, 25–49.

Gold, M. 2015. *People and State in Socialist Cuba: Ideas and practices of revolution.* New York: Palgrave Macmillan US.

Hamberg, J. 2012. 'Cuba opens to private housing but preserves housing rights', *Race, Poverty and the Environment,* 19 (1): 71–4.

Hernández, F., Kellett, P. and Allen, L. 2010. *Rethinking the Informal City: Critical perspectives from Latin America.* New York: Berghahn Books.

Holston, J. 2008. *Insurgent Citizenship: Disjunctions of democracy and modernity in Brazil.* Princeton: Princeton University Press.

Koont, S. 2011. *Sustainable Urban Agriculture in Cuba.* Gainesville: University Press of Florida.

Körner, I., Saborit-Sánchez, I. and Aguilera-Corrales, Y. 2008. 'Proposal for the integration of decentralised composting of the organic fraction of municipal solid waste into the waste management system of Cuba', *Waste Management,* 28 (1): 64–72.

Lefebvre, H. 2004. *Rhythmanalysis: Space, time and everyday life.* London: Continuum.

Lloréns, E., López Torres, M., Álvarez, H., Pellón Arrechea, A., García, J.A., Díaz Aguirre, S. and Fernández, A. 2008. 'Characterization of municipal solid waste from the main landfills of Havana City', *Waste Management,* 28 (10): 2013–21.

Mackie, E. 2017. 'Technological Disobedience: Ernesto Oroza', Assembly Papers. Accessed December 2021. https://assemblepapers.com.au/2017/04/28/technological-disobedience-ernesto-oroza/.

Neuwirth, R. 2006. *Shadow Cities: A billion squatters, a new urban world.* New York: Routledge.

Scarpaci, J.L., Segre, R. and Coyula, M. 2002. *Havana: Two faces of the Antillean metropolis.* Chapel Hill: University of North Carolina Press.

Smith, R.J. and Hetherington, K. 2013. 'Urban rhythms: mobilities, space and interaction in the contemporary city', *Sociological Review,* 61: 4–16.

Soto, H. de. 2000. *The Mystery of Capital: Why capitalism triumphs in the West and fails everywhere else.* New York: Basic Books.

Tablada, A., De Troyer, F., Blocken, B., Carmeliet, J. and Verschure, H. 2009. 'On natural ventilation and thermal comfort in compact urban environments – the old Havana case', *Building and Environment,* 44 (9): 1943–58.

Taylor, H.L. 2009. *Inside el Barrio: A bottom-up view of neighborhood life in Castro's Cuba.* Sterling, VA: Kumarian Press.

United States International Trade Commission. 2016. *Overview of Cuban Imports of Goods and Services and Effects of U.S. Restrictions.* Washington, DC: United States International Trade Commission.

Verde Olivo. 1992. *Con Nuestros Propios Esfuerzos: Algunas experiencias para enfrentar el período especial en tiempo de paz.* Havana: Editora Verde Olivo.

10
The death and life of Jian-Cheng Circle: a negative lesson for the built informality of urban places

Chin-Wei Chang

Jian-Cheng Circle – the oldest and largest night market in Taiwan – was a specific transplanted form of Japanese spatial colonisation located in Da-Dao-Cheng, Taipei. The market's origins can be traced to the period of Japanese colonisation, but it continued to thrive and expand in the postcolonial era, buffeted by political events and shaped by the cultures, cuisines and practices of the city's diverse immigrant communities. While the Jiang-Cheng Circle night market survived Japanese occupation, two world wars, an earthquake and two major fires, its redevelopment at the dawn of the twenty-first century precipitated a rapid decline. This chapter explores the distinct urbanity of Jian-Cheng Circle; how the process of congregating, exchanging and consuming food on open ground contributed to the production of urban space, engendered by and engendering new social relations.

'Informality plays a key role in all cities' (Dovey 2016: 218).

With the life and death of Jian-Cheng Circle, informality thrived and operated outside the control of the state within the urban marketplace. This chapter examines a trilogy of conceptual yet applicable themes; such a critical case study may contribute to a cross-dimensional understanding with implications for empirical research and service-learning practices in trans-cultural cities. Particular attention is given to socio-spatial conditions of their colonial histories, particularly in those cities of the Global South, which as Robert Neuwirth pointed out has seen more entrepreneurial flexibility, adaptation and creativity (Neuwirth 2012: 17–18).

Rather than adopting a chronological approach, I propose to use a thematic framework based on two factors, *event* and *space*, unique to the place-making narrative. The work was divided into two main aspects, and was then integrated into that of *place* to decipher the social production of spatial forms (Hubbard and Kitchin 2004: 101) in the urban place: Jian-Cheng Circle. In light of this, promoting a sustainable survival of place-making landscapes emerges from juxtaposing this inclusive local place with the exclusive nature of the concepts of global modernity.

In the second section of this chapter, the concept of *event* presents a story-telling narrative that is interrelated directly with the life and death of Jian-Cheng Circle. This section will provide a historical context of the Jian-Cheng Circle, which involves an introduction to the socio-political processes of urbanisation with its form, structure and transformation in Taiwan and the socio-economic specificities of survival throughout the country's development.

In the third section, the exploration of the concept of *space* illustrates the specific milieus involving building typologies and spatial patterns that sustained the vitality of the Jian-Cheng Circle. Considering not only the interactive relationships among stall men (sellers and vendors) but also the friendly amity between them and among customers (rural–urban immigrants and political refugees), Jian-Cheng Circle epitomised an unprecedented scene. This marketplace presented an overarching diversity of bottom-up place-making processes in the vacuum left by a weak state that failed in top-down governance.

The chapter concludes by discussing the idea of *place*: the prophetic endeavours and contemplative potential that Jian-Cheng Circle left posthumously, which can facilitate cross-cultural understanding through its distinctive social practice, political negotiation and spatial production. This was a hard-won lesson at the expense of the life of an urban place. The oldest and largest night market, full of tremendous historical value and collective memories, embedded the significance of local wisdom in pre- and post-Second World War Taipei and speaks to opportunities for local landscapes to be empowered and rearticulated in global visions.

The legendary birth of the Jian-Cheng Circle

Da-Dao-Cheng is one of the earliest developed villages, similar to Men-Gjia along the Tam-Sui River, whose inland banks were the origin of present-day Taipei. It was initially reclaimed by the Han during the Ching dynasty in the middle of the nineteenth century (Chen 1959). Like other original villages in west Taipei, Da-Dao-Cheng, where Jian-Cheng Circle was centrally located, later became an area that appealed to many Taiwanese people because of its vernacular temples and the development of local industries, mainly in the tea business (Li 2000).

Along with the Japanese colonial period of Taiwan (1895–1945), by the turn of the last century Da-Dao-Cheng had the largest population of Taiwanese people in Taipei (Wu 1958: 40–4). However, the location of today's Jian-Cheng Circle remained an empty space until Japanese colonisers carried out their primary 'Urban District Reform Plans', which transformed all of the demolished city walls and original gates, in 1910, into grand boulevards and urban circles (Su 2005; Wang 1989)

Jian-Cheng Circle[1], also formerly called 'Ri-Xin Ting Circle' according to the Japanese colonial land administration system, dates from 1908 and formed part of the reconstruction in the colonial capital aimed at severing the umbilical link between mainland China and Taiwan. It suffered less traffic pressure than other urban circles converted from original city enclosures, so that some residents started to take walks or rest on the friendly community-based open ground (Wang 1989).

After the implementation of the intensive 'Urban District Reform Plans', not only did the Japanese colonial municipality establish the official administrative institution for Taipei in 1920, equivalent to the Taipei City Government of today, but it also carried out another reformative land administration system in 1922 that renamed the area where Ri-Xin Ting Circle was located in Da-Dao-Cheng as 'Jian-Cheng Ting'. This is how Jian-Cheng Circle derived its present name (Li 2000).

Da-Dao-Cheng had owned its prosperous industries, including its internationally known and booming tea business, even before the reigns of the Han and the Japanese. As such, and later further emphasised by many modern development projects, Da-Dao-Cheng had already become one of the principal city gateways, with convenient transportation facilities and various entertainment fields when 'Taipei City' jurisdiction was officially instituted in 1920 (Li 2000).

With a population approaching 200,000 over the next five years according to the Japanese colonisers' estimation, the colonial municipality of Taipei City was prompted to put in place a legal city planning system characterised by a 'Park System', which addressed both the expansion of the city and the hierarchy of the roadways. This was a field of spatial governance in which the Japanese were relatively inexperienced in their motherland (Yeh 1993).

In 1935, a severe earthquake occurred in Taipei City, and Jian-Cheng Circle served as a shelter in the crisis. Thanks to its history as a haven in the tragedy and the fact that two-level housing structures had emerged around Jian-Cheng Circle (Kuo and Horigome 1994), the Japanese colonial municipality's city planning committee chose to delimit it as a miniature park, with the first city planning legislation for Taiwan promulgated in 1936 and put into practice the following year (Yeh 1993).

From miniature park to unprecedented marketplace

Legend has it that a fruit vendor taking a nap at Jian-Cheng Circle one afternoon was asked to sell his surplus by people strolling there. The vendor brought more goods to sell at the miniature park in the following days. This attracted other vendors to do businesses in the same place (Wang 1989). In addition to playing an essential role as a public space in Da-Dao-Cheng, Jian-Cheng Circle thus became a local afternoon market.

In response to increasing volumes of railway passengers and freight transportation, the Japanese colonial municipality undertook the construction of the railway connection between Taipei City and Tam-Sui Township, as well as the expansion of the original Taipei central station, originally built under authority of the first governor to Taiwan from China, Ming-Chuan Liu (1887–9). A later expansion, completed in 1939, was called 'Latter Station' and was oriented towards Da-Dao-Cheng, in contrast with the former one that mainly served the neighbourhood of Japanese colonisers, called Cheng-Nei (Li 2000).

As a result, the Latter Station area had attracted native and foreign investments in many clubs, restaurants and hotels, which served as a primary home base for business people and tourists who came to Taipei City seeking profit and excitement (Li 2000). Stall men who used to run the afternoon market at Jian-Cheng Circle extended their operating hours to meet the needs of those populations. Consequently, Jian-Cheng Circle became a thriving night market. It came to the notice of the Japanese colonial municipality, which led to constant policing by the Japanese.

The gradual evolution of stall equipment and different types of vending co-existing at Circle Night Market also challenged the Japanese colonial police efforts. The market became mobile by design and could therefore evade permanent destruction. This, combined with the general popularity of the food served, empowered the vendors. The Japanese colonial authorities accepted the proposal offered by Mr Wang on behalf of the stall men to establish the so-called 'Taipei Circle Night Market Commercial Association' (Kuo and Horigome 1994). This was how Jian-Cheng Circle formally became the first legal night market – albeit of informal origin – in Taiwan by the 1930s, despite efforts to quash it by the Japanese regime.

Saved at a critical moment

'Jian-Cheng Circle', regarded as a byword for the Circle Night Market in Da-Dao-Cheng, kept growing. It attracted nearby residents, passing travellers and Japanese colonisers diverted from the Xi-Men Night Market, a counterpart exclusively organised by their municipality. With the advent of the Second World War in 1941, however, Circle Night Market suffered a significant setback because of the Japanese colonial municipality's lighting restrictions and curfew policy enforced as a means of tactical defence.

In 1943, with the beginning of United States military air bombardment campaigns, the Japanese colonial municipality also implemented the strategic decision to resurrect Jian-Cheng Circle as an anti-aircraft battery, which at least temporarily sent the vendors away (Kuo and Horigome 1994). Switching to the square open space of a nearby pub diner, dedicated stall men changed their business plan to keep earning a living under the strains of war (Wu 1958).

Following Taiwan's retrocession to China, a period of calm came for the people of the city and Kuomintang, the Chinese Nationalist Party, regained sovereignty over Taiwan in 1945. In Nanjing, the central government designated Taiwan a province and made Taipei a provincial municipality. Within the old city boundaries Taipei was re-divided into 10 new districts, including 'Jian-Cheng District', named after the unique wheel-shaped space that had struggled for survival through colonial times in Taiwan, namely Circle Night Market or Jian-Cheng Circle.

Nevertheless, given the turbulent times of political and social upheaval in the Chinese Civil War, in 1949, Kuomintang left the People's Republic of China (PRC) for Taiwan and accordingly chose Taipei as its provisional capital. It launched a series of development projects, which accelerated the Jian-Cheng District into a progressively higher grade neighbourhood. For example, the filling and levelling of the anti-aircraft reservoir at Jian-Cheng Circle led not only to the original vendors coming back and rebuilding the Circle Night Market but a large number of newcomers also joined them, primarily political refugees from the PRC after the Civil War, migrating throughout the 1950s.

Contributor or tumour?

Generally, while most Taiwanese cities were mainly anti-communist military bases during the Cold War, the 1950s was regarded as the golden age of the Jian-Cheng Circle, as actual building typologies took shape amid the hundreds of stalls. In 1953, during the period of rapid reproduction the 'Circle Night Market Experience', which even sprawled into adjoining Chong-Qing North Road and Ning-Xia Road, the development came to be called 'Straight-linked Circle Night Market' (Wang 1989), and soon became the core of the so-called 'Circle Shopping District', despite the existence of illegally-built stalls among the legal ones.

With rapid economic development in the 1960s, which brought many more rural–urban migrants increasing pressure in terms of urbanisation, on 1 July 1967 Taipei City was elevated to the status of a special municipality, directly administered by central government. Driven by export-led processing industries for the world market, Taiwan, and specifically Taipei City, moved into the phase of planned modernist urbanisation as so-called 'National Economic Construction Planning' was urgently implemented with the aid of the US. Planning and discourse came from North America via United Nations consultants.

In contrast to the broadening of main roads and building public transportation, necessary infrastructure for a developing country, the revitalisation of Jian-Cheng Circle presented an embarrassment during the economic boom in Taiwan in the 1960s. Instead of being demolished without dispute, as were most urban circles left over from Japanese colonial times, the removal of Circle Night Market struck public opinion as controversial because of its great historical value and collective memory that embedded the local wisdom from pre- and post-Second World War Taipei.

At the hands of municipal officials and urban planners of the Taipei City Government – primarily technical professionals whose bias towards urban design was a by-product of their engineering education – Jian-Cheng Circle suffered suppression, including traffic control and the limiting of trading hours. Portrayed as a 'tumour on the city' in the context of the state-dominated bureaucratic city, the Circle Night Market still survived many carefully evaluated reconstruction proposals. These plans reflected the global modernist perspective and proposed incorporating the Circle Night Market into either an underground bazaar or a high-rise complex before the 1990s, but these were in vain.

Challenged by continual official scrutiny, the vendors of Circle Night Market kept up their legendary networking operation outside the boundaries of the legal system for more than half a century. This was until two accidental fires, in 1993 and 1999 respectively, gave planners opportunities to make inroads. Even though multiple disasters did not defeat the persistent stall holders working to earn a basic living in Jian-Cheng Circle over generations, their informal practice ultimately became the target of formalisation woven into the fibre of political discourse, attempting to reframe the market culture in the spirit of a capitalistic industrial process. Entering the twenty-first century, this problematic praxis seemed inevitable in the effort to forge a cosmopolitan identity as another imaginary world city: the product of the state institution of modernity.

Where creative destruction took place

Though partially surviving great fires twice, Jian-Cheng Circle suffered extreme difficulties including dilapidation and declining business. Nevertheless, on behalf of the Taipei City Government, Mayor Ying-Jiu Ma (who later served as the president of Taiwan from 2008 to 2016) decided in 1999 to demolish Circle Night Market in favour of a newly designed compact modern food court building – regardless of informal antecedents driven by subjective local wisdom – on the over-simplified basis of formal discourses little concerned with the urban landscape or public interest.

As a result of co-ordinated urban planning and design management efforts set in motion at the beginning of the twenty-first century, Jian-Cheng Circle was pulled down on 29 March 2001 and reopened to the public with a brand-new architectural design – based on the idea of 'Circle of Life' – by well-known Taiwanese architect Zu-Yuan Li on 4 October 2003. A glass curtain wall clad the ring-like food court building with two stories as its primary feature; there was only one perambulatory path around the vendors' area. With the updated title 'Jian-Cheng Circle Food Centre,' the new design was different from the original layout of the previous Circle Night Market.

When Jian-Cheng Circle Food Centre was reopened, the number of stalls decreased from 97 to 25; vendors' arguments about the entirely different design and its response to the actual networking reality were ignored. Only six original stall men, one-quarter of the original population, were involved in domestic and migrant culinary work at Jian-Cheng Circle and chose to stay at the location. The other vendors moved elsewhere and started their businesses again, or retired into obscurity.

The ultimate failure of the new Jian-Cheng Circle Food Centre undoubtedly proved the foresight of those vendors who chose to leave and seek survival elsewhere, as well as the hindsight of the stall men facing a waning period, during which those who remained traded barely passably for about one month while attempting to grapple with those newly acquainted with foreign foods. It continued to decline heavily without seeming to revive, and the Taipei City Government finally decided to shut down the legendary former food sanctuary on 2 July 2006. By then, it had operated in its new configuration for a mere four years.

At this stage, most of the disillusioned stall men retired one after another with an unsatisfactory subvention from the Taipei City Market Administration Office. During the whole tragic process they were also gradually deprived of their rights to all parts of the logistics of Circle Night Market by the state and local government. From the ill-advised formation to the distorted redevelopment of Jian-Cheng Circle, they remained outside the fray of what they could do best.

While Mayor Long-Bin Hao (2008–16) was in charge, ownership of Jian-Cheng Circle Food Centre was entirely given to a private entrepreneur without culinary experience based on a questionable nine-year management contract issued by the Taipei City Government in 2007. Ironically named 'Taipei Circle', a different dining style from the original accompanied by grotesquely offbeat live shows provides inescapable evidence of the demise of Jian-Cheng Circle, which can never be redeemed even today, when new Mayor Wen-Zhe Ke (2016–) demolished the much-debated glasshouse in 2017 without a more progressive redevelopment plan. Circle Night Market's posthumous glory is, as Dipesh Chakrabarty vividly reported, still left in the waiting room of history (Chakrabarty 2012: 8). According to this argument, formalisation converted informality into a version of this waiting room, whose coda had been written beforehand.

Fluid occupancy in the beginning

As mentioned above, Jian-Cheng Circle became a popular community base, which served as a public open space, a playground for neighbouring residents, the primary space being created during the initial stage of Japanese colonisation as part of a series of 'Urban

District Reform Plans'. According to a few records (Wang 1989), food vending took place after 1936 on that limited land, following the first city planning legislation for Taiwan carried out by the Japanese colonial municipality.

Although business transactions involving snacks and drinks were not legally authorised, the rapid development of Da-Dao-Cheng, where Jian-Cheng Circle was centrally located, ranged from transportation facilities to entertainment fields, and brought increasing numbers of vendors to the night market. With their unique way of fluid occupancy and high-frequency consumption in small quantities, it was as if they were playing cat-and-mouse with the Japanese police, engendering an intriguing consumption-based performance that played out daily between traders and regulators. The result, as Kim Dovey noted, was 'that traders [were] chased but not eradicated to keep profits flowing as part of a dynamic but resilient system' (Dovey 2016: 223).

However, growing tired of playing their cumbersome role while doing business under the scrutiny of the Japanese colonisers, the stall men were provoked to negotiate actively with the Japanese colonial municipality, fighting for their right to survive. In doing so, the 'Taipei Circle Night Market Commercial Association' was established in 1938 with rules establishing standardised operation and taxation. That is, formalising informalities through institutionalisation.

For example, the ringing of a bell signalled the opening and closing of operating hours from 5pm to midnight. Nevertheless, most vendors – if not all – carried on their business until 2 or 3am in response to demand from countless Taiwanese customers. A few intrigued Japanese intermingled in this colonial atmosphere. Compared with those manufacturing industries in the formal sector, this informal counterpart of local consumption was an ingenious realm of open-minded natives and a commercial circuit with loose boundaries, casual rather than formal, on a middle ground contextualised as an urban place *per se*.

Falling into spatial patterns

After enduring the Second World War, expelled stall men returned to Jian-Cheng Circle after war readiness measures were removed. At the same time, large-scale political immigration from post-1949 China added to the market population in Taiwan. Entering the purview of a relocated Republican government that failed to supply urban services, men, women with children, and the elderly who had given up posterity were transformed into waged labourers at Jian-Cheng Circle as part of an industrial reserve army in Taipei, a provisional capital in which the informal sector displaced the formal during the Cold War into the 1950s.

Unsurprisingly, those people who settled down at Jian-Cheng Circle ran longer operating hours, often, if not always, until daybreak. To ensure there would be sufficient space in the restricted area for aggressive business in a more and more competitive marketplace filled with burgeoning sellers, the original vendors, who had either carried a load with a carrying pole or pushed a mobile stall, ultimately transformed their stalls into stable occupancy instead of transient fluidity. Falling into spatial patterns in a particular setting, the socio-economic dynamics of well-prepared stall men triggered a whole new urban landscape overwhelmingly outside legal boundaries. The informality-driven revitalisation of Circle Night Market fell out of favour in terms of formal apparatus and protocol. However, it aligned well with inextricable informalities abreast of a pre-modern state after the Second World War. In the beginning, high-flown stall men, mainly from informal organisations and local gangs, used ropes bound around flour bags tied to banyan trees to encircle their area of the vending business in case of limited space, creating contention with others. With the population explosion at Circle Night Market, cutting down all trees became a matter-of-course way of solving the problem. Later, the fact that every vendor then asserted their ownership of space by digging in with bamboo and iron pipes meant Circle Night Market fell into chaotic patterns yet remained deep-rooted in a somewhat organised circularly centred way (Kuo and Horigome 1994).

Social practice of spatial production

Severe restrictions on opening hours were not now being imposed. Staying longer and longer at Circle Night Market disinclined most of the stall men from spending time hauling their bulky cooking utensils back and forth every day. Consequently, they decided to make an effort, unanimous in the midst of their previous rudimentary construction, to transform Jian-Cheng Circle into a permanent shelter from wind and drenching downpours. Most importantly, some vendors, especially those apprentices far from hometowns to hone their talent in cooking and serving, saw out the critical era by dwelling directly in Jian-Cheng Circle.

Putting up main beams made of wood and rooftops consisting of bisected bamboo, albeit formally censured from time to time, stall men worked together to frame their informal mechanism against state control over urban and industrial society, which was grounded in their everyday culinary practices and operational needs, rather than architectonic disciplines and structural calculations. Furthermore, when wind and rain let them know where the leaks were, if any, they would use various pre-existing components, such as flat pieces of asphalt skin and plastic surfboards (Kuo and Horigome 1994), to support not only their means of survival but also their unauthorised inhabitancy.

Building typologies take shape

As a result of the many roof layers stacked in the building above pathways, for a long time 'Circle Top' became a popular given name for Jian-Cheng Circle. Initially, the famous round operating area, with a diameter of about 100 feet, was divided into six sectors by two-metre-wide walkways for customers. Then, in the 1950s, there is evidence of three concentric extensions of the Circle Night Market, which enlarged the diameter of the extra-legal marketplace by 40 feet. This period was considered the golden age of Jian-Cheng Circle, with approximately 97 vendors (Kuo and Horigome 1994).

Each business sector included around 40 stalls that co-operated to satisfy on average 20,000 stomachs, from 10 in the morning to three hours before dawn every day, while some vendors even ran their businesses 24 hours. Miraculously, when it came to the atrium with a diameter of about 42 feet, located right at the centre of Jian-Cheng Circle, no matter how limited the quota of vending space was, none of the vendors dared occupy this core.

The central atrium, clear of vendors' occupancy, served as an important place for the surrounding stall men to wash their bowls and dishes after serving and for the customers, coming in an endless stream, to park their bicycles/or motorcycles before dining. In addition, public utilities, such as high-voltage towers and street lights, were installed in the central atrium under a common consensus of all the stall men (Kuo and Horigome 1994). Part of an informal agenda without formal regulation, the central atrium proved to be playing a crucial role akin to the service core of a modern building, and was defended as such by all the vendors.

Cultural representations of spatial practices: the interactive relationships between stall men

The vendors in Circle Night Market used to sell their snacks and drinks, usually recommended specialities of home-made cuisine cooked on-site, in relatively small portions. To avoid disappointment that food types would be monotonous or that their empty stomachs would not be filled, customers, especially those who frequently visited, were always in the habit of trying as many different kinds of foods as possible.

The compact but not strictly pigeon-holed arrangement of stalls in each sector spread out based on succinct concentric circles. This layout enabled customers to satisfy themselves by having many dishes in an efficient way. For example, customers could sit down at one stall to start and then order plates from nearby stalls. To accommodate this hotchpotch, vendors settled accounts among themselves by counting scales labelled by stall names at the end of each working day.

Friendly amity between vendors and customers

Because the allotment for each vendor was a single small stall, it was not uncommon to behold stall men working hard among customers almost face to face, nose to nose. Gobbling up foods and swigging drinks while chatting about everyday affairs with sweating vendors, busy themselves at cooking and serving, led to a sense of amity for customers: a hard-won atmosphere unavailable in traditional restaurants. Over generations, vendors and customers usually even became close friends. Overall, Jian-Cheng Circle became an urban place where stall men and veteran customers could recognise each other, not only for everyday dining but also as a source of identity for the city.

Risks and opportunities in trans-cultural cities: the synergy that sustained the Jian-Cheng Circle

The vendors and regulars at Jian-Cheng Circle, a specific transplanted spatial form of Japanese colonisation located in Da-Dao-Cheng, Taipei, Taiwan, developed their mode of congregating, consuming and exchanging prepared food from the colonial to the post-colonial period. Due to the absence of urban services in a developing capitalist economy, they laboured long hours for survival in an urban informal sector, while offering unparalleled place-making processes, in small and medium-sized economic circuits in Taiwan during its formal development.

With spatial production and a grassroots movement driven by the culinary culture of the rural–urban immigrants, Circle Night Market was the survival mechanism for people. It showcased an overarching diversity of an urban heritage that presented an unprecedented place-making scene for marketplaces. Accompanying the tenacious and flexible production network of vendors, whose interactions were frequent and confidence intense, customers were addicted to enjoying meals and spontaneously relaxing, hanging out in Jian-Cheng Circle. There has always been, according to Dovey, 'already a double or twofold condition of informality/formality' (Dovey 2016: 218). It was that mélange, also seen at the circle, which nowadays makes us reflect radically on how informalities serve the formal in the past and present.

Learning from Jian-Cheng Circle: the contributions towards cross-cultural understanding

Being neither part of the commercial functions of the state nor the trading facilities developed by private sectors, the cross-cultural consumption-based services provided by Jian-Cheng Circle, an urban informal industry rooted in community-based open ground, became one of the significant mechanisms maintaining the competitive edge of the Taiwanese economy for the world market. Unfortunately, Jian-Cheng Circle – the oldest and largest night market in Taiwan, was often portrayed as a 'tumour on the city' for consisting of informal economies and illegal buildings during the phase of rapid economic development after the 1960s in articulating global modernity.

With the heavy pressures of urban life and the emblematic urban governance relatively concentrated in Taipei City, Jian-Cheng Circle died due to modernist, exclusive design, without regard for the inclusive understanding reflected in its building typologies and spatial patterns. However, the place represented a unique urbanity in Taiwan with a particular socio-spatial dynamic informed by survival, namely the nuances of multiculturalism inherent in such a night market. That is, how those vendors were more than passive recipients of formal planning and were instead vital and legitimate agents in their informal masterfulness towards a real world city.

The lesson to be learnt in the ultimate failure that overtook this urban place speaks to a precipitous risk of our time in dire need of attention. It exemplifies how local landscapes can be rearticulated into global visions. All in all, the life and death of Jian-Cheng Circle, an inclusive local place set against exclusionary global modernity, calls stridently not just for a cross-border understanding of urban nature directed towards the survival of cultural landscapes. It also portends aspects of sustainable design that acknowledge the multifaceted interactions of different urban layers and scales in trans-cultural cities of the future.

Note

1 Japanese colonisers' primary 'Urban District Reform Plans' were driven by Western Europe- or North America-centred planning knowledge in Taipei City in the early 1900s and included demolishing all the city walls and creating nine urban circles in total as the city paths and nodes. Being different from the seven located at the original city gates that spread over demolished city walls, Jian-Cheng Circle and West-Gate Circle were relatively independent, responsible for connecting with Da-Dao-Cheng and Men-Gjia, two mainly Taiwanese areas in Taipei City during the Japanese colonial period.

References

Chakrabarty, D. 2012. *Provincializing Europe: Postcolonial thought and historical difference*. Princeton: Princeton University Press.
Chen, C.-H. 1959. *Geography of Taiwan*. Taipei: Fu-Ming Institute of Industrial Geography.
Dovey, K. 2016. *Urban Design Thinking: A conceptual toolkit*. New York: Bloomsbury Academic.
Hubbard, P. and Kitchin, R. (eds) 2004. *Key Thinkers on Space and Place*. London: Sage.
Kuo, C.-T. and Horigome, K. 1994. *Streets of Chinese People*. Translated by Feng-Kuei Pien. Taipei: Taipei City Archives.
Li, T.-M. 2000. *Eternal Light Line of the North*. Taipei: Yu-Shan Press.
Neuwirth, R. 2012. *Stealth of Nations: The global rise of the informal economy*. New York: Anchor Books.
Su, S.-P. 2005. *Invisible and Visible Taipei*. Taipei: Tso-An Press.
Wang, T.-K. 1989. 'A Study of Taipei Jian-Cheng Circle'. Unpublished Master's thesis, Tunghai University, Taichung, Taiwan.
Wu, Y.-T. 1958. 'First capital review of record', *Taipei Cultural Relics*, 7 (3): 40–4.

11
Informality as pedagogy: collective design in the Mariamma Nagar settlement
Nicola Antaki

Introduction

This chapter aims to contribute to the discussion on the notion of 'informality' in the built environment by suggesting it is a spatial, behavioural and pedagogical ingredient that enables urban learning. Between 2012 and 2017 a group of schoolchildren were involved in a 'collective design pedagogy', a series of workshops in which they could observe, assess, document and then transform their environment using design methods – borrowed from architectural practice – and local craft. They became actors in the fabrication of their urban realm. Beginning with a focus on the school building and classroom, they then attended to their home territory, Mariamma Nagar, an informal settlement in the heart of Mumbai.

    The chapter explores the informal processes present during two projects the class and facilitators undertook as part of the collective design pedagogy: the investigation of learning in Mariamma Nagar through the making of a map and the subsequent fabrication of a tapestry. Informality is understood as a term that applies to a variety of spatial and non-spatial practices, which are by nature relational. The distinction I am making between formal and informal is related to rules and skills on the one hand and spontaneity and exploration on the other. I investigate informal design practices that are based on intimate and intuitive ways of seeing; hands-on work, behaviour and communication, making with local resources and often through collaboration. I propose that the term informality can sometimes be translated by the Hindi word *jugaad*, which means innovative problem solving, in spontaneous or speculative ways in response to the unpredictable. The chapter also explores the multiple ways informality was a driver for learning during the interdisciplinary research project that explored design as a learning tool in the informal settlement. Informality as understood through this set of lenses is not defined by, or primarily in response to, the State.

I also aim to decipher in what way the practices that enabled the production of the children's map of learning and fabrication of the tapestry were informal. Furthermore, how have these informal practices, whether spatial or social, helped to create learning situations? And lastly, how does the representation of the neighbourhood in this way help in its analysis? First, I contextualise informality within socio-spatial discourse in relation to the Mariamma Nagar settlement. Then I briefly describe the pedagogical endeavour involving the class in exploring and documenting how they feel they learn in the neighbourhood. Next, I investigate the settlement itself through the children's map of learning: how does informality provide a space for 'entrepreneurial flexibility, adaptation and creativity' (Dovey 2012: 349)? Why does the porosity and interconnectivity of the informal settlement (or *basti* in Hindi) provide a rich space for learning? Lastly, I look at how the map made by the children was translated and interpreted into a locally produced artefact. How and why is craft a key informal practice in the settlement? And how does it impact learning? How does the tapestry represent informality as an artefact of *jugaad*?

The *basti* as abundant pedagogical ground

The city of Mumbai has a long history as an economically vibrant trading city, active port and centre for textiles, before, during and after colonial rule. Today it is a specialised economic city, globally important as a leader in finance and trade, high-ranking in economic, political and cultural terms, known to be 'the most cosmopolitan of Indian metropolises' (D'Monte 2011: 97). In the 1970s many migrated to Mumbai to work, following the famines in the northern state of Bihar and a more generalised shift towards urbanisation: settlements began to be informally constructed around the city. Many migrants found daily-wage jobs as labourers, maids and watchmen; however, within the migrant settlements themselves all kinds of economic activity began to develop as the settlements grew, in response to the needs of the city inhabitants and beyond. Mumbai is a city that presents global–local tensions across geographical, political, economic and social realms within which informality can be identified in a number of ways.

Since its creation as a theoretical debate in the 1960s, the discourse around informality has evolved over time following the widespread move of labour to cities in the 1950s and 1960s. After moving between continents and disciplines, in the last decade the discourse has become variegated and the understanding of the term more wide-reaching and interdisciplinary. Informality can be understood as 'that which exists outside of formal legal-juridical frameworks' (Boano 2013). Moreover, as Ananya Roy and AlSayyad explain, the difference between formal and informal emerges in practice: 'If formality operates through the fixing of value, including the mapping of spatial value, then informality operates through the constant negotiability of value', an approach applicable economically, socially and spatially (Roy and AlSayyad 2003: 5). In the context of the urban realm, geographer Colin McFarlane's description of informality is pertinent too. He explains that the 'formal–informal distinction is a multifaceted resource for naming, managing, governing, producing, and even critiquing contemporary cities' (McFarlane 2012a: 89). He also specifies that spatial, social and political distinctions of informality relate to 'urban territory (slum and non-slum), groups (labour), and governmentality (monitoring, naming and intervening)', and describes informal practices as activities of speculation, composition and bricolage. In the introduction to this volume Elorduy *et al.* suggest that informality viewed through the built environment can be understood as a relational concept, which reflects inequalities that are intrinsically linked to the physical manifestations of the built environment.

The study of informality by anthropologist Vyjayanthi Rao shows the informal settlement as an important 'theoretically productive spatial ecology', key to the development of urban theory and practice, and 'an invitation to think through both the material aspects and processes involved in contemporary urbanism, and the ethical and epistemological underpinnings of urban theory today' (Rao 2006: 228). She asks what cities south of the equator such as Mumbai, Lagos, São Paulo and Shanghai represent for the study of modernity and urbanism today, and presents the need for a philosophical 'debate on the relationship between conditions and possibilities' or an understanding of the possibilities of what she calls 'design action'. She also defines the informal settlement as 'a space "at risk" where risk is understood as a sense of threat and vulnerability [that] turns it into a space "of risk" where risk is understood as opportunity generated by volatility, flux and instability' (Rao 2006: 15).

The understanding of the term informal settlement, 'slum', *favela*, *bidonville*[1] or in India the *basti*, is often central to all urban logic rather than a marginal part of the city. Settlements increasingly provoke geopolitical debate on legality, humanity and practices of dwelling (Dicken 2005). A variety of practices have globally emerged on the one hand acknowledging informality as an organising principle but sometimes one that should be transcended, and on the other as an 'inventive urban form' that can inspire design (and art) practice. Many activist architects and urbanists have engaged with informality as a practice and as a setting 'positioned at the intersection of politics, design and research' (De Meuler and Shannon 2010: 5). But how can the informality of the *basti* contribute to contemporary education?

Indian scholar Gautam Bhan has written on informal practices relating specifically to Indian affordable housing as 'the dominant mode of producing and inhabiting the city for a majority of income-poor residents of India's cities' in terms of policy and citizenship (Bhan 2017: 589). He writes, 'seeing the *basti* as part of a mode of urbanization changes its signification. It no longer refers to just the materiality of its housing, a spatial form, or a planning category. It must be read instead as the territorialization of a set of political engagements within which urban residents negotiate – incrementally, over time, and continuously – their presence in as well as their right to the city'. The *basti* represents a practice of urban contestation. But, he argues, postcolonial debates on citizenship have not been attentive enough to spatial and urban citizenship in order to discuss spatial or social rights. I would extend this to argue that the *basti* is a fertile pedagogical ground for developing responsible modes of citizenship.

The *basti* creates a sense of locality that can be strongly identified and experienced through intensely dwelt spaces. First, there is a sense of boundary, whether felt or seen, which is often protecting the community within and the community without. The settlement sets apart from other urban formations through materiality, form and scale of dwellings; proximity of supplies and services for basic living imply a level of self-sufficiency. The density of population and a sense of convivial street life humanises the public realm. Other characters reinforce the settlement's visual identity: the porous and labyrinthine circulation and the presence of making and craft summon nostalgic impressions of traditional villages in rural territories (Roy 2003: 289).

Across the city, crafts such as tailoring, carpentry, metalwork, pottery, woodcarving, bamboo weaving, cane work and embroidery unite and help create local points of activity often in informal settlements.

Figure 11.1 Photograph showing the contextual plurality of the surroundings of Mariamma Nagar, Mumbai, India. Source: Antaki, 2018

Although craft in Mumbai is still a high-street activity in more traditional areas, the globalised city produces behaviours and materials that undermine traditional cultures of making. While religious, ethnic and economic localities are still prominent, those characterised by craft are beginning to disappear. However, informal settlements tend to provide spaces for making, demonstrated in the settlement of Mariamma Nagar.

Mariamma Nagar

The Mariamma Nagar neighbourhood (*Mariamma* is the name of a Dalit god and *Nagar* means 'place') is located close to the Muktangan school, and sits between two branches of the Love Grove Canal, in an area of approximately 24 square kilometres. It is centrally located in greater Mumbai with the Mahalaxmi racecourse and the Nehru Science Centre, a range of public and private owners, canals, pumping station and planetarium as neighbours. Quiet and surrounded on two sides by trees, the settlement is positioned in a complex 'plural' urban locality. Architect Rahul Mehrotra describes Mumbai as being 'characterised by intense duality where modernizing tradition, prosperity and acute poverty, communality and communalism, medieval society and cutting-edge information technology coalesce to create incomprehensible cities' (Mehrotra 2006: 166). The relationship between Mariamma Nagar and its neighbours exemplifies this urban complexity, geographically, politically, socially and spatially.

Near the settlement entrance, watchmen guard the Nehru Centre and planetarium gates, tempting passers-by with manicured lawns, gardens and large shady trees. The street area forms a taxi cross-over point, where drivers rest or hand over the car they have rented for their shift, convenient for many drivers living in Mariamma nearby. This public space forms the settlement threshold. Here, the city starts to change – a new sense of place begins to emerge: informal practices become spatial, and a place-making practice. The threshold between the more formal city and informal settlement exists in various ways: visual, implied and as an imaginary 'territoriality of place' (Harvey 2012). The visual threshold here is also exemplified by a change in design language and material culture creating Mariamma Nagar as a distinct place. Beyond, a new bridge crossing the Love Grove Canal has recently been built, which will bring vehicular access to the presently quiet area. Until now, the settlement could only be accessed on foot or by bike, which added to the particular sense of independence inhabitants had.

The Mariamma Nagar settlement was formed when inhabitants from informal settlements across the city were relocated due to site clearing for development in the 1980s. In Mumbai, settlement relocation occurs often in preparation for private development or SRA (Slum Rehabilitation Authority) projects. Although the settlement grew to around 15,000 inhabitants, further relocation and site clearing led to a decrease in number to around 5,000 in 2013. Intertwined with residential dwellings there is much economic activity and craft. Many of these activities are visible from the street, but countless are concealed behind closed doors: many tailors, bag makers and embroiderers work in this neighbourhood.

Informal practices in Mariamma Nagar can be identified as spatial and behavioural. First, spatial informal practices can be found within territorial formation, the fabrication, form and materiality of the assemblage of dwellings: Mariamma Nagar can be identified visually in contrast to the 'formal' modern city of concrete, glass and steel, roads and pavements defined and planned; as a visual material culture and form, a particularity of place. Guards, barriers and bridges visually separate 'formal' from 'informal' spaces. The ground is suddenly rough and winding lanes and bustling alleys replace the wider streets beyond.

Second, behavioural informality can be identified in the community that juxtaposes living, working and making, one that is transient and established, one that can be described as in a 'permanent temporariness', both a spatial and behavioural characteristic (Yiftachel 2009). For many inhabitants, it is one of two homes. The ancestral village represents family ties and rural territory, in contrast to the urban, Mumbai home. The organisation Urbz describes this social movement between homes as a 'circulatory journey', one that has more than one root, and an important territorial context within which to understand the settlement (Urbz 2017). Urbz explore the idea of 'belonging' where the village and the city constitute a 'simultaneous spatial logic' rather than a binary construct defined as past (rural) and the present (urban). They explain the village and city roots are both part of a 'dynamic present, defined by the lives of many types of people and generations' (Echanove and Srivastava 2014). The village forms part of the assemblage of urban informality, and should be taken into consideration as another simultaneous and symbiotic home and learning environment.

Pedagogical informality: mapping the Mariamma Nagar neighbourhood

In 2013, following a design project in and around the school building and classroom, the children (age 11) were asked these questions: How do you feel you learn in your home environment? What are the sources of learning? Who, when, where, how and why? Pupils, teachers and volunteers set off into the settlement to map learning happening in and around the home. Children organised themselves into groups, each equipped with cameras and questions to answer. They carried out a series of transect walks documenting the answers to their questions photographically.

The children gathered visual documentation of the settlement during a mapping project, which they would later use to create their interpretation of their neighbourhood. They had no set direction and were led by their curiosity, walking through lanes and down passages. They took photographs of people, animals, buildings, trees, likes and dislikes. They built a visual network of the informal settlement as a teacher, as an environment for learning. Architect Francesco Careri describes walking as an 'act of transversal, an instrument of phenomenological knowledge and symbolic interpretation of the territory', 'a form of psycho-geographical reading' of the landscape (Careri 2002: 11). In his work *Walkscapes*, he puts emphasis on the dynamism of the experiential mapping technique, underlining the 'revelatory power of this dynamism mobilizing the entire body – social as well as individual – in order to then transform the mind

Figure 11.2 Photograph showing children setting off on their neighbourhood walkabout. Source: Antaki, 2014

of he who knows how to look' (Careri 2002: 16). The physical nature of this informal exploration relates to the primal assessment of environment used for efficient survival and future knowledgeability: exploration is an informal (without known direction) activity of self-empowerment. I argue that experience is a characteristic of informality, and that informality is pedagogical in nature. The informality of this pedagogy was in part due to it taking place outside the classroom. But it is also due to the fact that the children were able to make their own decisions that oscillated between following rules (answering questions or taking photographs) and making spontaneous choices in the built environment (such as which route to take, what to photograph, who to speak to). Henri Lefebvre's view of experiencing the city is that it is a language and a practice (Lefebvre 1996: 143). He writes that 'only a *praxis* (…) can take charge of the possibility and demand of a synthesis: the gathering together of what gives itself as dispersed, dissociated, separated, and this in the form of simultaneity and

Figure 11.3 Two photographs showing the classroom where the class create their map of the settlement using printed photographs they had taken, drawings and annotations. Source: Antaki, 2014

encounters.' The children experienced a praxis, between action and reflection, utilising informal methods of *jugaad* to experience and document the settlement following, and breaking, its various and changeable rules. The informal pedagogy itself acts as a flow between assembled parts and interconnections between the children's lives, imaginations and learning in the settlement. It is informality that makes learning happen.

The schoolchildren built a geographically purposeful map in the classroom, from memory, of how they felt they learnt in their neighbourhood. They positioned their printed photographs and added drawn elements they felt were missing. Over a series of four weekly sessions their map took shape, until drawings, photographs and writing came together, to complete their representation of Mariamma Nagar.

Within the relatively formal pedagogic activity structure – loosely defined as action (settlement) and reflection (classroom) – the sessions oscillated between the two places and spatially represented modes of

Figure 11.4 Photograph of children's map of learning in Mariamma Nagar, made in cloth, ink and paper, 3x3m. Source: Antaki, 2014

practice and thinking. In the classroom, the practice was more structured. But settlement activities needed to adapt to the fluidity of exploration, in a dynamic and complex place with many opportunities for imagination and spontaneity, where the children could explore possible futures using design thinking and making.

The informal settlement is not often formally mapped within the city. The children's map not only shows an area that has not been mapped in so much detail before, but also represents an inventory or catalogue of the settlement's socio-spatial pedagogical characteristics. The map is rooted in time, locality and people: It is itself informal in its design language, production, imagination and the interconnectivity of its parts. This map is particular, not only to the time it was researched and created, but also to the specific occasion of our group outing, making it a unique representation of the distinctive production of the informal settlement as a pedagogical activity. As architect Aldo Van Eyck writes, '[w]hatever space and time mean, place and occasion mean more' (Van Eyck 1999: 471).

Informal craft: making a tapestry in the informal settlement

Urban informality in India, within its fluctuating levels of transience and resourceful political camouflage, is also linked to liberalisation, in the context of globalisation (Alsayyad 2003: 27). As a context for craft, the liberal global economy provides pocketed space for entrepreneurship and creativity. Across the informal boundary, the settlement is a centrally located hive of activity spatially separated by plots of unused land. As Dovey explains, 'High levels of informality enable micro-flows of information, goods, materials and practices that produce income and make life sustainable under conditions of poverty' and micro-spatial adaptations flourish under conditions of informal urbanism (Dovey 2013: 85). Survival strategies of informal settlement dwellers include integration into global supply chains – which transcend regional and national boundaries and politics. Yet these same strategies also expose them to neoliberal forces operating on a global scale. Textile-related craft in the Mariamma Nagar settlement particularly thrives. The small spaces and mobility of the necessary tools, the scale of products and proximity to resources and vendors make for good workshops. The network of bag makers, tailors and embroiderers fits together with the rest of the city in an environment that provides an assemblage of 'entrepreneurial flexibility, adaptation and creativity' (Dovey 2012: 349).

The children's map of learning was fragile and the collaged elements would not withstand the humidity for long. To reflect the local settlement craft palette that is predominantly textile based, and as a representation of the cultural meaning of cloth and embroidery embroiderers took on the project to interpret the children's map to create a tapestry. An embroidered tapestry would last, could be transported, and would represent the settlement material culture.

I brought the children's map to the workshop, located on the first floor of a settlement dwelling overlooking the stables and trees of the racecourse. The embroiderer interpreted the map his own way.

Figure 11.5 Four photographs depicting the process of making the children's map of learning in Mariamma Nagar, cloth, ink and paper, 3x3m. Source: Antaki, 2014

First, he traced it, decoding photographs drawings and text with single line drawings in pencil on a large roll of tracing paper. Then, he ran the tracing paper under the machine needle to create perforated dotted lines; a white chalky paste was wiped over the tracing paper perforations to create a temporary dotted line drawing that was to be used as a template for embroidery. He then followed this chalk line pattern and embroidered lines and infill. He picked the colours to match the children's original choices as closely as possible. He added designs he felt were missing: a signature green parrot, a moon and their names (along with the children's) within the map border.

Today in India, handicrafts are often practised within informal settlements. Scholar Singanapalli Balaram writes that 'In India, craft is not a thing of the past, but a thing of the present as well as of the future. With nearly 23 million craftspersons still practising, craft is as contemporary as mass production, showing a great promise in the globalized world of the future' (Balaram 2005: 13). Moreover, a large proportion of craft is informal, thriving on the assembled nature of the settlement as a creative environment. Mariamma Nagar exemplifies the translocality of this urban activity: despite its small area, the porosity and dynamism of the settlement is revealed in the multitude of crafts practised there. In Mariamma Nagar, embroidery is predominant: both hand embroidery and machine embroidery work of varying qualities is carried out within hutments. Craft requires a number of social and spatial characteristics; the unwritten rules and material languages need space for focus and experimentation within workshop spaces. The informal settlement provides the tools necessary for the flexibility of craft practice, and proximity to a variety of other crafts, density of accommodation, and visibility/accessibility of workshops allows a spontaneity that helps create a dynamic space for making.

However, the living situation of many craftspeople in urban and rural environments in India is difficult: poverty, lack of access to social services, illiteracy, exploitation by middlemen and low social status are among some of the most notable issues. Although craft in India is often informal, there are many disadvantages to this form of economic activity. For instance, often a 'total lack of civic, professional, and social service infrastructure', and 'irregular electricity, lack of good roads, and absence of transportation facilities are professional problems as well as daily aggravations. (…) And social services infrastructure – insurance, pension plans, medical care – is something beyond hope' particularly in more rural conditions (Liebl and Roy 2004: 53). In addition, there exists a paradox attached to craftspeople who live in poverty whereas their work supports prosperous domestic and export trade as a result of complex, varied and persistent problems that affect the crafts sector in India. Informal practices are a way of surviving these contexts with resilience. But as Dovey points out, '[i]nformality is not to be confused with poverty; it is indeed a resource for managing poverty' (Dovey 2013: 85).

Although the crafting of the tapestry can be described as a representation of the material culture of the settlement, it is also a conversation with the settlement: as anthropologist Tim Ingold writes, making is correspondence and that 'to correspond with the world, in short, is not to describe it, or to represent it, but to *answer* to it' (Ingold 2013: 108). The tapestry is both an informal and formal response to the children's map. The craftsperson used informal practices of 'composition', 'speculation' and 'bricolage' (McFarlane 2011: 38) to interpret the children's design drawings and photographs. But they also used formal techniques – particular stitches, use of tools and learnt skills – of embroidery as a craft.

The production of the tapestry presented a method for exploration and engagement with the settlement, using agency and economic activity; a negotiated route through the settlement, in which I as a mediator also experienced the adaptation of behaviour necessary to fit in using

Figure 11.6 The finished tapestry. Source: Antaki, 2014

practices of *jugaad*. The crafted interpretation smoothed the children's collection of photographs and drawings. The making of the tapestry is a translation, using relational informal and formal craft techniques and therefore a representation of both informal and formal processes. Although embroidery as a craft uses many rules and skills, the methods used to translate photographs and drawings into stitches were taken in an unplanned but experienced way, a craftsperson's spontaneous act of creativity. The embroidered translation of photographs picks out certain elements – people, lines, colours and materials of everyday spaces and activities in Mariamma Nagar. The tapestry represents a 'plane section' of life in the settlement, simultaneously reducing down and bringing out the topological nature of learning situations, giving even but subjective detail to each item. Here, the embroiderer is crafting his own unique interpretation of the children's map. The tapestry pictorially represents parts of the settlement as an assembled, speculative and 'bricolaged' composition.

Conclusion

The Mariamma Nagar settlement situates multiple informal practices: the spatial, behavioural and pedagogical informal practices identified here have contributed towards the co-creation of an informal learning environment for the children who live there. The children's map contained many layers of information and facets of enquiry, demonstrating in the first instance how the children experience the informal settlement as an informal learning setting. Subsequently, through the formal and informal practices of craft to transform their map into a tapestry, the neighbourhood and specific local informal practices found there now find themselves represented in the particularity of the embroidered work. The tapestry presents a reflection of the assembled nature of the settlement, and the rhizomic and creative structures of informality, in spatial, behavioural but also pedagogical ways.

Craft represents both formal and informal characteristics within the settlement: it is a practice of interconnection and conversation between rules, skills, spontaneity and innovation. The oscillation between informal and formal practices of craft transformed the children's map into a territorial artefact. During this project, many informal practices helped create dynamic learning situations, by providing opportunities to improvise, speculate and compose. Informal practices of *jugaad* combine with design language, behaviour and imagination, intertwining to create an assemblage of informal learning.

In Mumbai, informality manifests as a social and spatial practice, but also as a design problem and a theoretical ecology, as Rao indicates (Rao 2006: 229). It is plural: it is both a practice and a setting, an activity and an environment. I argued that informal practices can be found in urban formation, behaviour, pedagogy and learning. Rao also highlights that the informal settlement is a space at risk, and of risk (Rao 2006). In Mariamma Nagar opportunities for exploration and design action are linked to instability and flux, which makes it a fertile ground for learning through experimentation. Further, I propose that design activities in education can be informed by informality, as bricolage, speculation and composition (McFarlane 2012a: 89) as design naturally incorporates a movement between formal and informal practice.

The making of the map and tapestry was part of a 'collective design pedagogy', one that thrives on the informal, as a setting and as a practice. Informality is a learning method beyond the particular setting of Mariamma Nagar. Informal spatial practices often demonstrate high levels of dexterity in negotiating the (often difficult to disentwine) formal and informal powers that frame and regulate. McFarlane describes informality as an urban development practice (McFarlane 2012b), but I would go so far as to say it is a design practice. Informal design practices are based on intimate and intuitive ways of seeing; hands-on work, behaviour and communication; making with local resources and often through collaboration. I propose that informality as a setting and a practice is an advantageous environment and activity for the development of a collaborative type of learning that involves the socio-spatial politics, materials and economies of locality. This research has suggested that the informal settlement Mariamma Nagar provided lateral and spontaneous opportunities for an education of making and craft that is culturally rooted and socially connected with people and places. In a collective design pedagogy informality is a pedagogical ingredient: it leaves opportunity for the use of the imagination of both facilitator and learner. Its rhizomic nature leaves chances for engaging curiosity, empathy, possible futures and narratives; leaving open opportunities for spontaneity, agency, entrepreneurship and innovation. I argue for the value of informal environments with particular opportunities for learning and making, and informal practices of design.

Note

1 *Bidonville* is the French word for slum or informal settlement, due to the use of recuperated materials, some of which were 'bidons', or jerrycans.

References

AlSayyad, N. 2003. 'Urban informality as a "new" way of Life'. In Roy, A. and AlSayyad, N. (eds), *Urban Informality: Transnational perspectives from the Middle East, Latin America, and South Asia*. Lanham, MD: Lexington Books, 7–32.
Balaram, S. 2005. 'Design pedagogy in India: a perspective', *Design Issues*, 21 (4): 11–22.
Bhan, G. 2017. 'From the basti to the 'house': socio-spatial readings of housing policy in India', *Current Sociology Monograph*, 65 (4): 587–602.
Boano, C. 2013. Architecture must be defended: informality and the agency of space. London: OpenDemocracy.
Careri, F. 2002. *Walkscapes: El Andar como Practica Estética* [Walkscapes: Walking as an Aesthetic Practice]. Barcelona: Editorial Gustavo Gili.
De Meuler, B. and Shannon, K. 2010. *Human Settlements: Formulations and (re)calibrations*. Amsterdam: SUN Architecture Publishers.
Dicken, B. 2005. 'City of God', *City*, 9 (3): 207–320.
D'Monte, D. 2011. 'A matter of people'. In Burdett, R. and Sudjic, D. (eds.), *Living in the Endless City*. London: Phaidon.
Dovey, K. 2012. 'Informal urbanism and complex adaptive assemblage', *International Development Planning Review*, 34 (4): 371–89.
Dovey, K. 2013. 'Informalising architecture: the challenge of informal settlements', *Architectural Design: The Architecture of Transgression*, 83 (6): 82–9.
Echanove, M. and Srivastava, R. 2014. 'Mumbai's circulatory urbanism'. In Angelil, M. and Hehl, R. (eds.), *Empower! Essays on the Political Economy of Urban Form*, Vol. 3. Zurich: Ruby Press, 82–113.
Harvey, D. 2012. 'From space to place and back again: reflections on the condition of postmodernity'. In Bird, J., Curtis, B., Putnam, T. and Tickner, L. (eds.), *Mapping the Futures: Local cultures, global change*. London: Routledge 2–29.
Ingold, T. 2013. *Making: Anthropology, archaeology, art and architecture*. London: Routledge.
Lefebvre, H. 1996. *Writings on Cities*. Kofman, E. and Lebas, E. (eds. and trans.). Oxford: Blackwell.
Liebl, M. and Roy, T. 2004. 'Handmade in India: traditional craft skills in a changing world'. In Finger, J.M. and Schuler, P. (eds.), *Poor People's Knowledge*. Washington, DC: World Bank Publications, 53–74.
McFarlane, C. 2011. *Learning the City: Knowledge and translocal assemblage*. Oxford: Wiley.
McFarlane, C. 2012a. 'Rethinking informality: politics, crisis, and the city', *Planning Theory and Practice*, 13 (1): 89–108.
McFarlane, C. 2012b. 'The entrepreneurial slum: civil society, mobility and the co-production of urban development', *Urban Studies*, 49 (13): 2795–816.
Mehrotra, R. 2006. 'Learning from Mumbai'. In *Mumbai Reader 06*. Mumbai: Urban Design Research Institute.
Rao, V. 2006. 'Slum as theory', *International Journal of Urban and Regional Research*, 30 (1): 225–32.
Roy, A. 2003. 'Transnational trespassings: the geopolitics of urban informality'. In Roy, A. and AlSayyad, N. (eds), *Urban Informality: Transnational perspectives from the Middle East, Latin America, and South Asia*. Lanham, MD: Lexington Books, 289–318.
Roy, A. and AlSayyad, N. 2003. 'Urban informality: crossing borders'. In Roy, A. and AlSayyad, N. (eds.), *Urban Informality: Transnational perspectives from the Middle East, Latin America, and South Asia*. Lanham, MD: Lexington Books, 1–6.
Urbz. 2017. 'Circulatory lives', Urbz.net, 25 July. http://www.urbz.net/projects/circulatory-lives.html.
Van Eyck, A. 1999. *Aldo van Eyck: Works, 1944–1998*. Ligtelijn, V. and Strauven, F. (eds). Basel: Birkhäuser.
Yiftachel, O. 2009. 'Theoretical notes on "gray spaces": the coming of urban Apartheid?', *Planning Theory*, 8 (1): 88–100.

12
Informality as an urban trend in mainstream architectural publications
Fani Kostourou and Paul Goodship

Informality has grown in dominance as a type of urban production and as a theoretical thesis of its own concrete substance. This chapter explores its transformation from marginalised urbanisation of, for and by the poor to an emerging practice in the making of the built environment in contemporary cities.

Due to the wide variety of definitions and conceptual understandings, few studies have attempted any chronological overviews of informality. Moreover, the state-centric and dualist approaches to study urban informality's explorations usually focus on its specific contexts and aspects such as economy, society, policy or infrastructure. In Brazil, for example, urban informality has been mainly discussed through the lens of urbanism, policies and the question of housing, while in India, as Swati Chattopadhyay recounts here (Chapter 2), it has encompassed physical and social infrastructures appropriated as tools of rebellion against colonial practices and control.

This chapter seeks to contribute to a less-researched angle in urban informality, the evolution of the term in architectural mainstream publications. These publications are an infrastructure of knowledge and theorisation that most architects and planners use to inform their decision-making and influence the way others see the built environment. This is true especially in the case of architects and planners with construction duties and tight weekly schedules, who rarely get the opportunity to delve into complex socio-spatial issues and therefore have to rely on quick reads and easily accessible media. As infrastructures that enable contemplation and debates on formal and informal urbanscapes, these publications engage with and reflect the developments in the making of the built environment, the image of cities, and the exchanges that take place in them, and in turn influence critical discourse and city development in the present and future.

The rise of an urban trend

In August 1963 *Architectural Design* published the hugely influential 'Dwelling Resources in South America' edition of its magazine, co-edited by John Turner (Turner et al. 1963). The edition reflected upon much of Turner's experiences from the *barriadas* of Peru, along with others' similar experiences across the world, where informal urbanisation and methods of self-construction from the Global South were discussed as an alternative to top-down mass interventions. Turner's work provided the opportunity to start formulating the idea that self-built homes and communities could work better than those conceived and designed by architects and other built environment professionals (Turner and Fichter 1972). The publication was one of the first examples of a mainstream architectural magazine that published the phenomenon of informality and opened up the image of urban informality to a broader audience for discussion, many of whom would never have seen this side of the city before. Since then, academics, architects, urban designers, researchers and professionals within the built environment have become fascinated by the idea of learning from informality.

The term *informal* was first developed in the early 1970s, most noticeably by Keith Hart in 1972 as previously discussed by Fran Tonkiss (see Chapter 3), to 'describe a set of socio-economic and spatial processes, which combined irregularity with deficient levels of productivity in the production of goods, services and the built environment' (Fiori 2013: 40).

In recent times, built environment professionals have started 'acknowledging the informal as a vital part of the city's ecosystem [which] has been the great U-turn of urban policy over the last two decades' (McGuirk 2014: 25); and a growing number of architectural publications picked up the discussion. This led, more recently, to high-profile architects addressing the subject in their work, including the 2016 Pritzker Prize winner, Chilean architect Alejandro Aravena. The rise in the popularity of informality in the built environment has seen it transform into an urban trend, resulting in a noticeable increase of both conceptual projects and real architectural interventions for the urban environment.

The chapter follows the diachronic appearance of the terminology used to describe informal settlements throughout the second half of the twentieth century. It examines the changes in the frequency of the use of terms in seven European and North American architectural publications and tests the hypothesis that since the 1960s, a phenomenon that mostly affects the Global South has attracted the attention of and been debated by the Global North. The argument is structured in three parts. The first part seeks to answer when, how often and to what extent the mainstream architectural press has discussed informality in the built environment. The second part interrogates how the mainstream architectural press has over time perceived informality as an inherent characteristic of cities, whereas the third part links historical trends to relevant historical developments and local and global socio-political events. The final discussion hints at the role of these publications in constructing the image of informal settlements and in establishing a linguistic precedent for recognising their subalternity, despite their refusal to be described and represented.

Data and methodology

The timeline of our investigation is between 1960 and 2015, with the 1960s – as we saw before – being a radical moment in the conceptualisation of informality in the built environment. The selection of publications was based on a list indexed by the British Architectural Library of RIBA,[1] which catalogues most periodicals related to the built environment. We established a set of three criteria: 1) the periodicals had to actively publish between 1960 and 2015, 2) the periodicals could not be exclusive to scientific or professional fields other than architecture, and 3) the periodicals had to be written in English, which constitutes a disparity of its own. From a total of 207 journals, seven magazines were selected: *Architects' Journal* (AJ), *Architectural Design* (AD), *Architectural Record* (ARec), *Architectural Review* (AR), *Domus*, *RIBA Journal* (RIBAJ) and *Ekistics*.[2]

The seven magazines are based in the UK (AJ, AD, AR, RIBAJ), USA (ARec), Italy (*Domus*) and Greece (*Ekistics*), revealing a European and American bias of the international architectural press, which coincides chronologically with moments of decolonisation for a large part of the world. Furthermore, the historical context, as well as the founding dates[3] of these magazines, also hints at their publishing pretext and aims. Still, the RIBA Library regards five out of these journals (AJ, ARec, AR, *Domus*

Magazines	N° of Issues 1960–2015	Year Founded	Country of Origin
Architects' Journal	1,344	1895	UK
Architectural Design	336	1930	UK
Architectural Record	672	1891	USA
Architectural Review	672	1896	UK
Domus	672	1928	Italy
Ekistics	397	1955	Greece
RIBA Journal	672	1893	UK

Table 12.1 Table showing list of the selected seven magazines with their estimated total number of issues for the period 1960–2015. The table includes the year each magazine was founded and its country of origin. Source: Authors.

and RIBAJ) as 'the most important and most representative journals from their countries and are (or are likely to be) the most asked for by our [their] readers' (RIBA 2015: 6). Furthermore, together all seven reach a circulation spectrum of more than 140 countries, being distributed to all habitable continents and received by educational and research institutions, practitioners as well as international organisations (Table 12.1) (Athens Center of Ekistics 1959).

Qualitative meta-research

The journals' content was analysed through a qualitative meta-research, composed of a meta-data-analysis and a brief meta-synthesis (Paterson *et al.* 2001). The first consisted of a secondary data analysis of the databases centred on an online search of keywords associated with urban informality, while the second focused on the synthesis and assessment of these findings per publication and time.

For the identification of keywords, we looked at relevant literature[4] and other official documents such as the UN-Habitat's list of 'the words that describe the slums' (Moreno 2003: 30) and Mike Davis's (2006) influential *Planet of Slums*. This search gave us a total of 70 keywords, including the primary *slums* and *informality*[5]. The list of keywords, while not exhaustive, is extensive enough to allow specific patterns to emerge. For instance, according to *Lotus* magazine (issue 143, 2010) 60 out of the 70 keywords are geographically specific words found in different languages.

Three limitations are apparent in our methodology. Firstly, specific continents, such as Oceania, are entirely excluded from our study. Secondly, some countries with big landmass like Canada or China are missing and thirdly, the featured regions such as the Middle East, Asia, Europe and Africa are unequally represented by the keyword selection. This once again highlights the Eurocentric and English-language bias among these architectural publications, allowing us to infer that the image of urban informality is partially created from a part of the world that has little to no experience of this urban reality. This bias is a finding on its own, since these publications are the primary source of information for the majority of built environment professionals globally, and thus have a pivotal role in shaping views, decision-making and policies beyond national borders.

Linguistic trends in mainstream media

The peaks and troughs of the graph (Figure 12.1) indicate how discussions related to informal settlements started to rise from the beginning of the 1960s, experiencing a drop in the 1970s and 1980s only to increase in popularity from 1990 to 2011 and thinning out again in the last four years of the investigation period.[6] Interestingly enough, the average trendline deviates significantly from the absolute numbers as far as the recent years are concerned. This means that while in recent times mainstream magazines have been found to discuss issues of built informality more often, this represents just a fraction of what they publish in total (number of search results).

The trend changes drastically when the analysis is broken down into its parts, and this sheds light on the differences between the seven publications. While most of them show a steady rise in the use of keywords with the majority peaking between the end of the 1990s and 2014, *Ekistics* is the only one that has a descending gradient (Figure 12.2). The disparity in outcome between *Ekistics* and the other journals can be explained in that it is a more scholarly than mainstream journal and its influence has declined over the years[7]. Should *Ekistics* be omitted from the ensemble, a clear trend appears: urban informality as a topic was not much debated before the 1990s – except for the mid-1970s as an after effect of a few scholars' activities – but became extremely popular towards recent years.

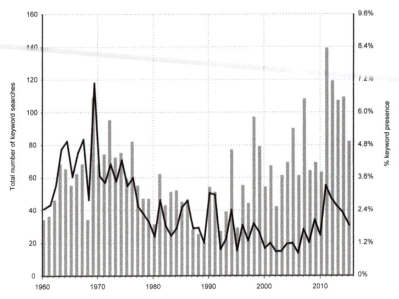

Figure 12.1 Graph showing the evolution of the total number of keyword searches for all magazines selected between 1960 and 2015 (in absolute numbers). Superimposed is the average frequency trend line showing percentage of keywords present among total number of results. Source: Authors.

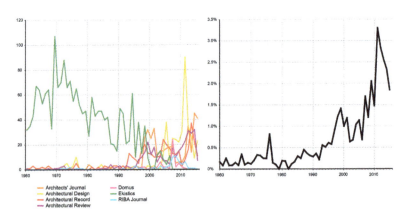

Figure 12.2 (Left) Graph showing the evolution of the total number of keyword searches for all magazines selected between 1960 and 2015 broken down to each of the seven mainstream magazines. (Right) Graph showing the average evolution of the concurrence of keywords (percentage) in six mainstream magazines between 1960 and 2015 (excluding *Ekistics*). Source: Authors.

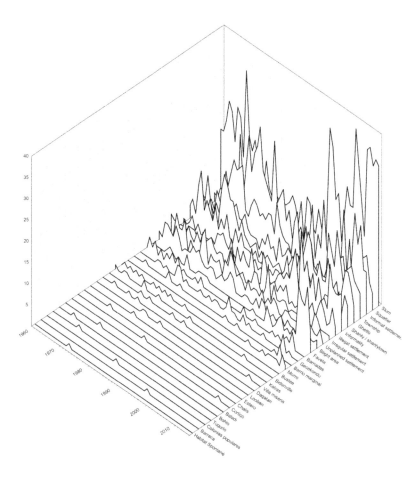

Figure 12.3 Area graphs for 31 keywords referenced between 1960 and 2015 (absolute numbers). Source: Authors.

The analysis also shows that generic and commonly used terms such as slum, squatter, informal settlement, shantytown, irregular/illegal/unplanned settlement and informality constitute a constant word concurrence pattern across all publications (Figure 12.3). Some journals demonstrate a greater variety of keywords than others, with *Ekistics* being the leading one in referencing geographically specific keywords (18), followed by the AD (11) and ARec (6). This is consistent with the initial scope of *Ekistics* to address experts in developing – and previously colonised – countries, using the local terminology instead. It is the only journal mentioning the keywords *habitat spontané* (North-West Africa),

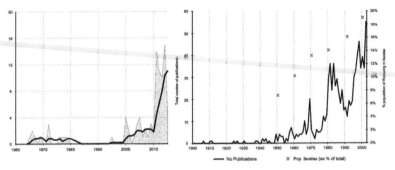

Figure 12.4 (Left) Graph showing the concurrence of the *favela* keyword in seven mainstream magazines between 1960 and 2015. (Right) Graph showing bibliography on the *favelas* of Rio de Janeiro together with number of publications per year between 1900 and 2002. Sources: (left) Authors; (right) Valladares, 2008 using data from URBANDATA, Brazil, 2004.

colonias populares (Mexico), *tugurio* (Peru, Venezuela and Costa Rica), *chalis, katras, bustee* (India), *estero* and *looban* (Philippines). Here, the appearance of different words for different geographies, while raising issues of non-translatability, is seen as a tool to drift away from the legacy of colonialism.

Still, slum is by far the most popular keyword, scoring highest in every periodical search – followed by the terms ghetto and township, which, however, have different meanings contextually depending on where or when each are used. This popularity may relate to the fact that the United Nations officially adopted the term slum 'to publicise the seriousness of the urban problem and to improve its ability to attract funding' and despite the subsequent establishment of specific terminologies, the same generic terms continued being employed with impunity to discuss a variety of social and spatial morphologies, typologies and processes (Gilbert 2007: 697). Scholars have already condemned such semantic generalisations, arguing that the word slum should not be used as an umbrella to represent every other urban reality, meaning the *bidonville*, ghetto, *taudis*, and *favela* among others (Valladares 2008). Dovey in his essay states that 'many dwellings in informal settlements are not slums' and a key distinction between the informal settlement and the slum is the material outcome of poverty while informality is best seen as a resource – a means of managing poverty. Hence, a dictation by the media to perceive all informal settlements as slums can create a negative image of urban informality for the broad audience.

From the geographically specific words, the most popular is *favela*, a Portuguese word used to describe slums in Brazil. The first *favelas* appeared in the late nineteenth century and have been a part of Brazilian cities ever since. In 2008, Licia Valladares juxtaposed the bibliography on the *favelas* of Rio de Janeiro with the total number of publications per year and the population of Rio living in them for the period 1900–2000 (Figure 12.4). She argued that three periods are evident. Between 1900 and 1940 *favelas* are *silenced* by most publications reflecting the formal consideration of *favelas* as 'ephemeral place[s] that would soon disappear from the urban landscape' (Novaes 2014: 207). In the following years, *favelas* are *highlighted* as illegal and socially problematic areas, still unknown though to most readers. This situation changes rapidly because of the formal recognition of *favelas*' existence (late 1960s), the introduction of anti-*favela* policies to eradicate them (early 1970s) and the launch of new less radical governmental programmes, such as the *Favela-Bairro*, to research *favelas* (spike of late 1990s). This also ties in with the period that the above Eurocentric magazines moved away from simplistic terminologies, like slum, and started to acknowledge more appropriate terms.

Essentially, the discussion around *favela* or *morro* took off when Brazil hosted the 2014 World Cup and the 2016 Olympic Games. This was a time when the rest of the world, especially European magazines, started to take more notice of Brazil. Similarly, *township* became a hot topic around the time South Africa hosted the 2010 World Cup, while *blight area* became fashionable in the 1960s and 1970s during the expansion of Los Angeles with high-speed infrastructure and residential displacements as well as in 1984 when the city hosted the summer Olympic Games for the second time.

Therefore the spikes in the graph are often linked to local social, economic and cultural events that spotlight the country of origin and the less visible parts of its urban landscape. This suggests efforts of urban branding and the development of urban spectacles that aim to boost the economic capital of the cities, unsettling informal sites as prime development opportunities. This is accompanied by a growing 'interest for slums' in mainstream media, which is essentially a political act and raises questions whether the portrayed image is a fair representation of the poverty on the ground.

A chronological overview: the emergence of a concept, 1960–79

The clearest spike in the graph is detected over the last 20 years, confirming our initial hypothesis that urban informality has become hugely popular in recent times (Figure 12.5). Other peaks are also observed in 1974, 1976 and 1980. We believe this relates to the latest large cycle of decolonisation and the post-modernism era, when avant-garde groups reacted to the top-down planning of cities and looked for inspiration away from past colonial practices. International organisations like the UN General Assembly, established the United Nations Habitat and Human Settlements Foundation (UNHHSF), the first official UN body dedicated to urbanisation. Traditional architecture schools integrated in their curricula new subjects related to informality. Notably, the Architectural Association in the United Kingdom introduced Urban Poverty within the newly formed Department of Development and Tropical Studies, which later moved to UCL and formed the Bartlett's current Development Planning Unit. Meanwhile other disciplines brought forward new radical ideas inspired by the social capital of informal settlements. In the words of sociologist Henri Lefebvre (1995: 279), 'can people who populate them [buildings], who live in them, who shape them according to their need, also create them, or will that remain the prerogative of the small group which plans, builds and organises them? Up until now, the answer has been no, and this failure is the crucial problem.' The image of informality in the built environment would never be the same again.

Figure 12.5 Standardised line graphs of the evolution of informality as an urban trend in the mainstream press (average without taking into consideration *Ekistics*). Source: Authors.

The subsidence of informality as a spatial practice, 1980–95

In the next 15 years, the interest by the media drops followed by a plateau phase until 1993. This ties in with what Jorge Fiori (2013) and Mariana Dias Simpson (2013) call the neoliberal period when a change in international policies not only influenced the way projects were managed in the Global South but also shifted much attention away from state-funded projects in the West, towards more privately funded projects. In the UK for example, after 1979 and the birth of the Thatcher era, there was an 'ideological shift away from state intervention and towards private enterprise and competition', which resulted in a massive sell-off of public sector housing (Brand and Thomas 2005: 114). Likewise, when the Washington Consensus, a controversial series of macroeconomic policies including the privatisation of public utilities, trade liberalisation and deregulation, was implemented in Latin America in the 1980s and 1990s, upgrading projects slowed down or came to a halt (Fabricius 2011). Meanwhile, brutal dictatorships, such as the 17 years military government of Augusto Pinochet (1973–90) in Chile, would 'maintain strict control over land invasions and limit the informal growth of the periphery' (Jirón 2010: 75), while the debt crisis of 1982 would prevent countries such as Brazil, Argentina and Mexico from providing funds for public upgrading projects. Due to the lack of financial support from the state, many established architectural practices gave up on socially orientated projects and the architectural press turned its attention away from issues related to informality and towards the private sector and profitable initiatives.

However, the neoliberal strategies quickly led to an increase in levels of urban poverty and the widening of social gaps, and throughout the next years 'the informal kept growing in size, diversity, and complexity' (Fiori 2013: 42). As a result, discussions about informal settlements were revived after 1990. It is interesting, for instance, that during the Structural Adjustment Policies (SAP) programmes in Africa and Latin America, as peasants and workers were pushed out of work (Bolivia and Senegal) and off the land (Mexico) and governments divested their social programme, much of the life world of the poor was left in the hands of NGOs that were to rediscover informality as something noble and worthy of support to fight the misery imposed on them by the global neoliberal regime. This revival of interest also marks the shift towards a 'comprehensive approach to poverty' (Simpson 2013: 11), which as Simpson argues, focused on the upgrading and urbanisation processes of informal urban areas through integrated, multi-scale and participatory approaches. Different from all previous periods, 'poverty [now] began to be understood as a multidimensional phenomenon that must be addressed comprehensively', economically as well as socially (Simpson 2013: 11).

The surge of an urban trend, 1996-2010

By the end of the 1990s, a massive boom in the popularity of informality occurs, creating what we call an urban trend. This coincides with the introduction of the internet in the 1990s, followed by a widespread technological revolution, which improved – and democratised to a certain extent – access to information. Until then, the architectural press had a massive responsibility in distributing the news to its readers, who would rely almost exclusively on them for information and knowledge building[8]. With the new technologies, professionals could update themselves quickly, easily and at will. This brought to the fore less well-known aspects of the unregulated built environments, such as their adaptive processes or their practices of production and distribution of resources, goods and services.

Meanwhile, there was a more extensive mobilisation of international organisations on issues relating to urban poverty and the emergence of new megacities. An illustrative example is that the 1996 Habitat Agenda document contained more than 100 commitments and 600 recommendations and was adopted by 171 countries[9]. The growing acceptance of informality within established organisations encouraged the setting out of targets like the Millennium Development Goals[10], which ambitiously defined eight goals to be achieved by 2015, 'targeting the alleviation of poverty and cutting the proportion of people living in extreme poverty in half' (Davis 2006: 200). While the outcomes of these efforts can be questioned, they helped bring issues of informality to the forefront of international development and recognise the need to reduce poverty globally. At the same time, new economic allyships emerged such as the BRIC block in 2009, with the aim of rivalling traditional western nations leading a 'new phase of global capitalism [to] take-off' (Sassen 2015: 45).

Internationally recognised individuals then followed suit to celebrate urban informality and inspire newer generations. Star architects like Rem Koolhaas glorified the informality of Lagos, describing the city as 'powerful, inspiring and brutal' (Koolhaas *et al.* 2000: 652) and argued that all cities might look like this one day and therefore informality should be embraced. Furthermore, the Urban Think-Tank design practice dedicated itself to social architecture and informal development, providing an alternative for architects being non-conformists and activists (McGuirk 2014). Additionally, recognisable TV presenters and architectural commentators such as Kevin McCloud lauded the community spirit and togetherness of Dharavi in his 2010 documentary 'Slumming It'[11]. While the above can be seen as patronising to some extent, they helped put informality at the forefront of architectural and urban discourse, contributing one way or another to the transformation of a previous subaltern – invisible, peripheral and illegible – built reality into a recognisable and at times appraisable possibility.

The beginning of the fall, 2011–

One last remark can be made on the plateauing of the interest in informality after 2011, which coincides with what Simpson (2013: 17) calls a return to the 'failed "conventional" housing policies implemented in the past'. Under the umbrella of formal state intervention, the new spatial practice consists of state-funded housing projects built in vast volumes in countries such as Brazil, Chile and Mexico[12]. In Brazil only, the 'Minha Casa, Niha Vida' programme started with the aim 'to deliver 1 million ready-to-occupy units for middle and low-income households throughout the country while fuelling economic growth through the construction industry' (Simpson 2013: 17). The language that comes with this is, as it should be, no longer affiliated with the informal side of the built environment.

Conclusion: the realities of an urban trend

Through a qualitative meta-research of keyword search in mainstream architectural magazines this chapter recognised the gradual establishment of the informal built environment as an urban trend over 55 years. The discussion provided the opportunity to link fluctuations in the 'interest in the informal' to local and global socio-economic and political events. We saw that as a concept informality in the built environment is highly contextual and as such its perception and cognitive understanding changes over time. Architecture like any discipline unfolds in the background of and in interaction with larger social and political dynamics, and if informality constitutes a central issue within broader geopolitical agendas and power relations, it is only natural that the built environment professionals and their journals would engage and reflect on these debates as they unfold over time.

On the one hand, engagement and reflection are often influenced by internal factors, for example magazines' managing editors, thematic focus, circulation capacity, as well as by external events, such as global economic and political regimes, colonial legacies, overpowering governments or the agency of a few empowered individuals. On the other hand, they have the power to influence the ways informal settlements and urban informality are seen and conceived by the formal city. As Dovey argues the formal/informal distinction is a constructed framework created by economies and governments. We argue that it is also broadcasted and sustained to a certain degree by the media and other information technologies. Our work shows that the mainstream architectural media have the power to transform the image of urban informality expressed in the built environment and provide a language to describe and distinguish previously subaltern morphologies and forms of social capital. Those are the ones who among others help informal practices and forms gain visibility even if by doing so they threaten the very exchanges that take place within them and the infrastructures that support them. They are the ones responsible for bringing to the cognitive map of broader audiences the issues at stake in the 'other' half of cities.

Notes

1. The Royal Institute of British Architects (RIBA) is the professional body of architects primarily from the UK. The list was available at https://www.architecture.com/RIBA/Visitus/Library/Assets/Files/Collections/JournalsIndexed.pdf and has currently transferred to https://riba-prd-assets.azureedge.net/-/media/Files/Resources/RIBA-indexed-journals.pdf.
2. While the magazines' hard copies are fully archived in libraries, for practical reasons we only considered digital data and used the online databases of EBSCOhost, JSTOR, ProQuest, Nexus and Wiley. Even then, the digital accessibility of the seven magazines varied significantly. The non-digitalised early editions of AJ (before 1979) and AD (before 1969) were missing, and the oldest issues sometimes supplied only the articles' titles and abstracts. As a consequence, specific databases were prioritised, resulting in data merging based on data accessibility, extent and accuracy.
3. The AJ, ARec, AR and RIBAJ journals started circulating at the end of nineteenth century after the Industrial Revolution and the transition to machine production methods. Their initial aim was to provide information and give insight into all aspects of the construction industry and the building market, which was experiencing radical changes. AD and *Domus* are among those journals that became famous for reporting from the avant-garde forefront of the profession. After the fall of the modernist paradigm, publications such as *Ekistics* emerged with the aim of reflecting a rather pragmatic and multi-disciplinary approach towards architectural and urban production.

4   We used the most common publications found in Google Books when searching for the keyword *slum*. Slum is the most commonly used word by the RIBA Library to classify articles relating to informality.
5   The 59 keywords from UN-Habitat are informality, slum, bidonvilles, taudis, habitat précaire, habitat spontané, asentimientos irregulares, barrio marginal, barraca, conventillos, colonias populares, tugurio, solares, bohios, cuarterias, villa miseria, mudun safi, lahbach, brarek, medina achouaia, foundouks, karyan, carton, safeih, ishash, galoos, shammasa, tanake, aashwa'i, baladi, hrushebi, baraks, favela, morro, cortiço, comunidade, loteamento, hood, blight areas, chawls, chalis, ahatas, katras, bustee, zopadpattis, cheris, katchi abadis, iskwater, estero, eskinita, looban, dagat-dagatan, umjondolo, watta, pelpath, udukku, pelli gewal, museques and chereka bete. The 11 additional keywords are informal settlement, irregular settlement, unplanned settlement, illegal settlement, shanty/shantytown, squatter, ghetto, townships, barriadas, gecekondu. Four keywords from the UN-Habitat's list – solares, carton, baraks and hood – were excluded, as they were often associated with other topics not related to informality.
6   From the 70 terms initially searched, only 31 were included in the graph, those that appeared at least once in the keyword search.
7   The abnormality of *Ekistics* can be explained by the turbulent life of the magazine and its clear early focus on issues related to informality. From its beginning in 1955, *Ekistics* aimed at keeping housing and planning experts in developing countries up to date with the latest news and urban theories. This is why the graph peaks in 1969 where a number of annual issues were devoted to topics like self-built housing, social actions and human settlements, urban and economic development as well as urbanisation patterns. After 1995, when a drop in the trendline is observed, the publication was only producing three issues per year (previously monthly) until it ceased its publishing activity in 2007. This explains why it has such a contrasting trend to the other magazines, yet this publication has arguably done more than any other to push forward our understanding of informality.
8   Reading architectural magazines is recognised by the RIBA as part of the 35 hours annual continuing professional development required of all registered architects.
9   In 1996, the United Nations held a second conference on cities – Habitat II – in Istanbul, Turkey, to assess two decades of progress since Habitat I in Vancouver and to set fresh goals for the new millennium.
10 In September 2000, the largest gathering of world leaders in history adopted the UN-Millennium Declaration, this later became known as the Millennium Development Goals.
11 This is a cultural and socio-political documentary published by UK's Channel 4 in 2010.
12 This refers to Brazil's *Minha Casa, Minha Vida*, Chile's *Un Techo para mi País* and Mexico's *Two Million Homes* mass housing programmes for low-income population groups.

References

Athens Center of Ekistics. 1959. 'The readership of ekistics', *Ekistics*, 8 (47): 155–8.
Brand, P. and Thomas, M. 2005. 'Urban environmentalism in action 1: competitiveness and the quality of life in Birmingham, UK'. In Brand, P. and Thomas, M. (eds.), *Urban Environmentalism: Global change and the mediation of local conflict*. London: Routledge: 111–47.
Davis, M. 2006. *Planet of Slums*. New York: Verso.
Fabricius, D. 2011. 'Looking beyond informality', *Architectural Design*, 81 (3): 144–9.
Fiori, J. 2013. 'Informal city: design as political engagement'. In Verebes, T. (ed.), *Masterplanning the Adaptive City: Computational urbanism in the twenty-first century*. London: Routledge, 40–8.
Gilbert, A. 2007. 'The return of the slum: does language matter?', *International Journal of Urban and Regional Research*, 31 (4): 697–713.
Jirón, P. 2010. 'The evolution of the informal settlements in Chile: improving housing conditions in cities'. In Hernández, F., Kellett, P. and Allen, L.K. (eds.), *Rethinking the Informal City: Critical perspectives from Latin America*. New York: Berghahn Books, 71–90.
Koolhaas, R. 2000. 'Harvard project on the city'. In *Mutations*. Bordeaux: Arc en rêve centre d'architecture.

Lefebvre, H. 1995. *Introduction to Modernity: Twelve Preludes September 1959–May 1961* (trans. John Moore). London: Verso.

Lotus (magazine). 2010. 'Learning from favelas', *Lotus*, 143: 1.

McGuirk, J. 2014. *Radical Cities: Across Latin America in search of a new architecture*. London: Verso Books.

Moreno, E.L. 2003. 'Slums of the world: the face of urban poverty in the new millennium? Monitoring the millennium development goal, target 11: world-wide slum dweller estimation'. Working paper. Nairobi: UN Habitat.

Novaes, A.R. 2014. 'Favelas and the divided city: mapping silences and calculations in Rio de Janeiro's journalistic cartography', *Social and Cultural Geography*, 15 (2): 201–25.

Paterson, B.L., Thorne, S.E., Canam, C. and Jillings, C. 2001. 'Meta-synthesis'. In Paterson, B.L., Thorne, S.E., Canam, C. and Jillings, C., *Meta-study of Qualitative Health Research*. Thousand Oaks, CA: Sage, 109–23.

Royal Institute of British Architects (RIBA). 2015. 'List of journals indexed by the Library', January 2015. https://riba-prd-assets.azureedge.net/-/media/Files/Resources/RIBA-indexed-journals.pdf.

Sassen, S. 2015. 'Shrinking economies, growing expulsions'. In Mörtenböck, P., Mooshammer, H., Cruz, T. and Forman, F. (eds.), *Informal Market Worlds Reader: The architecture of economic pressure*. Rotterdam: NAi010 Publishers: 45–54.

Simpson, M.D. 2013. 'Urbanising favelas, overlooking people: regressive housing policies in Rio de Janeiro's progressive slum upgrading initiatives'. Working paper. Development Planning Unit, University College London.

Turner, J.C. 1963. 'Dwelling resources in South America', *Ekistics*, 16 (97): 361–74.

Turner, J.F. and Fichter, R. 1972. *Freedom to Build: Dweller control of the housing process*. New York: Macmillan.

Valladares, L. 2008. 'Social science representations of favelas in Rio de Janeiro: a historical perspective', *LLILAS Visiting Resource Professors Papers*, 9 (3): 1–31.

13
Conclusion: foregrounding positionality

Nerea Amorós Elorduy, Nikhilesh Sinha and Colin Marx

This book has revisited the relationships between urban informality and the built environment. Our argument rests on two considerations: that the built environment is always already political, and that the State, while ever-present, need not be analytically central to all readings of urban informality. These two considerations drive the analysis we present of the chapters, authors, topics and geographies contained in this book, which shows a richness of relationships and associated inequalities. This analysis can be applicable at different scales and sites. Our approach contributes to understanding how injustices are created and sustained in urban environments globally, and it adds further nuance to conceptualisations of urban informality.

This final chapter begins by reviewing how we have approached the study of the politicised built environment concerning urban informality. We then consider what this means for conceptualisations of urban informality before reflecting on the value added from our perspective. In this process, we move from foregrounding the built environment in the introductory chapter to foregrounding issues of positionality in this concluding chapter. The interrogation of positionality is prompted partially by our diverse disciplinary backgrounds, architecture, economics and geography, and partially with a view to questioning whether the relational approach adopted unsettles how the study of informality is positioned within the field of built environment studies.

Three lenses on the built environment: infrastructure, exchange and image

Initially we posited the built environment as 'all the physical elements constructed by humans to interact with each other and their surroundings, constituting overlapping social, economic and physical relations' (p. 5). However, to operationalise this understanding, we needed a more refined categorisation to counter the shallowness of banal erudition. Our response was to think of the built environment through three lenses: infrastructures, exchanges and image.

While these three represent seemingly arbitrary entry points, they reflect critical concerns of the authors and editors, weaving the book together thematically and conceptually. They are aspects of, and constitutive of, the built environment – in that they are relational concepts. They are at the same time evaluative criteria, inviting discourses around uses, processes of human interaction and aesthetics. To create alternative viewpoints from where to consider informality from beyond, or alongside, the State, it is also necessary to disentangle our evaluative criteria from notions that are based on the formal. While this is a much grander project, the attempt to open concepts of infrastructure, exchange and image through exploring the relational nature of the informal built environment is, we hope, a step in the right direction.

Infrastructures: platforms of diverse power and agency

Chattopadhyay elucidates how infrastructure enables both exchange and appropriation and how the physical form of infrastructures are based on a particular modelling of space and time. The appropriation of infrastructures for unintended uses transforms both this vocabulary and the landscape. Equally, looking beyond the formal vocabulary of infrastructure allows the recognition of physical and intangible infrastructures created, transformed and managed by multiple and diverse actors, highlighting transversal and non-linear organising logics, as well as various typologies of power and agency.

One such instance is Dino's study of Tirana's urban evolution, which documents how citizens, private companies and individuals transformed a planned city with segregated, discrete, single-purpose blocks into a rich, mixed-use fluid urban space. Specifically, in Shallvaret, the rapid densification accompanied by a spontaneous fluidity of purpose involves a distinct set of actors comprising the urban middle class and elites, real estate developers and private banks. These emergent phenomena arise from, and cater to, transactions between non-state actors, a set of social relations populating the interstices left vacant by formal planning and regulation. In contrast to the notion of informality from above where fluidity is usually seen to serve the interests of the State, the reconfiguration of Tirana's urban blocks represents a repurposing of the city for and by private actors. Dino explains how individual citizens and private developers have slowly transformed the city's housing infrastructure by tackling the city block.

While she stresses the dynamism of informal processes in the transformation of post-socialist Tirana, a significant caveat lies in the nature of the actors engaged in and benefiting from these transformations and their place within local, regional and global power structures. In Tirana, the 'acupuncture' interventions have quite literally opened doors leading to new ways of imagining and inhabiting the city, though, in this case, unequally and only for those able to pay the high rents, or shop in the high-end boutiques of Shallvaret.

Fitzgerald's study in La Habana Vieja focuses on the reuse of leftover spaces and decrepit buildings, a crumbling urban infrastructure. In her rhythmanalysis of Julio's garden, the ebb and flow of daily activities around this garden is reminiscent of Jane Jacobs's sidewalk ballet of Hudson Street, recognised as maintaining the safety and freedom of the city. As Jacobs explains, the ballet of a good city sidewalk does not repeat itself from place to place and 'in any one place is replete with new improvisations' (Jacobs 1961, 50). In the same vein, the daily reinvention of the urban infrastructure that Fitzgerald describes is rich and varied, is time and place-specific, and situated. The overloaded infrastructure brings an opportunity for a citizen-led medicinal and urban agriculture – informal infrastructure that provides social cohesion, food security and income.

Starting from Chattopadhyay's understanding of infrastructure as sinews of power, we can explore Kostourou and Goodship's analysis of architectural academic and mainstream literature as an infrastructure of knowledge. It is an infrastructure that directly affects the physicality of urban developments, the politics of the categorisation and the transformation of whole urban swathes under the flag of formalisation. In their chapter analysing the birth and uses of informality labels in the architectural and urban discourse, Kostourou and Goodship unveil how geopolitical events globally influenced different uses of the label informality and its diverse contextualised interpretations. Who first started to use the word slum? How did it spread to gain such relevance? And, why did it have its diverse taints and meanings across the years and for different actors?

Through built environment-centred urban informality lenses, unequal reinvention, reuse, richness and complexity are highlighted in contrast with the opacity afforded by a top-down view. This view liberates these new uses from state-centric or opposed-to-formal judgements; these reinventions are not automatically categorised and hence understood as rebellions by oppressed subaltern populations or illegal appropriations. They, therefore, lend themselves to a more open analysis.

Exchanges: customs, spaces and inventions

In her chapter, Tonkiss suggests three categorisations of urban informality as orders of exchange. This refers to a typology of exchange ordered by custom and convention such as those presented by Cerrada Morato in Galicia; spaces of exchange, which refers to those material spaces that facilitate exchanges such as those offered by Chang, Tunnacliffe or Gutiérrez; and intersections of informality, which focuses on those exchanges related to innovation such as those presented by Fitzgerald, Antaki and Kostourou and Goodship.

Cerrada Morato's depiction of *traídas* highlights how formal market logics fail to capture the richness and complexity of co-operative modes of production and service provision. Faced with a choice between centralised water provision and the labour-intensive upkeep of the traditional *traída* system, residents of Pedruozos question the notions that water can be commodified and the quality of municipal water. The unwritten arrangements that underpin the functioning of the *traída* system, specifying limits on usage, frequency of maintenance, and how costs of repair will be shared, reflect a recognition of a precious shared resource and responsibilities, which inform and shape the nature of these exchanges.

Chang's chapter is underpinned by the idea of 'spaces of exchange', describing how Jian-Cheng Circle's night market's built environment was configured by the social relations between stall owners and customers – the two-metre-wide walkways for accessing porous boundaries between cooking and serving areas. The proximity of stalls and permeable boundaries fostered, or at least allowed for, collaborative practices with customers ordering from multiple stalls and stall owners settling accounts at the end of the day. Similarly in Tunnacliffe and Gutiérrez, the material form of the built environment provides the canvas and sites for artistic exchange and care respectively. Each of these instances illustrates how the built environment structures or is transformed to permit certain forms of social exchange, which are site-specific, emerging from and contiguous with social relations.

The third of Tonkiss's categories relates to exchanges at the intersections of informalities, and indeed between formal and informal, which can be read as innovative or entrepreneurial. Antaki's association of informality with *jugaad*, translated as 'innovative problem solving, in spontaneous or speculative ways in response to the unpredictable' (Chapter 11, p. 156) frames informality as an entrepreneurial response to adversity. This framing shifts focus from its relation with the State, locating the informal within global supply chains and the interplay of neoliberal forces. While reading informality as entrepreneurial risks conflating the speculative activities of privileged members of society with a struggle to meet basic needs, it recognises the agency of actors, however asymmetric and limited their power.

These notions of exchange encourage a dynamic processual reading of informality, emerging from and co-evolving with custom, material form and material conditions. While these negotiations may in some cases involve and be mediated by the State, the processes, meanings and values of the exchanges are determined in relation to a multiplicity of other actors.

Image: moving beyond aesthetics and colonial hangover into the politics of visibility

Dovey highlights in his chapter how the flexibility and mobility of capital, the growth of tourism (pre-pandemic) and the expansion of the information economy has augmented the web of relations that interact with and shape the perception of urban built environments. New middle-class housing that towers above low-rise settlements increases visibility and potential for conflict between competing visions of the city. Chattopadhyay refers to the power of image as she refers to the desire for international translatability, which drives certain kinds of urban development projects. Conversely or perversely, the foreign, exotic aspect of urban informality attracts a particular type of attention. Dovey and King (2011) refer to that as 'a quest for authenticity, the shock of the real and the aesthetic of the sublime' – which, in the words of Dovey, says more about the tourist than the settlement, creating a complex relational encounter. Equally, this activity establishes, reproduces and alters links between informal spaces and the global economy in ways in which a state-centric approach may be ill-equipped to capture.

Using these lenses, one can analyse how the image of the various actors shifts. Thinking of image as political, many of the actors involved in informal urban processes change from vulnerable and powerless victims, receivers of aid and services, and rebellious subaltern populations to become service providers, transformers, managers and makers. Inequalities are still present but relate to different dynamics. This view is shown in the chapters of Cerrada Morato, Gutiérrez and Fitzgerald; developers as is the case of Tirana shown by Dino; teachers and co-creators of knowledge and innovative pedagogies as explained by Antaki; and artists as is demonstrated in Tunnacliffe's chapter.

Our approach contributes to changing the perception of the spaces rendered visible, enhancing those as grey and complex. Many are the examples of change in perception in this book. In the case of Old Havana, Fitzgerald takes us from a ruin and a reflection of state limitations to urban heritage, a productive space, a place for innovation and community-making. Another example is the one that Antaki explores where Mariamma Nagar in Mumbai is seen as an open-air school, as a space for pedagogical and progressive education, for co-creation and collaboration rather than only as an economically poor neighbourhood, with overcrowding and sanitation issues in need of top-down formalisation.

The perspective put forward by Cerrada Morato does not classify its actors as rebels as state-led perspectives would. Instead, her view of informality highlights the *traídas* and their managers as safeguards of tradition, cultural heritage and a potentially more affordable and sustainable service provision for this type of built environment. To a similar effect, Tunnacliffe presents the walls of Accra in Ghana not only as private property but as a canvas for art and public expression, and their artists as such, rather than only as rebellious youth. One of the most direct affronts on state-led views of informality is that presented by Chang, where the night market in Taipei changes from being labelled a cancer of the city to a lively cultural exchange and a fascinating hub where economic, culinary and artistic transactions take place.

Locating, location and being located

We turn to consider the value our perspective adds. If we take a step back to think of the bigger picture, we are arguing for the value of a new location in the in/formal binary. While 'research is largely about location' notes Simone (2011, 205) of 'the location of things in cells, curves, correlations, indicators, regressions and context specificities' – to locate causes and effects is also to locate oneself and be located. The concept of positionality seeks to account for all three aspects: locating, location and being located. We therefore conclude by considering how this collection raises questions about positionality.

Working from existing scholarship, we consider urban informality as an organising logic that is fundamentally relational, and hence a phenomenon with intelligibility and intentionality that is located and locates. Such an understanding immediately raises questions about positionality: where do we need to be (analytically) to interpret this intelligibility? How do particular understandings locate us? What can we discern from such a location?

The strong sense that urban informality has already been understood relationally has always meant that positionality is essential. Scholars have conceptually situated themselves between informal phenomena and an ostensibly (but neither exhaustively nor consistently) formal State. From this vantage point of being able to look both ways – towards, and/or from, the formal State and/or towards/from the informal urban phenomenon – analysts have developed rich insights that could be operationalised into activism against injustices. Taking its cue from such traditions of an in-between positionality, this edited collection situates itself in between urban informality and the built environment. We work between the always already political built environment and urban informality. As referred to throughout the book, such a positionality has also involved decentring the State in the analysis.

Situatedness and positionality cannot be escaped. Thus, attentiveness to positionality cannot reduce partiality since it merely reproduces other forms. Our hope can only be that these brief disjunctures in positionality alert us to the benefits and consequences of views. In this collection, we have highlighted the benefits of analysing different social relations without automatically understanding them concerning the State. And, we show how attentiveness to positionality can allow for diverse voices to come into range.

One benefit of the contributions is that, while inequality is a constant theme, people also want other things and act convivially, collaboratively and communally for identity and social standing. However, conviviality, collaboration and community are not marked off beyond inequality, and the relations with the built environment can be just as constitutive of inequality as straightforward exploitative transactions.

The works in this volume examine diverse types of power, which challenge a reading of power relations that are automatically read vertically through the State. In the book, these challenges are highlighted in the examples of citizen-led service provision and welfare infrastructures where the built environment has a lead role in providing a critical service for a group or population. We present examples drawing on the *traídas* of Galicia, learning from/in Mariamma Nagar, the street art of Accra, and social infrastructures of care in post-crisis Athens.

Citizen-led infrastructures and transversal exchanges

In Galicia, the communal water access infrastructures in the territories in between rural and urban areas allowed entire swathes of the population to collaborate and organise access to this essential resource on their own terms. These communal means of water access pre-date state-sponsored private water infrastructures. Cerrada Morato posits, through the different lens of this book, these infrastructures are environmentally and socially sustainable, affordable and culturally relevant in Galicia's in-between territories. Thus, Cerrada Morato explains how the state-centric informal label presents these infrastructures as unco-operative to state-law, unsanitary and unregulated, needing centralisation and state formalisation – formalisation here understood as regulated by the State. The built-environment lenses allow Cerrada Morato to understand their existence in relation to the climate, the culture and the history of the region. As Fran Tonkiss observes, they exist due to the exchanges that urban informality enables. In a region where central infrastructure was not available, unaffordable and unsustainable, *traídas* provide just those exchanges. In this case, decentring the State in the understanding of urban informality allows us to see the richness of service provision options that are not opposed to but are a complement to the state-centralised and regulated systems.

Another example is an innovative pedagogy tested by Antaki in Mariamma Nagar in Mumbai. This progressive, co-created, and context-specific learning process could only exist in the tight-knit and dense neighbourhood where it was developed. This test for a networked pedagogy, one that uses the social and physical relationships of the settlement as educators, relied on learning from the surrounding built environment, getting the buy-in from the neighbours and especially establishing a flourishing collaboration with the craftspeople of the surrounding buildings. Again, this neighbourhood is labelled a slum through a state-centric lens, an improper space that needs formalisation to achieve a certain quality of life. Yet, foregrounding the built environment and its relationality, using the exchanges and infrastructures allows another image to be created and new inequalities in educational practices to be analysed.

Gutiérrez's analysis of informal structures of welfare in Athens post-crisis highlights the relational and contingent nature of informality, that is dependent on context – in this case intensifying the awareness of interconnection and expanding the sense of implicit obligation to others while reinforcing the need to embrace the contingency of unequal material conditions. In the section titled 'Spatial imprint: considerations on informality in space-making practices' Gutiérrez describes how the hotel in Central Plaza is transformed into a multi-use facility offering accommodation and healthcare, with shared spaces being used as playgrounds, classrooms and spaces for film screenings, assemblies and celebrations. One way to understand these transformations is to acknowledge that social relations that compose and give meaning to the built environment can be reconfigured through artistic endeavour, as illustrated by Tunnacliffe or in response to the community's changing needs. The physical changes that were made signifying only one aspect of the more fundamental shift in the way people saw and utilised the spaces – this fluidity being a response to and a manifestation of the uncertainties of the crisis. Viewing these transformations through the lens of the built environment and underlying social relations reveals the dynamics of informal logics, adaptive and resilient, repurposive yet circumscribed by the larger context of the unequal material conditions.

Attentiveness to positionality and the disjunctures created when positionalities shift also has the consequence of allowing different voices to be heard: the school children and artisans of Mariamma Nagar, the stall owners and diverse customer base of Jian-Cheng Circle night market, the entrepreneurs and middle-class residents of Shallvaret, and the contributors to the mainstream architectural press who have helped shaped discourse and practice. A particularly vibrant example of the many voices making and remaking the urban experience globally are the street artists in Accra, Ghana.

Tunnacliffe studies an all-encompassing and inexhaustive category of urban inscriptions, which include the commercial, political, social and religious forms of social relations that make up the city's fabric. At the same time, she suggests that the particularity of graffiti and street art offers a way of taking ownership of the city, suggesting a mutability of social relations that composes the built environment, that these may not be concrete. The process of obtaining permission, and the transactions/negotiations illustrate how these urban inscriptions recognise, re-affirm, contest and reconstitute social relations that compose the built environment. Tunnacliffe suggests that by renegotiating the relationship between formal and informal, street art and graffiti reveal the power dynamics that play out on the city's surface while also revealing and transforming the underlying relations that compose the built environment. In these contributions, we see different connections, hear diverse voices, and see how they are constitutive of inequality even if they are not routed through the State and formality.

The urgency of the urban challenge is matched by its magnitude and multidimensionality. Informality has been characterised as problem and solution, entangled in power hierarchies, injustice and deprivation but equally resilience, innovation and hope. The articulation of a view grounded in the relationality of the built environment, and decentring the State, offers a perspective that makes visible transversal and non-linear organising logics, incorporating multiple sets of actors and relations. While no single analytical framework or lens can or should be cast as authoritative, approaching informality through the built environment opens new pathways for scholarship and practice by allowing us to ask different questions. We aim to add nuance and richness, to test new approaches and methods that can work across a range of contexts without automatically reverting to a general view of urban informality defined in terms of the purported formality of a located (Western) state.

References

Dovey, K. and King, R. 2011. 'Forms of informality: morphology and visibility of informal settlements', *Built Environment*, 37 (1): 11–29.

Jacobs, J. 1961. *The Death and Life of Great American Cities*. Toronto: Random House.

Simone, A. 2012. 'Screen'. In Lury, C. and Wakeford, N. (eds), *Inventive Methods*. Abingdon: Routledge, 202–18.

Index

access 6, 9, 13, 22, 26, 29, 77, 86, 91, 97–8, 101, 125–6, 135, 138–9, 160, 167, 173, 184, 192, 196
Accra 10, 13, 37, 49–69, 196, 197
activity 4, 10, 35, 101, 158, 165, 169, 170
  artistic 61
  commercial 98, 104
  economic 13, 33–4, 38, 39, 156, 160, 167
  façade 99, 104
  high-street 159
  informal 162
  pedagogicic/pedagogical 163
  residential 104
  retail 99
  solidarity 112
  social 95
  urban 51, 166
activism, social 54
adaptation 37, 45, 60, 89, 91, 92, 101, 122, 141, 156, 165, 167
adversity 193
aestheticisation of poverty 2, 7, 44
aesthetics 14–16, 44, 190, 193
agency 5, 21, 35, 58, 167, 170, 186, 190, 193
  economic 35
agents 13, 119, 121, 153
agreements 13, 56, 81, 108, 112, 116, 118, 119
Airbnb 38
Albania 8, 90–5, 97–9, 101–3
analysis/analyses 2–4, 6, 20–3, 33, 100, 156, 177, 179, 189, 191–2, 195, 197
  Conzenian plan 94–5
  critical 37
  data 176
  discourse 45
  economic 35, 94
  land-use 99
  meta-data 176
  rhythmanalysis 126, 139, 191
  space syntax 16, 95
  spatial 10, 16,
Anderson, B. 45
Anglo-American academics 4
Antaki, Nicola 10, 11, 15, 16, 155–69, 192–4, 196
approach, interdisciplinary 96
appropriation 7, 10, 16, 50, 51, 56, 94, 103, 108, 190, 192
Architects' Journal (AJ) 175
Architectural Design (AD) 14, 174, 175
Architectural Record (ARec) 175

Architectural Review (AR) 175
architecture 10–12, 14, 35–7, 42, 64, 90, 91, 110, 147, 155, 173–86, 189, 191, 197
  contemporary 90
  formal 37
  informal 42
  literature 11
  practice 11, 155, 183
  social 36, 64, 68, 185
  of social care 110
  traditional 182
aspects 5–6, 10, 14, 21–2, 111, 142, 173, 184, 190, 193, 195, 197
  economic 1
  governance 1
  material 157
  political 1
  qualitative 154
  relational 6–7
  social 109
assemblage 42, 45, 64, 160–1, 165, 169
Athens 9, 13, 36, 37, 107–23, 196, 197
  crisis-ridden city 107
Athens Community Polyclinic and Pharmacy (ACP&P) 107, 111–12, 116, 117, 119
austerity 13, 37, 39, 107–10, 112, 122, 123

Balaram, Singanapalli 166
Balkanisation 91
Banerjee, Prathama 24, 28
Bangkok 44
barriadas 14, 174
basti/bustee 15, 156–9
Batty, M. 101
behaviours 12, 15, 33, 34, 107, 155, 159, 160, 161, 167, 169, 170
Bhunyas (bhuiyas) 28
billboards 13, 52, 53, 56
  religious 67
boom 143, 184
  economic 146
Boudreau, J. A. 6
Bourriaud, N. 56
Brahmanical rituals 27
bricolage 157, 167, 169, 170
built environment 1–17, 52, 57, 68, 90, 100, 101, 155, 157, 162, 163, 173–5, 177, 182, 184, 185, 189–98
  citizen-led infrastructures/transversal exchanges 196–8
  exchanges 192–3

image 193–4
infrastructures 190–2
location 195–6
physical elements 190

Caldeira, T. P. R. 2, 81
capital (city) 90, 109–10, 145, 150
　administrative 90
　colonial 143
capital (social/economic) 13, 30, 36, 38, 43–4, 52, 93, 193
　capital-intensive 19
　economic 181
　formal 92
　political 43
　social 11, 43–4, 79, 182, 186
　symbolic 8, 43–4
capitalism 38, 184
capitalist 76, 77, 86, 103, 109, 147, 152
care 34, 36, 193
　collective 110
　infrastructure of 196
　medical 167
　mutual 119, 122
　social 36, 37, 110
Careri, F. 161, 162
centralized 9, 12, 73–5, 78, 90, 130, 192, 196
ceremony/ceremonies
　religious 128
change 2, 28, 58, 61, 63, 66–69, 81, 87, 120, 160, 183, 194
　democratic 57
　material 139
　regime 96–7, 104
　social 101
　socio-spatial 46
　urban 91, 101
change maker painters 65–7
chaos 22, 44, 89, 150
Chattopadhyay, Swati 7–11, 15, 16, 19–31, 50, 51, 63, 64, 68, 126, 173, 190, 191, 193
China, People's Republic of (PRC) 145
Chin-Wei Chang 141–54
Circle Top 151
circuits 4, 107, 110, 122
　commercial 149
　economic 153
citizen 8, 10, 107, 112, 130, 134, 158, 190, 191
citizen-led 9, 107, 108, 110, 191, 196
City Plaza 116, 118
City Plaza Refugee Accommodation Centre 107
class 22
　middle 5, 7, 20, 41, 44, 46, 51, 92, 191, 193, 197
　political 110
　social 12, 43, 46
classroom 119, 131, 155, 161–4, 168, 197
collaboration 28, 155, 170, 194, 196, 197
colonialism 2, 7, 12, 23–9, 45, 63, 138, 141, 143–6, 149, 152, 156, 173, 180, 182, 193
　colonial English law, formality of 29
　colonial governance, infrastructure of 28
commodification 73, 82, 85, 86, 192
common spaces 33, 119–20
communication 10, 25, 26, 28, 57, 62, 111, 114, 118, 120, 155, 170

community 28, 45, 50, 53, 58–61, 64, 66, 78–81, 126, 128–9, 131, 133–5, 138–9, 143, 158, 160, 185, 196
　imagined 8, 45
　local 58, 66
　multi-ethnic 59
　tribal 28
　wellbeing 58
community-based initiatives
　open ground 143, 153
　water supply infrastructures 73
community-led
　infrastructures 78, 80–1, 86
　water supply systems 73
Confederaciones de Aguas 82
Con nuestros propios esfuerzos: algunas experiencias para enfrentar el período especial en tiempo de paz 133
context 3, 9–10, 16, 50, 54, 69, 78, 80, 86–7, 108, 122–3, 125, 146, 157, 165, 195, 197
　Albanian 95
　family 35
　geographical 91
　global 43
　historical 142, 176
　planning 44
　territorial 161
　urban 45
corporation-led centralised modes of water access 73
cosmopolitanism 147, 156
Coxapo 78–82; *see also traídas*
　constitution of 79
　governmental *laissez-faire* approach 79
　traída A Malata 80
craft 15, 66, 145, 155, 156, 158–60, 165–9
creativity 22, 46, 50, 58, 60, 61, 125, 139, 141, 156, 165, 168
crisis 13, 36, 37, 102, 107–10, 112, 118–23, 144, 183, 196, 197
　economic 91, 102, 109, 110
　financial 13, 36–7,
Cuba 8, 15, 125–38
custom 12, 14, 28, 34, 128–31, 138, 142, 149, 151–3, 192, 193, 197

Da-Dao-Cheng 141–5, 149, 152, 154n1
damin boundary 24
Damin-i-koh 24, 26
Davis, D. E. 3, 6
Davis, M. 46, 176
design 14, 33, 46, 54, 80, 83, 90, 103, 126, 128, 144–7, 155–70, 174, 175, 185
development 10, 37, 44, 46, 54, 60, 78, 90, 93–5, 103–4, 120, 142–3, 145–6, 149, 157, 160, 170, 181, 184
　city 174
　economic 39, 146, 153
　formal 153
　informal 91, 185
　post-communist/post-socialist 91, 95
　private 160
　slum 89
　spatial 33
　urban 10, 43–4, 89–92, 96, 100, 121, 170, 193

200　URBAN INFORMALITY

development planning unit 182
Dharavi, slum tours of 44
diku 28
Dino, B. 10, 16, 89–106, 190, 191, 194
discourse 7, 11, 14, 19, 30, 45, 46, 58, 74, 126, 146, 147, 156, 157, 174, 185, 190, 191, 197
   critical 174
   interdisciplinary 157
   political 147
   socio-spatial 156
   urban 185, 191
Domus 175
Dovey, K. 14, 15, 36, 41, 64
Durga Puja 27
dwelling 22, 42, 53, 128, 134, 150, 158, 160, 165, 174, 180
dynamics 1, 4, 96, 120, 122, 149, 150, 153, 161, 164, 167, 193, 194, 197

economics 35, 42, 89–91, 139, 189
   development 33
Ekistics 175, 177, 179
elites 108, 191
Elorduy, N. A. 1–18, 157, 189–98
empowerment 56, 60
endeavour 122
   artistic 197
   pedagogical 156
enterprise 34, 37–8, 139
   ethnic 33
   private 183
entrepreneurship 22, 37, 43, 60, 125, 126, 134, 139, 141, 156, 165, 193
epistemic injustice 2, 7
ethnicity 43, 46
event 23, 26, 43, 79, 80, 114, 116, 118, 141, 142, 175, 181, 185, 186, 191
eviction 42, 43, 46
exchange
   artistic 192
   economic 9, 16, 20, 34–6, 38, 39, 64
   financial 130
   marketplaces 38
   orders of 35–6
   social 35, 193
   spaces 36–7, 62
expression 64, 68, 90
   artistic 13, 60
   public 194

favela 15, 41, 44, 125, 158, 180, 181
favela tours, in Rio 44
festivals 56
   religious 21
   urban 10, 50
finance 156
Fitzgerald, S. 13, 15, 16, 125–39, 191, 192, 194
flexibility 43, 60, 141, 156, 165, 167, 193
fluid 13, 15, 121, 130, 148–50, 164, 190, 191, 197
food market 147–9
footprint, geographical 93
formality 1, 3, 4, 6, 8, 9, 11, 13, 16, 19–24, 27, 30, 35–9, 41–6, 58–9, 63, 64, 68, 82, 84–6, 89, 94, 123, 126–7, 147, 149–51, 155, 157, 160, 163, 167–70, 173, 181, 185, 190–3, 195, 198
formalisation 34, 42, 64, 116–18, 147–9, 191, 194, 196, 197
framework 2, 45–6, 64, 78, 119, 123
   analytical 198
   constructed 186
   economic 46
   institutional 117
   formal/informal 42
   governance 81, 84
   legal-judicial 157
   legislative 82, 85
   public–private 84
   state-centric 4
   thematic 142
framing places 45
FRINGE series 3
future 1–2, 24, 53, 56, 81–2, 85, 86, 125–6, 133, 138–9, 154, 162, 164, 166, 170, 174

Galicia 9, 12, 73–87, 192, 196
Galicia–north Portugal, Atlantic axis of 77
Ganges river 28
garbage dumpsters 133
garden 110, 125–35, 138, 160, 191
geographical information systems (GIS)
   software 96
Ghertner, D. A. 2
Global South 20, 46, 51, 59, 141, 174, 175, 183
global supply chain 15, 165, 193
Goodship, P. 11, 14, 173–88, 191, 192
Google 11
governance 1, 2, 4, 12, 26, 28, 43, 73, 78–85, 87, 142, 143, 153
gowalas (milkmen) 28
graffiti 10, 13, 15, 49–69, 198
Greece 8, 107–9, 112, 113, 115, 175, 176
   austerity programmes 107
green medicine 126, 128, 129, 131, 133, 138
groups 3, 10, 24, 59, 79, 110, 114, 117, 121–3, 131, 157, 161
   avant-garde 182
   civil society 82
   ethnic 22
   large 138
   low-caste 28
   marginal 27–8
   religious 22
   self-organised 122
   small 28
   social 1
   subaltern 63
   working 114, 116, 118
growth 8, 14, 43, 50, 58, 60, 76, 100, 102, 193
   continuous 78
   economic 76, 185
   explosive 76
   GDP 108
   informal 89, 183
   urban 96, 101
Gutiérrez, I. 9, 13, 16, 36, 37, 107–24, 192, 194, 197

Habana Vieja 126–32, 136, 137, 191
Havana 15, 125–39, 194
Healey, P. 6
heritage 78, 153, 194
Hillier, B. 95, 100, 103
Hirt, S. 91–2, 94, 102, 103
household economies 35
household water, photograph of 75
housing 6, 22, 33, 43, 47, 59, 91, 100, 109, 128, 144, 173, 191
　affordable 158
　census 93
　informal 22, 36, 42, 89, 92
　low-income 59
　middle-class 193
　policies 185
　public sector 183
　refugee 117
　self-built 14
　self-funded 114
　social 91
Hunter, W. 29
hypervisibility 8, 19, 22, 63

illegality 5, 12, 13, 22, 35, 37, 39, 42, 53, 58, 59, 74, 86, 117, 146, 153, 179, 181, 192
illegibility 19, 22, 23, 63
image 2, 3, 5–11, 14–16, 19, 41–7, 50–3, 60, 63–5, 68–9, 174, 175, 177, 180–2, 186, 190–4, 197
　cross-cutting theme 14–16
in-between territories 73–87, 196
　suburban renascence 84–6
incremental 42, 47, 89, 158
India 8, 22, 23, 158, 159, 165–7, 173, 180
　urban informality 165
Indonesia, *kampung* improvement programme 43
industrialisation 75
industry 44, 75, 78, 96, 97, 143, 146, 147, 149–51, 153, 185
inequality 1, 6, 59, 91, 157, 189, 196–8
informal economy 13, 21, 33, 34, 36–9, 93, 130, 153
informal infrastructures, governance paradigm 81–4
informality 37, 51
　Antaki's conception of 15
　basti, as abundant pedagogical ground 156–9
　collective design pedagogy 155
　definition of 108
　economic 38
　informal craft 165–9
　insurgency, as infrastructure 27–9
　intersections of 37–9
　laws and regulations 29–30
　learning/fabrication 156
　Mariamma Nagar 159–61
　pedagogical informality 161–5
　politics of 114–19
　reading 19–23
　Santal Rebellion 24–6
　switching codes 26–7
　urban trend 182; *see also* urban trend

informal settlement 1, 8, 10, 13–15, 19, 37, 41–7, 50, 52, 58, 59, 64, 67–9, 155–61, 164–9, 175, 177, 179, 180, 182, 183, 186
informal urbanism, place identity of 16
infrastructure
　hybrid 86
　insurgency as 27–9
　optical 8, 10, 50, 59, 63, 64, 68
　social 8, 10, 11, 28, 59, 64, 173, 196
　tangible 190
　water 9, 12, 73–86, 196
ingenuity 134
injustice 1, 2, 7, 59, 118, 189, 195, 198
innovation 12, 13, 35, 37, 38, 86, 139, 170, 192, 194, 198
inscriptions
　hybrid surface 50, 64
　urban 50–6, 67, 198
institutions 6, 14, 21, 35, 74, 80, 82, 96, 109, 112, 119
　administrative 143
　European 108
　formal 78, 117
　international 16
　official 107, 120, 123
　officially recognised 116
　public 118, 123
　research 176
　state 5, 147
insurgent/insurgency 26–9
　as infrastructure 27–9
intelligibility 195
intentionality 195
interaction (s) 11–12, 24, 34–7, 42, 46, 58, 67, 139, 153, 107,117–18, 185
　daily 126
　economic 12, 35
　face-to-face 114
　human 190
　informal 86, 114, 122
　multi-faceted 154
　personal 111
　social 6, 12–13, 120, 134
interests 14, 23, 33, 60, 68, 94, 128, 133, 181, 183, 185, 191
　commercial 13
　community 58
　economic 42, 64, 86
　private 78, 82, 119
　public 82, 147
　speculative 120
interconnectivity 156, 164
interstices, social 56, 61–2
inventar, phenomenon of 13, 133–5
invisibility 8, 23, 43, 81
issues 15, 44, 46, 50, 66–8, 116, 167, 177, 186
　aesthetics and image 15, 44
　economic 68
　environmental 68
　everyday 138
　image and meaning 45, 65
　informality 183, 184
　non-translatability 180
　positionality 189
　sanitation 194
　socio-spatial 173

202　　URBAN INFORMALITY

urban poverty 184

Japanese colonisers 12, 143–5, 149, 154n1
Jian-Cheng Circle 12, 14, 141–54, 192, 197
   building typologies 151
   Circle Night Market 145
   contributor/tumour 146–7
   creative destruction 147–8
   critical moment 145
   cultural representations 152
   fluid occupancy, in beginning 148–9
   learning 153–4
   legendary birth of 142–4
   market 12
   miniature park, to unprecedented market place 144–5
   night market 14
   risks/opportunities, in trans-cultural cities 152–3
   spatial patterns, falling into 149–50
   spatial production, social practice of 150–1
   vendors/customers, friendly amity 152
Jian-Cheng Circle Food Centre 147–8
Jugaad 156, 163, 168, 169, 193
Julio's garden, in Habana Vieja 130, 132

Kelling, E. 3, 6
King, R. 14, 36, 42, 44, 90, 91, 102, 193
kitchens, social 111–23
Klongs, of Bangkok 44
knowledgeability 162
knowledge transfer 15, 138–9
Kostourou, F. 173–88

learning 10, 11, 52, 132, 153–6, 161, 163–6, 174, 196, 197
   dynamic 169
Lefebvre, H. 126, 162, 182
legality 5, 12, 22, 33, 34, 35, 38, 39, 46, 53, 56, 58, 59, 78, 85, 94, 117, 118, 123, 130, 143, 145–7, 150, 151, 157, 158
'Let's Talk Sh*t' project 61
liberalisation 108, 183
LIFE grant/project 82–3
Lima 14
lives 4, 12, 14, 27, 56, 59, 61, 66, 67, 82, 92, 109, 114, 120, 131, 141–2, 154, 161, 165, 169
   children's 163
   collective 120–1
   daily 139
   economic 34–5, 37, 64
   everyday 27, 45–6, 60, 63, 109–10, 114, 116, 120, 122–3, 127, 139
   evolving 126
   quality of 197
   quotidian 125
   religious 20
   social 5, 11, 20
   spiritual 54
   street 158
   urban 4, 7, 9, 20, 33, 52, 65, 96, 123, 126, 153
   world (s) 23, 183
location 8, 59, 80, 98, 99, 101, 120, 128, 133, 135, 141, 143, 148, 151, 152, 165, 195–8

central 15, 149, 159, 165
convenience 77
geographical 92
locality 10, 16, 158, 164, 170
   economic 159
   ethnic 159
   religious 159
   translocality 166
   urban 159
lohars (blacksmiths) 28
Long-Bin Hao 148

magazines, keyword searches 178, 180
managing 42, 47, 80, 81, 157, 167, 180, 186
Manhattan 19
manufacturing 149
map(s) 15, 43, 61, 77, 96, 101, 155, 156, 161, 163–7, 169
marginalised populations, cultural production of 23
Mariamma Nagar 10, 15, 155–70, 194, 196, 197
market
   logics 78192
   market-led 73, 86, 87
Marx, C. 1–17, 109, 189–98
material conditions 111, 193, 197
mayors
   Long-Bin Hao 148
   Tomiño 84
   Wen-Zhe Ke 148
   Ying-Jiu Ma 147
McCloud, Kevin 185
McFarlane, Colin 84, 157, 167, 170
message 34, 52, 64
   economic 67
   political 63
   religious 53
migrants 9
mobilisation 110, 184
model 20, 73, 84, 90
   business 8
   capitalist 103
   consumerist 87
   development 92
   economic 96, 126
   mono-centric city 91
   planning 91
   social 96
   Stalinist 90
   unregulated 93
modernity/modernism 9, 46, 77, 78, 90, 142, 146–7, 153, 157, 159, 182
moneylenders 28
Morato, L. C. 9, 12, 16, 73–88, 192, 194, 196
morphology 2, 8, 10–12, 14–16, 37, 41, 43, 94–7, 99–101, 128, 180, 186
movements 50, 54, 67
   progressive 84
   social 122, 153, 161
   street art 62, 69
Movement of the Squares 13, 37, 110, 120
multiculturalism 153
Mumbai 10, 15, 44, 155–7, 159–61, 169, 194, 196
Myers, Garth 59, 60

neighbourhood 10, 12, 52, 59, 90, 96, 112, 116, 125–7, 129, 133–9, 144–5, 156, 159–63, 169, 197
    dense 196
    economically poor 194
    eighteenth-century 128
    elite 92
    informal 6
    inner 100
    negotiation 7, 8, 10, 11, 13, 16, 50, 52, 73, 121, 127, 134, 142, 149, 158, 167, 170, 193, 198
neoliberal strategies 183
network 13, 20, 26, 44, 45, 73–84, 87, 90, 95, 96, 99, 100, 107, 110, 112, 122, 130, 136, 137, 153, 161, 165
    economic 13
    historical 76
    informal 45
    market-led 73
    municipal 80
    production 153
    regional 82–3
    social 13
    spatial 26
    visual 161
New York graffiti style 54
night market 12, 14, 141, 142, 144–53, 192, 194, 197
Nima Muhinmanchi Art Collective (NMA) 56
    change maker painters 66
non-regulation district 29
non-regulation tracts 30
norms 27, 116, 121, 123, 134
    behavioural 33
    cultural 95
    group 36
    infrastructural 20
    relational 39
    social 12, 34, 36

Olympic Games 181
opacity 20, 22, 192
    of informality practices 16
    strategy based on 118
    of urban informality 14
opportunity 11, 12, 13, 50, 57, 61, 62, 64, 65, 84, 87, 133, 135, 142, 147, 152, 157, 164, 169, 170, 173, 174, 185, 191
    development 44, 181
    economic 37
    learning 132
orders of exchange 35–6

painters, change maker 65–7
parking space, photograph of 93
peaceful elections, photograph of wall art 65
pedagogical/pedagogy 10, 15, 155–70, 194, 196, 197
Pedrouzo's community 74
periphery 73, 74, 76, 89, 183
perspective 6, 7, 8, 15, 45, 63, 69, 79, 89, 94, 189, 194, 195, 198
    Anglo-Saxon 85
    economic 79
    historical 90

modernist 146
regional 82
state-led 194
phenomena 191
    informal 4, 5, 7, 21, 195
    social 3, 6
    urban 2
place 6, 44, 51, 54, 59, 62, 63, 121, 125–6, 133, 139, 142, 144
    geographical 87
    identity 15–16, 41–3, 46
    inclusive 142, 154
    making 50, 56–8, 60, 67–8, 142, 153
    urban 142, 149, 152, 154
place-led transformation 50, 57–8, 62
place-making 142, 153, 160
Planet of Slums 176
planning 1, 9, 20, 33, 37, 44–6, 76, 78, 84, 85, 90–4, 143, 144, 146, 147, 149, 153, 158, 182, 191
plants 128–33
    religious 126, 133
    water-intensive 128
political economy 1, 2, 22, 42, 45, 46
politics 9, 10, 12, 21, 28, 42–6, 51–3, 56, 64, 67, 74, 85, 89, 91, 96, 103, 107–8, 121–2, 126–7, 138, 141–2, 145, 149, 156–8, 165, 174–5, 181, 185–6, 189, 191, 193–5, 198
    austerity 110
    elite 13, 37
    party 21
    of eviction 42, 46
    of informality 37, 114-119, 123, 139
    socio-spatial 170
popular culture 23
Population and Housing Census (2001) 93
porosity 45, 156, 166
positionality 17, 189–98
post-socialist urbanisation 91
power 2–6, 8–12, 14–16, 20, 22, 24, 26, 27, 34, 36, 44, 45, 52, 58, 62–6, 68–9, 108, 117–18, 134, 161, 170, 190–3, 196, 198
    dyamic(s) 30, 53, 68, 69, 198
power imbalances 15, 118
practice 10, 13–16, 21–2, 26–7, 33–9, 43, 45, 54, 57–8, 67, 78, 85–7, 108, 111, 116–17, 119–21, 125, 127, 133–4, 138, 141–2, 144, 147, 150–2, 155–8, 160, 162, 164, 167–9, 173, 182–6, 192, 197
    economic 35, 39
    social 30
Pritzker Prize (2016) 174
privatization 43, 73, 92, 100, 108–10, 112, 121, 183, 198
problem 8, 15, 19, 22, 23, 25–7, 44, 46, 60, 63, 69, 94, 118, 128, 150, 167, 182
    design 169
    social 14
    solving 156, 193, 198
    urban 180
process 4, 7, 10–12, 19, 21, 38, 73, 82, 86, 89, 109, 119, 141, 180, 198
    adaptive 41, 184
    alienating 62
    building 94

204   URBAN INFORMALITY

bureaucratic 84
collaborative 58
development 96
dynamic 45
empowering 57
formal 168
industrial 147
informal 1, 8, 16, 89–92, 104, 155, 191, 194
learning 10, 196
local 95
map-making 15
modernisation 78
participatory 83, 86
relational 16–17
self-regulating 101
spatial 174
urban 7, 194
provision 9, 33, 74, 78, 80–2, 91, 107
infrastructure 84
service 73, 79, 86, 192, 194, 196
social 13, 37
socialised 35
state 35
water 74, 81–3, 192
welfare 122
public space 13, 20, 21, 36, 37, 53, 56–8, 62, 67, 93, 94, 100, 103, 110, 120, 121, 128, 160
public telephones 133

Rajmahal hills 29
realm 149, 157
informal 27, 85
economic 35, 157
public 103, 158
social 110, 157
urban 155, 157
rebellion 23–30, 173, 192
refugees 8–9, 12, 110, 114, 117, 119, 142, 145
regional water institute 82
regulation 1, 3, 29–30, 38, 39, 45, 79, 80, 82, 92, 94, 151, 191
relationality 2, 3, 5–7, 16–17, 52, 56, 62–4, 68, 111, 155, 157, 168, 189, 190, 194, 195, 197–8
relations 2, 3–7, 9, 10, 36, 37, 68, 86, 114, 122, 190, 196
contractual 116
diplomatic 90
economic 2, 7
physical 190
political 22
power 4, 12, 22, 186, 196
religious 198
social 2, 7, 11, 14–15, 81, 141, 191–3, 195, 197–8
socio-spatial 21, 191
urban informality 6
relationship/s 2, 4–7, 9, 13, 38, 42, 45, 50, 56–62, 64, 68, 73, 78, 79, 81, 82, 84, 86, 109, 111, 116, 126, 135, 142, 152, 157, 160, 189, 197, 198
religious plants 133
reproduction
social 9, 107, 108-111, 116, 120-123

research 3, 41, 44–6, 95, 139, 156, 158, 170, 181, 195
empirical 141
interdisciplinary 156
morphological 101
qualitative 176, 185
resilience 13, 22, 167, 198
resistance 13, 22, 27, 73, 75, 82, 86, 87, 110, 120, 167, 198
resources 1, 9, 13, 22, 35, 42–3, 73–4, 76, 79, 81–2, 84–5, 89, 110–11, 116, 118–19, 133, 139, 155, 157, 165, 167, 170, 174, 180, 184, 192, 196
returns, economic 138
rhythms, graphic representation of 136, 137
RIBA Journal (RIBAJ) 175
Riggle, N. 53
right to the city 158
rights 110, 148
citizenship 119
democratic 109
discretionary 24
human 114
irregular 33
land 20
refugee 114
social 158
Rio de Janeiro 41, 180, 181
Risk 22, 86, 134, 152–4, 157, 169, 193
Ri-Xin Ting Circle 143
role 5, 12, 34, 50, 68–9, 78, 82, 111, 116, 141, 149, 151, 175
ambassador 61
of the artist 60–1
of the built environment 196
city 51, 69
of communities 84
Coxapo 80
economic 41
of media 175–7
non-state actors 15
social norms 12
of *traídas* 83
urban informality 73, 141,
urban space 108
Roy, A. 2, 4, 44, 46, 84, 92, 157, 158, 167
rules 3, 22, 36, 60, 90, 95, 111, 116–18, 155–6, 162, 163, 167–9
local 95
social 95
tacit 36
universal 111
unwritten 167
rules of the game 4
rural–urban migrants 146

Sánchez, Isabel Gutiérrez 9, 107–24
Santal
administrators 26
British administrator 24, 30
colonial authorities 28
in colonial India 23, 27
cultural codes 27
damin 24
insurrectionary tactics 28
peaceful 29

INDEX 205

Santal Parganas 29–30
Santal prisoners 28
Santal Rebellion (1855–6) 23–6
self-consciously mimicked 27
sympathy 28
tribal Santals 29
Sassen, S. 20, 33, 38, 184
scenario 86
  hybrid 73
  spatio-temporal 120
sector(s) 151–2
  business 151
  construction 93
  controversial 130
  crafts 167
  economic 33
  financial 108
  formal 149
  healthcare 112
  informal 34, 38, 102, 150, 153
  market 131
  organised 19
  private 92, 108, 153, 183
  public 79, 84, 183
  service 38
self-built structures 2, 14, 16, 74, 93, 174
self-construction 110, 174
service 6, 9, 22, 34–5, 43, 49, 52, 58, 74, 77–9, 81–2, 91, 96, 99, 100, 109–10, 112, 120, 130, 141, 149, 151–3, 158, 167, 174, 184
  religious 52
  social 167
Settle, A. 5
Shallvaret, case study 98–100
shantytown 179
shelter 37, 114, 144, 150
Sinha, N. 1–18, 189–98
skills 155, 167–9
slum tourist 44
slums 14, 15, 19, 22, 42, 44–7, 58, 89, 157, 158, 160, 176, 179–81, 185, 192, 197
social reproduction, crisis of 108–11
socio-economic exchange 36
socio-political relational power 2
solidarity initiatives 107
Solidarity Movement 110
  Athens Community Polyclinic and Pharmacy (ACP&P) 112–14
  City Plaza Refugee Accommodation Centre 114
  O Allos Anthropos Social Kitchen 111–13
  urban instances 111–14
South Asia 34
space(s) 1, 3–5, 7, 8, 10, 12, 19–21, 24–9, 35–7, 42–6, 50–1, 64, 65, 91, 93–5, 99, 107, 110–12, 114, 116, 118–23, 125, 127, 130, 132, 134–5, 138–9, 141–5, 148, 150–1, 156–60, 165–9, 190–2, 194, 197
  intimate 120
  social 110
  see also public space
Spain 9, 73, 75–7, 80, 83, 85
spatial governance 143
spontaneity 13, 125, 153, 155, 156, 162, 164, 167–70, 179, 190, 193

squatter 19, 22, 42, 46, 179
SRA (Slum Rehabilitation Authority) projects 160
Stanllos, It. 91, 100, 102, 103
state-centredness 3–5, 16, 63, 69, 84, 86, 173, 192, 194, 197
state-centric lens, challenges 5
state-led 9, 80, 194
Statistical Account of Bengal 29
status 87, 100, 146
  legal 94
  non-formalised 117
  ownership 138
  social 167
Stavrides, Stavros 119
strategy 4, 14, 20, 27, 41, 45, 46, 50, 85, 102, 110, 118, 125, 134, 145, 165, 183
street art 10, 13, 15, 16, 49–67, 196–8
struggle 1, 78, 110, 120, 123, 128, 139, 145, 193, 194
subaltern 10, 15, 21, 23, 45, 50, 62, 63, 175, 185, 186, 192, 194
Sub-Saharan Africa 34
supply 9, 12, 15, 30, 73, 78, 79, 81, 84, 93, 109, 126, 128, 149, 165, 193
suppression 146
survival 89, 119, 134, 142, 145, 148, 153, 154, 162, 165
sustainability 1, 78, 85, 87, 139, 142, 165, 194, 196
switching codes 26–7
Sztompka, P. 102

Taipei 12, 141–50, 152, 153, 194
Taipei Circle Night Market Commercial Association 149
tea plantations 30
telis (oilmen) 28
territory 25, 28, 76, 155, 157, 161
ties 5
  commercial 12
  domestic 35
  economic 5
  family 161
  social 7, 12
theory
  assemblage 45, 64
  social 44,
  urban 46, 157
Tirana 10, 16, 89–104, 190, 191, 194
  demand for commercial units 102
  non-domestic land 102
  photograph of 103
  urban growth in 1989 and 2016 101
Tonkiss, F. 8, 11–13, 16, 33–40, 64, 81, 86, 92, 94, 102, 174, 192, 193, 196
traídas 75, 86, 192, 194
  association 79
  Cerrada Morato's depiction of 92
  collective water deposits 76
  communities/local government, relationship 84
  Coxapo 80, 83; *see also* Coxapo
  defined 73
  economic contributions 81
  European subsidy 81

206   URBAN INFORMALITY

in Galicia 84, 196
legal representation 78, 85
municipal network 80
Pedrouzo's community 74
resources/plan 87
in Tomiño 12, 79
traditional 81
transforming 78
urban informality 84
users of 82
water supply networks 73
transaction 5, 6, 11, 12, 16, 24, 35, 134, 149, 191, 194, 196
artistic 194
economic 6, 194
translation 20, 23, 51, 54, 111, 122, 156, 168, 180, 193
Tunnacliffe, Claire 10, 15–16, 49

Uber 38
UN-Habitat 42, 176
understanding, cross-cultural 142
United Nations Habitat and Human Settlements Foundation (UNHHSF) 182
unsustainability 9, 22, 85, 154, 196
urban agriculture 15, 125–7, 131, 135, 138, 191
urban branding 46, 181
urban dynamics 6
urban economic exchange 34
urban food production 13
urban informality 1–8, 10, 11, 14–17, 23, 30, 41–2, 46–7, 52, 63, 68–9, 89, 92, 94, 100, 125–39, 161, 173–4, 176–7, 180, 182, 184, 189, 192, 195–6, 198
in Brazil 173
built environment/relationality 5–7, 189
definition 1
exchanges 11–13
exploration of 125–39
global imaginations challenges 69
image 14–16
in India 165
moving past state-centrism 3
notion of exchange 11
relational nature 16–17, 63
scholarship/activism of 1
socio-political relational power 2
visual appearance of 8
urbanisation 62, 76, 78, 85, 91–4, 96, 100, 142, 146, 156, 174, 182, 184
urban poverty 182
urban reproduction, crisis of 108–11
urban spectacle 42, 43, 46, 52, 181
urban territory 157
urban theory 46, 157
urban transformation 16
urban trend
chronological overview 182
data/methodology 175–6

fall, beginning of 185
informality 173, 183–4
linguistic trends, in mainstream media 177–81
qualitative meta-research 176–7
realities of 185–6
research 173
rise of 174–5
surge of 184–5
utilities 6, 151, 183

value 3, 5, 6, 38, 53, 62, 67, 68, 74, 77, 84, 87, 118, 125, 131, 133, 134, 142, 146, 157, 170, 189, 193, 195
historical 142, 146
social 62
spatial 157
vehicle circulation 97–8
Vieja, La Habana 126–32, 136, 137, 191
visibility 14, 22, 37, 42–4, 46, 60, 64, 68, 99, 167, 186, 193
vital/vitality 5, 142, 146, 150, 153, 174
vocabulary 20, 63, 190
volatility 157
vulnerability 118, 157

wall art
'African unity' 61
photograph of 49, 51, 55
war
Chinese Civil War 145
Cold War 146, 150
ethnic 91
Second World War 90, 142, 145–6, 149, 150
water 9, 12, 20, 42, 45, 73–87, 108, 109, 125–8, 132, 135, 139, 192, 196
Water Act (LAG 9/2010) 78
water supply 9, 73, 78–9, 84, 109, 128
community-based 73
community-led 73
hybrid 73
non-centralised 81
welfare 9, 36, 37, 107–23, 196, 197
work bench, photograph of 57
workers 22, 96, 131, 183
own account 38
railway 128
self-employed 130
social 112
World Cup 181

Xie, Y. 101

Yiftachel, O. 2, 4, 161

Zakari, R. 67
zamindars (landlords), *cutcherries* (offices) of 26